MW00528439

WHY
WE
LOVE
FOOTBALL

WHY WE LOVE FOOTBALL

— A HISTORY IN **100** MOMENTS —

JOE POSNANSKI

DUTTON

DUTTON

An imprint of Penguin Random House LLC
penguinrandomhouse.com

LIBRARY OF CONGRESS CATALOGING-IN-PUBLICATION DATA
Names: Posnanski, Joe, author.
Title: Why we love football: a history in 100 moments / Joe Posnanski.
Other titles: History in one hundred moments
Description: [New York] : Dutton, [2024] | Includes index. |
Summary: "A moving celebration of the history of
American football"—Provided by publisher.
Identifiers: LCCN 2024011336 (print) | LCCN 2024011337 (ebook) |
ISBN 9780593475522 (hardcover) | ISBN 9780593475539 (epub)
Subjects: LCSH: Football—United States—History. |
Sports journalism—Authorship.
Classification: LCC GV950 .P67 2024 (print) | LCC GV950 (ebook) |
DDC 796.33209—dc23/eng/20240706
LC record available at https://lccn.loc.gov/2024011336
LC ebook record available at https://lccn.loc.gov/2024011337

Printed in the United States of America

1st Printing

BOOK DESIGN BY LORIE PAGNOZZI

TO MARGO, ELIZABETH, AND KATIE . . .
AND TAYLOR SWIFT, WHO SOMEHOW BRINGS
THEM ALL TOGETHER

CONTENTS

I think now of a football story.

In 1976, the fierce linebacker Dick Butkus—to the surprise of almost everybody—started to make a small name for himself as an actor. He played an ambulance driver in the black comedy *Mother, Jugs & Speed*. At the same time, he had a critically acclaimed role* in the movie *Gus*, about a Yugoslavian mule who kicked 100-yard field goals.

His decision to become an actor after years of being the single most violent and terrifying force in football left sportswriters and players fairly astonished and uncertain.

"The Dick Butkus who graduated magna cum grouch from Illinois is an actor now?" asked Chicago columnist Bob Verdi.

He was. How tough a player was Dick Butkus? His name, *Los Angeles Times* columnist Jim Murray wrote, constituted "syllables of doom." Butkus played middle linebacker nine years for the Chicago Bears, during which time, in the memorable phrase of football's bawdy poet Dan Jenkins, he "mashed runners into curious shapes."

"He went after you like he hated you from the old neighborhood," running back Paul Hornung said.

"Dick Butkus hated everybody," Deacon Jones added. "I think he even hated himself."

"I never set out to hurt anyone deliberately," Butkus protested. "Unless it was, you know, important, like a league game or something."

How tough? One event can stand for many: Once, during a game against the Broncos, Butkus hit running back Floyd Little so hard that after the game, Little said, "My body almost liquified." After the play, the normally merciless Butkus went over to Little to see if he was OK.

---

* "*Gus* won't be a career maker for any of its large cast of jocks and comics," wrote the Buffalo film critic Hal Crowther. "Personally, though, I think Dick Butkus shows faint signs of talent and could be very funny in the right script."

"Of course," Little said, surprised that Butkus cared.

"Then why are you in our huddle?" Butkus asked.

No player in the history of professional football took meanness and fury quite to the level Butkus did. But that was the football player Dick Butkus. The thespian Dick Butkus was entirely different. His costar in *Mother, Jugs & Speed*, Raquel Welch, just adored him. She was baffled why anyone would have anything bad to say about him.

"I love everything about Butkus," she said. "He's funny. He's charming. Why do people say such mean things about him?"

At which point a member of the crew said: "Yeah. Don't pick up a football."

INTRODUCTION

"Baseball begins in the spring, the season of new life.
Football begins in the fall, when everything's dying."

—GEORGE CARLIN

I live a double life. On the outside, in public, I am a full-blooded base-ball fan—mild mannered, somewhat cultured, fascinated by po-etry, swayed by romance, a student of history.

"Stan Musial, you say?" I might remark at a party while wearing a tweed jacket with patches on the elbows. "Why, did you know that Stan Musial had exactly 1,815 hits both at home and on the road? Doesn't that just speak directly to the mathematical rhythms of baseball and life?"

"Did I hear you arguing about the designated hitter?" I might inter-ject as I pass a conversation at the cheese board. "Funny thing: Did you know that there were efforts to add the designated hitter to baseball going as far back as 1891? Ha! I believe it was Harry Truman who said, 'There is nothing new in the world except the history you do not know.' And, oh, did you know that Truman was the first president to throw a ceremonial first pitch left-handed?"*

---

* Harry Truman actually threw out pitches both right-handed and left-handed. Truman also attended more baseball games than any other president while in office (16) and this includes the biggest baseball fans to ever be presidents, Richard Nixon (11) and George W. Bush (10).

Wow, it's hitting me now: I'm actually quite annoying as a baseball fan.

But this is only the face I show the world.

I have another face, another side, a part of me that, as Jack Nicholson says in *A Few Good Men*, I don't talk about at parties. This is a part of me that prefers gray days, that feels most alive as the days grow short, that feels like barking at a television set or gnawing on barbecue in a stadium parking lot or screaming about John Elway or falling into an angry sleep by counting the number of starting quarterbacks my hometown Cleveland Browns have had since the turn of the century.

Yes, I am a football fan. I am . . .

. . . No, wait. Now I can't get it out of my head, all those tragic Browns quarterbacks. The Browns left Cleveland after the 1995 season to go play in Baltimore. I was at that last home game. What was it like? It was like watching your own open-heart surgery without anesthesia.

They came back, though, in 1999—well, a new team called the Browns came to town (the freshly named "Ravens" stayed in Baltimore), and since 1999, the Browns have been such a wreck that they have had at starting quarterback—deep breath now—Tim Couch (who was the first pick in the draft) and Ty Detmer and Doug Pederson (who would later coach the Philadelphia Eagles to a Super Bowl victory) and Kelly Holcomb and Luke McCown and also his brother Josh McCown (Josh was actually the good McCown, and he should be listed first) and Jeff Garcia and Trent Dilfer and Charlie Frye and Derek Anderson and Ken Dorsey and Brady Quinn and Bruce Gradkowski. Whew. That's a mouthful.

But we're only getting started. They also had Colt McCoy and Jake Delhomme and Seneca Wallace and fellow philosopher Thaddeus Lewis and Brandon Weeden and Jason Campbell and Brian Hoyer and Spergon Wynn (probably the best Spergon ever to play in the NFL) and Connor Shaw and Johnny Football himself, Johnny Manziel (whom they drafted on the advice of a homeless person),* and Robert Griffin III and Cody Kessler. That's absurd, right?

Oh, sorry, also DeShone Kiser and Kevin Hogan and Tyrod Taylor and Baker Mayfield (who did lots of fun television commercials) and Case Keenum and Nick Mullens and Jacoby Brissett and Deshaun Watson (don't get me started on him) and Jeff Driskel and Dorian Thompson-Robinson and P. J. Walker and Joe Flacco.

I think that's all of them. I'll save you the trouble of counting: That's thirty-seven different quarterbacks. . . . Wait, no, it's actually thirty-eight. I forgot about Austin Davis. How could I have forgotten Austin Davis? Made two starts in 2015. Lost them both.

By the time you read this, the Browns will probably add a couple more.

Yes, I'm a bit more fatalistic as a football fan. All football fans, I think, are at least a little bit fatalistic. Carlin was right. Baseball is about new life; Opening Day is about fresh beginnings. Football . . . not so much. In baseball, there's always hope, as best described in the poem "Casey at the Bat" when things looked bleak for the Mudville nine.

A straggling few got up to go in deep despair. The rest
Clung to the hope which springs eternal in the human breast . . .

That would have been a *very* different poem if it had been "Casey Drops Back to Throw."

A straggling few got up to boo, their faces red with dread.
The rest, depressed, blamed the refs and called for the coach's head . . .

Carlin got so much right in his famous "Baseball and Football" routine. Baseball has a seventh-inning stretch, football a two-minute

---

* This is not a joke. The team owner really drafted Johnny Manziel on the advice of someone who was lying down on the street in front of draft headquarters.

warning. Football is about downs (What down is it?) and baseball is about ups (Who's up?)

And then there's this marvelous comparison:

- In baseball, during the game, there's kind of a picnic feeling in the stands. Emotions may run high or low, but there's not too much unpleasantness.

- In football, during the game, you can be sure that at least twenty-seven times you're capable of taking the life of a fellow human being in the stands.

It feels so true. And yet there's something hard to explain. Every year during the 2000s, I would go out as a reporter to see at least one Oakland A's baseball game. And the place felt sunny. The A's uniforms glowed green and gold, and there were kids running around, and the fans were welcoming and friendly. It really was a picnic feeling. One fan actually offered to buy me a beer.

Also, every year, I would go out as a reporter to see at least one Oakland Raiders football game, and the place felt dark, foreboding, a *Mad Max* sort of hellscape. People dressed up as pirates and marauders. Spikes came out of their shoulders. More than one threw a beer at me.

Baseball and football, right?

Except—and it took way too long for me to have this epiphany—these were the *same people*. Baseball fans *are* football fans. Football fans *are* baseball fans.

Lots of us are living double lives.

EVERY CHILDHOOD HAS ITS OWN MYTHOLOGY, I SUPPOSE, AND A key point in my own is that I was born on the day of Super Bowl I. As the story was told again and again, I was born first in my family, not only ahead of my brothers but also ahead of all my cousins, and as such there were nerves galore throughout the family network. Relatives on multiple continents paced and worried and waited anxiously for news on that January day in 1967.

All, that is, except my father, who, as family legend has it, sat unbothered in the waiting room, watching that first Super Bowl* between the Green Bay Packers and Kansas City Chiefs.

"How can you sit there and watch football?" my maternal grandmother somewhat famously yelled at him—famous in our family legend anyway—at which point Dad said something to the effect of it not just being any football game but the Super Bowl.

This story was used often to explain why I grew up such a fanatic about football. What could you expect? My father was watching the Super Bowl when I was born. My mother's father—a Holocaust survivor who despised all games so intensely that he used to carefully pull out the sports section every morning so that he could happily jam it in the kitchen trash bin before beginning reading the real news—could never understand why his oldest grandchild would waste his time and energy on such nonsense, such *mishegoss*, as he called it.

I don't think he ever fully forgave my father for watching the Super Bowl when he should have been properly pacing back and forth, nervously awaiting my birth.

But here's the thing, the M. Night Shyamalan twist.

I wasn't born on the day of the first Super Bowl.

I didn't find this out until I was in college. I was raised on the certainty that the first Super Bowl was the day I was born. It was tops among my catalog of remembered historic dates. The moon landing

---

* It wasn't officially called the Super Bowl yet, though there were already those referring to it that way. The name was hatched by Kansas City Chiefs founder Lamar Hunt, who saw his daughter playing with a Super Ball and thought that would make a great name for the pro football championship. But the NFL commissioner, Pete Rozelle, thought the name was ridiculous—"Pete just didn't like the word 'Super,'" his longtime aide Don Weiss said—and refused to endorse it. By Super Bowl III, though, the name had become so ubiquitous that Rozelle simply gave in.

was on July 20, 1969. President Kennedy was shot on November 22, 1963. Pearl Harbor was bombed on December 7, 1941.

And the first Super Bowl was on my birth date, January 8, 1967.

Only, it wasn't. The first Super Bowl was one week later, January 15, 1967.

When I confronted my family with this shattering news—was everything a lie?—they insisted that my father WAS watching football when I was born. But how could that be? I was born in the bye week before the Super Bowl. There was no football on television. And this is when I learned, for the first time, that from 1960 to 1969, the NFL—to provide counterprogramming to the upstart American Football League—created a consolation game they played in Miami called the the "Playoff Bowl."

This game matched up the second-place teams in each conference.

Vince Lombardi called it "a losers' bowl for losers."

That's the day I was born in Cleveland, Ohio, on the day of the losers' bowl for losers. And my dad was attentively watching that pointless game. What chance did I even have?

From my earliest memory, I marked my life with football. I loved baseball, sure, basketball too, tennis, soccer—any sport, really. But my relationship with football was something bigger and more complicated than love. The first season I remember was 1975. I was eight years old. The Browns lost their first nine games of the season.

On the day before a sixth-grade science exam I had not studied for in 1977, the Browns almost came back and beat the Pittsburgh Steelers behind a backup quarterback and full-time dentist, Dr. Dave Mays. Almost. The loss sent me into a tailspin. I failed that test.

When I was twelve years old, I "had" to go with my father to a school-sponsored sex-education class. All I remember is racing to the car afterward and listening as Don Cockroft kicked a field goal with one second left on the clock to give the Browns a 13–10 victory over the Colts.

Nothing mattered to me as much as football. In 1980, a classmate invited me to some sort of memorial for John Lennon, who had been killed earlier that week. As I recall, he said a girl I had a crush on would be there. I passed and instead watched the Browns lose to the Vikings when Ahmad Rashad caught a Hail Mary pass as time expired.

When I was a sophomore in high school, I skipped a debate—costing me two letter grades in my debate class—so that I could watch (on television) the Browns lose 14–13 to the New York Jets. It didn't matter. The Browns had been eliminated from playoff consideration weeks earlier.

I thought about football—specifically the Browns but also everything else football—more or less every minute of every day. During boring classes (and I found just about all my classes boring), I would write long football stories just to make the time go by. I'd predict champions, celebrate moments, salute players and coaches, unleash anger. I never even thought of showing these stories to anyone. They weren't for reading.

Those stories just poured out of me. Football just poured out of me.

Over the years, much of that obsession has faded. Football can be a hard sport to love for any number of reasons, particularly the violence and danger. When I told a friend, television producer Michael Schur, that I was writing a book called *Why We Love Football*, he said: "Is it a one-word book and is that word 'bloodlust'?"

But even Mike can't quit football. It's inside us. Writing this book—writing about all these incredible moments and players and miracles—I felt like I was back in high school, and football poured out of me again. I lost myself countless times. Perhaps the only difference is that when I emerged from this latest trance of football writing, I wasn't sitting in front of an algebra quiz that made no sense to me.

THIS BOOK COMES WITH NO INSTRUCTIONS. YOU CAN READ IT any way you like—front to back, back to front, open up to any page and just start. Inside, you will find a hundred reasons why we love football, from throughout football history—not just pro football but also college football, high school football, lots of other bonus stuff that comes free with the purchase of this book!* Well, you'll see.

I think these also are the game's hundred greatest moments, and I use the word "greatest" as a generality. I was looking for something very specific with these moments. When I chose the moments for my last book, *Why We Love Baseball*, I used a formula of sorts:

$$(I+D+E) \times A = \textit{Great Moment Score!}$$

I represented the Importance of the play. D stood for its Distinctiveness: Was the play unique somehow? E stood for Emotion. And finally, A was for Awesomeness.

For football, essentially, emotion was the whole deal. Football is a game of constant emotion, skyscraper highs, subterranean lows, boiling rage, gasps of relief, irrepressible joy that is immediately repressed because there was a flag on the play.

During a baseball game, you relax, chat with friends, reminisce. . . .

During a football game, you live and die and live and die again.

My friend Michael Mulvihill, president of Insights and Analysis over at Fox, explained this best:

"What," he asked me, "do you think the biggest off-the-field event is in baseball?"

After thinking about it, I said: "It's probably the Hall of Fame induction in Cooperstown every year." The Baseball Hall of Fame is, by far, the most talked-about, argued-about, cherished, and celebrated hall of fame in all of sports. Every year, tens of thousands of people show up in this hard-to-get-to little village in New York so that they can salute

---

* Because you came down to read this footnote—thanks for doing that!—I'll fill you in on the biggest Easter eggs in this book. You will notice that the hundredth moment is simply titled "Aaron Donald"—it is about Donald's incredible final two plays in the Super Bowl. And the ninetieth moment is simply titled "Anthony Muñoz." And the eightieth moment is simply titled "Sammy Baugh." This will continue all the way to No. 10. Why? Within this larger countdown, I have secretly weaved in a countdown of the ten greatest players in pro football history. In order. So, yeah, you can scream at me about that too if you want.

their heroes and remember their childhoods and be a part of baseball history.

"Right," he said. "It has to be the Hall of Fame induction. Now, what do you think is the biggest off-the-field event in football?"

That was even easier to answer than the baseball question. "The draft," I said instantly. The NFL Draft is not only the biggest off-the-field sporting event in football; it probably draws more interest than anything in any other sport. The NFL claimed that 54.4 million people watched the 2023 NFL Draft at some point during the three days. More than 300,000 people attended the draft live in Kansas City.

"Of course," Michael said. "It's the draft."

"So, it seems to me that's the biggest difference between baseball and football. In baseball, fans look back. And in football, fans look forward."

I do hope you'll join me in looking back a bit.

ONE LAST THING: IN *WHY WE LOVE BASEBALL*, I WROTE ABOUT beating my friend Jim Banks in the most important Strat-O-Matic World Series ever played. It made me so happy to enshrine in the permanent record my glorious victory and the role that Red Sox star Dwight Evans played in it.

But . . . fair is fair. Strat-O-Matic, a tabletop sport-simulation board game, has a football version, which we were every bit as obsessed with as baseball. And in our biggest football game, I was coaching the Oakland Raiders, and he was coaching the San Diego Chargers, and I was leading by five with only time for one more play. His greatest player, by far, was wide receiver Wes Chandler, and so using all the tools Strat-O-Matic offered, I essentially put my entire defense on Wes Chandler.

His quarterback Dan Fouts threw the Hail Mary touchdown pass to Chandler anyway.

This is only one of the many football heartbreaks I will never, ever live down.

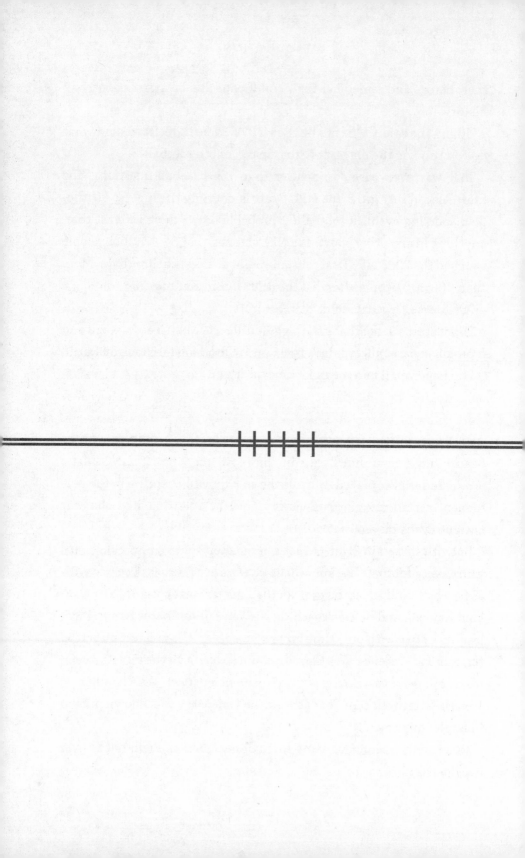

NO. 100:

AARON DONALD

"You're supposed to win the one-on-ones."

—AARON DONALD

—

FEBRUARY 13, 2022

In the moment, the key moment, the winning moment, only one thought raced through the mind of Los Angeles Rams coach Sean McVay: "Aaron Donald is going to make a play."

The thought so surged through him that he almost involuntarily said it out loud for all of his coaches and players (and, later, the television audience for the NFL Films recap) to hear. He did not say it as a wish or a prayer but as a simple truth, the sort of thing you say to remind yourself of something important.

Don't forget to get milk.

Be sure to turn left after the gas station.

Augusta is the capital of Maine.

Aaron Donald is going to make a play.

In truth, Aaron Donald had *just made a play*, a nearly impossible one. With less than a minute left in Super Bowl LVI, Donald's Rams led the Cincinnati Bengals by three, 23–20. But the Bengals and their irrepressible quarterback, Joe Burrow, were driving. They moved the ball into Rams territory and were 10 or 15 yards from field goal range. On third and 1, Burrow handed off the ball to Samaje Perine, a 240-pound monster truck of a man.

There was nothing in front of Perine but green and the first-down line.

Much of watching football is built around expectation. You see Perine in the clear; you see the first down; you expect the first down.

That's how it goes every time. The monster truck men *always* get the first down when there isn't a defender standing between them and the line.

Only this is what Aaron Donald did: On the snap, he smashed into Cincinnati's right guard Hakeem Adeniji, a 6-foot-4, 315-pound bruiser. Donald spun him around like he was a revolving door and grabbed a sprinting Perine from behind.

From behind. Any rudimentary understanding of mass in motion will tell you that Donald could not stop Perine's forward motion from behind him any more than someone could grab the caboose of a moving train and stop it from rolling forward. Nobody is that strong without CGI.

Only Aaron Donald is, in fact, that strong. Two Archies made him so. When Aaron was growing up in Pittsburgh, his father, Archie Sr., worried about him being undisciplined. "He was kind of chubby," Archie Sr. said. Father and son cut a deal: Every day before school they worked out together. These sessions evolved into massive two-hour workouts beginning at four thirty a.m.

This made the body strong. Aaron's older brother, Archie Jr., strengthened the mind. Aaron could never remember a time that he didn't idolize his brother. Archie played linebacker at the University of Toledo, where he was among the nation's leading tacklers. He was all heart. "You gotta put every single thing you have into every play," Archie Jr. said.

"I just want to play like my brother," Aaron said whenever anyone asked about his football goals. "I just want to have an attitude like him."

Here at the Super Bowl, third down and 1, he combined the life lessons of the Archies and pulled Samaje Perine back before he could get the first down.

"That," Al Michaels said on the broadcast, "is why people say he's the best player in the league."

Now the Bengals faced fourth down and 1 with the game in the balance.

And Sean McVay said, out loud, to everyone and no one at the same time: "Aaron Donald is going to make a play."

| | | | | |

HERE'S SOMETHING KIND OF FUNNY: THE ULTIMATE COMPLI-
ment a football coach can offer—the highest commendation, the most
stirring tribute, the grandest praise—is to call a football player "a football player."

That probably doesn't look like much when you put it quite that way.
It doesn't really work the same way when you say, *Tom right there is an
electrician,* or *Sally does our taxes and—let me tell you—she's an accountant.*

But football coaches have a way of saying "football player" just so—
in hushed tones, with bowed heads—and it is clear that they are reach-
ing for something beyond words. A "football player," in coach-speak, is
a player who lives up to the coach's most soaring ideals, someone who
works harder than others, plays smarter than others, takes the blame,
shares the credit, and, more than anything, yes, makes the play when
a play is needed most. Aaron Donald is a football player. He's one of the
footballest football players in the history of the sport.

The strange part is . . . for so long, very few people saw it. None of the
big-time colleges wanted him. No Alabama. No Georgia. No Ohio State.
No Michigan. No Texas. No Notre Dame. They apparently thought him
too small—at 6-foot-1, 260 pounds—to be a starting interior lineman
at the highest level of college football. Akron wanted him. Toledo. Rutgers. Schools like that.

Fortunately for Donald, about twelve miles away from his high
school, the head coach at the University of Pittsburgh, Dave Wannstedt, saw film of Donald. Western Pennsylvania is sacred football
country—it's the home of Unitas, Montana, Ditka, Dorsett, Huff,
Ham, Namath, on and on—and Wannstedt is as Western Pennsylvania as you can get.* He watched Donald make five plays. That's all it
took.

---

* You can tell this because, like other Western Pennsylvania men like Mike Ditka and Bill
Cowher, he grew a Western Pennsylvania mustache when he became a coach.

This guy, Wannstedt thought, *is a football player.*

Donald was incredible at Pittsburgh. As a senior in 2013, he won the Bednarik Award as the nation's best defensive player, the Nagurski Award as the nation's best defensive player, the Lombardi Award for being the best defensive lineman or linebacker, and the Outland Trophy for being the most outstanding interior lineman. There were no more trophies to give a defensive player. He made more tackles for loss than any player in America. He then went to the NFL Combine and ran the fastest time any interior lineman had ever run.

He still was not taken until the thirteenth pick of the 2014 draft. Scouts were mixed. "Lacks ideal height and has short arms," the *St. Louis Post Dispatch* wrote.

But, again, people missed it. They missed that with Aaron Donald you didn't measure his arms or his height or his weight. He was something new. You couldn't block him no matter how many blockers you used. You couldn't keep him out of the backfield no matter what schemes you designed. By his second year, Pro Football Focus wrote that he was the best player in the NFL. Not the best interior defensive lineman. Not the best defensive player. The best. All of it.

In his fourth season, he won his first of three Defensive Player of the Year awards. In his fifth season, he became the first defensive tackle ever to record twenty sacks in a season. In his first ten seasons, he had forty more tackles for loss than any other player in the NFL.

There has never been another one like him.

So, yeah, Sean McVay knew what everyone knew: Aaron Donald would make the play.

SUPER BOWL LVI, FOURTH DOWN, 1 YARD TO GO FOR THE BEN- gals, and Aaron Donald was thinking about confetti. Three years earlier, the Rams had played in the Super Bowl against New England, and Donald was so confident the Rams would win that he promised his five-year-old daughter, Jaeda, that after the game they would lie down in the confetti and make snow angels.

The Patriots won that game instead—the Rams only managed to score 3 points—and Donald was devastated by the loss. But it got worse after the game when he was hugging his sobbing daughter and she said, "I thought we were going to get to play in the confetti." That just about broke him.

Donald lined up, expecting another run. Then he saw Burrow in the shotgun, and he shouted out: "They're throwing the ball." The Bengals had two blockers ready for him, obviously. Left guard Quinton Spain had the main assignment and center Trey Hopkins was supposed to slide over to help.

But Donald's speed is perpetually stunning. No matter how many times you face him, it comes as a jolt. He broke right and left Spain standing like someone who missed a bus. Hopkins was not nearly quick enough to get over in time. By the time Burrow tried the pump fake that was meant to slow him down, Donald was already behind him. Donald grabbed Burrow and spun him around like they were square-dancing. He then laid Burrow on the ground.

He made the play. The Rams won the Super Bowl. And when a reporter came up to him for a postgame interview, Donald saw his children, saw Jaeda, and smiled.

"Excuse me," he told the interviewer. "We're going to play in the con-fetti for a minute, man."

NO. 99:

FANTASTIC FINISHES

[*Drumroll. Wa-wa-wa-wa, wa-wa-wa, wa-wa-wa, WAH!*]
"Alcoa presents Fantastic Finishes!"

—ANNOUNCER HARRY KALAS

—

SEPTEMBER 7, 1980

Can you hear it? Can you hear the trumpets blaring? They never sounded entirely in tune; there was always something of an underwater quality about them. But, oh, that sound still came crashing through. Can you hear it? More than forty years have drifted by, so there's a good chance you cannot hear it, a good chance that all this happened long before your time.

But if you are old enough, you surely still hear the trumpets of Alcoa's Fantastic Finishes.

"Alcoa presents Fantastic Finishes!" announcer Harry Kalas would say then. "1967. Johnny Unitas and the Baltimore Colts trail Green Bay 10–0 with just fifty-one seconds left. First, Unitas arches a perfect pass to Jimmy Orr. Then a successful onside kick and *here come the Colts again*! Unitas fires a strike to Willie Richardson, a 13–10 victory delivered by Johnny U!"

Or this: "Alcoa presents Fantastic Finishes! 1980. Bart Starr's Packers have a chance to beat the Bears in overtime. Chester Marcol's kick is up . . . *and blocked*! The ball bounces back into Marcol's hands. There's nothing for Chester to do now but tuck it in and run. He picks up a needed block along the way and cruises 25 yards into the end zone. The Packers win 12–6 on their own blocked field goal on the game's final play!"

Or this: "Alcoa presents Fantastic Finishes! 1975. Bum Phillips versus Don Shula. Needing more than a field goal, Dan Pastorini hands off to Ronnie Coleman. He cuts back inside one tackler, breaks outside, then rumbles over a second tackler, sidesteps a third, breaks the grip of a fourth, and powers his way through tacklers five, six, and seven. Houston wins 20–19!"

I still feel goose bumps . . . and something else, something harder to describe.

I still feel the sadness of another Sunday dying.

***

SURELY, EVERY GENERATION HAS ITS OWN CONNECTION TO PRO football. For my childhood household, well, our lives revolved around six hours on fall Sundays, from one p.m. to seven p.m. Eastern. That was the whole deal. There was no *Sunday Night Football*. There certainly was no *Thursday Night Football*, except on Thanksgiving. There *was* *Monday Night Football*, yes, but that was its own thing, a Howard Cosell and Don Meredith variety show, and by then the school week had begun and bedtime was no later than halftime.

Sunday was everything. Everything, all week long, pointed to Sunday. The hours leading up to kickoff were the worst, the clock barely moving as if, in the wonderful words of Georgia announcer Larry Munson, someone had poured molasses on it. And when the games ended, all that was left was darkness and unfinished homework and unresolved drama and the raging fear of alarm clocks blasting.

But those six hours in between? Heaven. Hell. Bliss. Pain. Escape. It felt like leaving the world for a short while, which is all I ever wanted to do at thirteen years old.

In those days, all the Sunday games were on either NBC or CBS, and we concentrated so fully that we could recognize differences in production. The NBC games always seemed more colorful; the CBS games were darker and starker. This lent a gravitas to CBS games. They always felt a little bit more important. The NBC games seemed more fun, though.

The days ended with *60 Minutes*. When you heard that ticking stopwatch that kicked off the show, you knew: Football was over. Sunday was over. Happiness was over. Monday was upon us. It felt a little bit like dying each and every week.

THE STORY OF ALCOA'S FANTASTIC FINISHES IS A STORY OF THAT time. This was the late 1970s, and America was in the middle of an energy crisis. You couldn't even buy gas every day. You had to go on an even or odd day, depending on the last digit on your license plate. My father once ran out of gas while in a long line to buy gas.

And so, Alcoa had a problem.

Regular folks didn't have any idea who or what Alcoa was, which was totally fine with the Alcoa executives. They were the world's leading producer of aluminum. Everybody needed aluminum. Alcoa was content to stay in the background and do their thing.

But the energy crisis was making it hard to be unnoticed. See, Alcoa—one company—used *4 percent* of America's energy. With costs skyrocketing and gas lines getting longer and President Jimmy Carter calling on Americans to turn their thermostats to "65 degrees in the daytime and lower at night," well, you didn't have to be a genius to see where this was going.

"They were worried people would say, 'Wait a minute, let me get this straight: I'm on a gas line at four a.m. so you can drink soda out of a can?" Alan Linderman, media director for the HBM/Creamer ad agency, said to me. "They were right to worry."

Alcoa gave Linderman and his group a $10 million budget to get the word out about the necessity of aluminum. Lindeman wanted to reach America's most influential people—business leaders, local politicians, the people who called in to talk radio shows, the presidents of Optimists and Kiwanis clubs, etc. In that spirit, he planned to plaster advertisements throughout business magazines like *Forbes* and *Business Week*.

Only, here's what he found: The people they wanted were not all reading *Forbes*. They were not all poring through newspapers. They were not all watching prime-time television.

But they were all watching NFL football on Sunday.

And so, Alan Linderman had this brainstorm: What if, during the two-minute warning, he ran an ad celebrating the wonders of aluminum? That was when the game was likely at its most dramatic, when the most people would be paying attention.

Trouble was: You couldn't just *buy* the two-minute warning. Nobody got to choose the time slot of their ad. Companies spending much, much more than Alcoa had no say in such matters. Also, the two-minute warning was sixty seconds long and Alcoa had offered only enough money for a thirty-second spot.

That's when creative director John Waldron and Linderman approached NFL Films' president Steve Sabol and asked about pairing a thirty-second Alcoa commercial with a thirty-second NFL clip, one featuring, yes, a fantastic finish.

The rest was magic.

"It was such a simple but beautiful idea," Sabol told me. "It would be the last two minutes of a game and then you would watch a Fantastic Finish. And, man, you were really pumped up after seeing that."

Alcoa's first Fantastic Finish was in 1980, its last somewhere around 1986—nobody seems exactly sure anymore when they stopped. But Alcoa kept a metric of how people perceived aluminum, and their approval rating skyrocketed to over 70 percent after the Fantastic Finishes.

Even more, my generation's memories of football revolve around those trumpets. And, yes, I still hear them.

NO. 98:

TEBOW'S PROMISE

"I promise you one thing: A lot of good will come out of this."

—TIM TEBOW

SEPTEMBER 27, 2008

The second-most-famous post-loss comment in history probably happened on November 25, 2001, when the San Francisco 49ers mashed the Indianapolis Colts 41–20. After the game, which included four interceptions thrown by quarterback Peyton Manning, the Colts coach Jim Mora walked into the postgame press conference and said: "That was a disgraceful performance."

And then he took questions.

"Hey," a local television reporter named Tim Bragg said, "you're probably going to have to win out to make the playoffs."

Mora looked at Bragg with a baffled look on his face. "What's that?"

"You're probably going to have to win out to make the playoffs," Bragg said.

"Playoffs? You talkin' about . . . *PLAYOFFS*? You kidding me? Playoffs? I just hope we can win a game."*

Needless to say: The Colts did not make the playoffs.†

And that's why it's only the second-greatest post-loss comment. The best one changed a whole season.

---

* As famous as this rant has become, I don't even think it was Mora's best. That came when he was coaching New Orleans in 1996. After a 19–7 loss to Carolina, he said: "We couldn't do diddly poo offensively, we couldn't make a first down, we couldn't run the ball, we didn't try to run the ball, we couldn't complete a pass, we sucked."

† Another wonderful post-loss comment came from Detroit Lions coach Bobby Ross: "I'm getting all the damn heat with each and every one of you hammering my tail. I'm tired of taking the blame. I really am. . . . You think I coach that stuff? I don't coach that stuff."

‖ ‖ ‖ ‖

IN 2008, THE UNIVERSITY OF MISSISSIPPI STUNNED THE UNI-
versity of Florida 31–30 in front of more than ninety thousand Florida
fans at a stadium they call the "Swamp." The Gators had come into that
game with national championship hopes led by their Heisman Trophy–
winning quarterback, Tim Tebow. Ole Miss, meanwhile, had lost nine
consecutive conference games. Florida was a 23-point favorite.

Mississippi's players were inspired that day, and with less than a
minute left in the fourth quarter, they stuffed Tim Tebow on fourth
down and 1, something nobody thought possible, least of all Tebow
himself. He was 6-foot-2, 240 pounds, and his whole life he *always* got
the yard. As a sophomore, he had scored a conference record 23 touchdowns.

But this time, Tebow took the snap, ran right, and was met at the
line by Ole Miss's Greg Hardy, who would go on to a Pro Bowl career in
the NFL, during which he would call himself the "Kraken."* Several
other Mississippi defenders, including defensive end Kentrell Lockett,
piled on.

"I got it! I got it!" Tebow yelled out as the official blew the whistle.

"No," Lockett said happily. "You didn't."

He didn't. It was unfathomable. "I got blown up," Tebow would say.
"It was shocking. It was devastating." The Gators lost.

"The Legend Crumbles" was the headline in the *Orlando Sentinel*.

As he stepped to the microphone in the postgame press conference,
he could barely speak, he was so torn apart. He went through some rote

---

* The nickname came to be when he was playing for Carolina, and before a *Sunday Night
Football* game, he was asked to introduce himself on camera and say his alma mater.
Hardy said, simply, "Kraken. Hogwarts." "I can do whatever I want," he later explained.
"I'm the Kraken. If you feel like you can ask the Kraken personally where he goes to
school, well, you can't."

explanations—"We turned the ball over," and "We didn't play like the Florida Gators"—and then he said this:

"I just want to say one thing to the fans and everybody in Gator Nation. Um. [Long pause.] I'm sorry. I'm extremely sorry. We were hoping for an undefeated season. That was my goal, something before never done here. [Another long pause.]

"But I promise you one thing: A lot of good will come out of this. You will never have seen any player in the entire country play as hard as I will play for the rest of the season, and you will never see someone push the rest of the team as hard as I will push everybody the rest of the season. And you will never see a team play harder than we will the rest of the season. God bless."

What happened next is mind-boggling: For the next ten games, Florida played as well as any team in the history of college football. They destroyed Arkansas by 31, then crushed No. 3 LSU by 30. They beat Kentucky 63–5 and No. 8 Georgia 49–10. They blasted a good South Carolina team by 50 points, pounded their statewide rival, Florida State, by 30, and scored two fourth-quarter touchdowns to come from behind and beat No. 1 Alabama in the SEC Championship Game. Tebow was named the MVP of that game.

In the National Championship Game, Florida played Oklahoma. At halftime, with the scored tied, Tebow asked the coaches to let him run the ball more. In the second half, he smashed into the line again and again, willing his team, and late in the fourth quarter, he threw the touchdown pass that clinched the 24–14 win.

"Tebow," his teammate Percy Harvin said. "Just call him Superman."

"Promise delivered" was the opening sentence in Antonya English's *Tampa Bay Times* game story. The second: "Promise kept."

NO. 97:

THE MIAMI MIRACLE

"I looked up and saw Gronk. And I was kind of like,
'What are you doing out here'?"

—KENYAN DRAKE

—

DECEMBER 9, 2018

Biblical scholars generally agree that there are thirty-seven miracles of Jesus recorded in the Gospels. Some go with thirty-eight. I've seen some stretch the definition of "miracle" and come up with forty miracles. But the consensus is that Jesus performed thirty-seven miracles, ranging from turning water into wine at a wedding to the miraculous catching of 153 fish.

Football, remarkably, has more miracles than the Gospels.

How many football miracles are there? There's no way to count. Every week or two, some team will pull off some unlikely feat that is promptly called a miracle by the coaches, the fans, the media. There is no room in this book for all of football's miracles, not even all of those that are specifically labeled as such, including the Miracle at the Met, the Miracle on the Mount, the Monday Miracle, the Miracle of Miami (not to be confused with the Miami Miracle, which we're about to get into), the Miracle in Missoula, the Miracle in Missouri, etc.

But there are lots of miracles in this book.

You'll find them on the sevens in the same way that you get your traffic report on the nines on morning radio.

THERE WERE NINE SECONDS LEFT IN THIS 2018 NFL REGULAR-
season game between Miami and New England. The Patriots led 33–28

because of course they did; the Patriots just about always beat the Dolphins in those days. From 2001 to 2018—eighteen seasons—the Patriots had won the AFC East division sixteen times and had finished with a worse record than the Dolphins exactly zero times. The Patriots would go on that year to win the Super Bowl. The Dolphins would go on to a losing record for the tenth time in fifteen years.

The Dolphins had time for one, maybe two plays. New England coach Bill Belichick, believing that the Dolphins' only hope was some desperation heave toward the end zone, put his colossal tight end, 6-foot-6 Rob Gronkowski, back near the end zone to swat away any last-gasp pass.

But the Dolphins tried something else. Quarterback Ryan Tannehill tossed a short pass to receiver Kenny Stills, who shook off New England's Jonathan Jones and then lateraled the ball back to DeVante Parker.

Ah, so this was their game—the Dolphins would try to keep lateraling the ball in an effort to keep the game alive. Such desperate ploys have worked at various times but not in pro football and certainly not against Belichick's famously disciplined defense. Parker pitched the ball to Kenyan Drake, who was sprinting down the sidelines. New England's Kyle Van Noy dived at Drake's legs but was unable to bring him down.

Then Drake paused for just an instant and took stock of his dilemma. There were Patriots all around him, but he quickly realized that only two were a direct threat. One, standing directly in front of him, was safety Patrick Chung, a longtime Patriots stalwart and a sure tackler. The other, Stephon Gilmore—who just one year later would be named NFL Defensive Player of the Year—was off to his left, waiting to pounce.

Drake also saw there was no one left to pitch the ball to. The clock had run out. He decided to make a break for it. And the most wonderful and unexpected thing happened. Chung was knocked out of the play by Dolphins guard Ted Larsen, who had run downfield to help.

And Gilmore ran the wrong way; he had expected another lateral.

And suddenly Kenyan Drake was in the clear. He could see the end zone. It was impossible, but he could see the end zone. All he had to do was get by one more Patriots player, just one more, and that player was . . .

"What's Gronk doing back there?" Dolphins fan and legendary golfer Jack Nicklaus shouted out from the stands.

Right. Except for Rob Gronkowski.

If I get tackled by Gronk, Drake thought to himself as he saw the end zone, *I'm never going to hear the end of it.*

There was no danger of that. Gronk had been put back there to knock down a pass and not to tackle a speedy running back like Drake. Gronk stumbled as he tried to chase Drake, but you kind of got the sense he wouldn't have known what to do even if he had kept his balance. "Gronkowski!" broadcaster Ian Eagle shouted in real time. "Didn't have the angle!"

And when Drake scored the touchdown, he threw the ball into the stands in triumph.

"Miraculous in Miami!" Eagle shouted.

"Gronk is obviously going to be a first-ballot Hall of Famer," Drake said. "But not for tackling somebody."

After the game, Gronk—who in his normal role as tight end had caught eight passes for more than 100 yards and a touchdown—stood behind a lectern and took the hard questions he knew were coming his way.

"It's sucky" was his final summation.

NO. 96:

GRONK!

"I still don't know how he caught that."

—TOM BRADY TO ROB GRONKOWSKI

NOVEMBER 2, 2014

For as long as Bill Belichick coached the New England Patriots, he was infatuated with an idea. He wanted a big, strong, overpowering tight end who could pancake linebackers and make absurd catches in traffic and blast through tackles. He searched the land for one of these rare creatures. He drafted a tight end named Dave Stachelski, whose name sounded perfect for a tight end, and he drafted Jabari Holloway and also Daniel Graham and Ben Watson and David Thomas.

Some proved better than others—Graham and Watson played on Super Bowl–winning teams—but none filled that giant vision in Belichick's mind.

Then, in 2010, Bill saw two tight ends in the draft who got his heart racing. One turned out to be a tragic story. Aaron Hernandez was a terrific player and a deeply troubled person; after being found guilty of first-degree murder and sentenced to life in prison, he was found dead in his cell after hanging himself with bedsheets.

The other tight end was a big lug who played at the University of Arizona and was named Rob Gronkowski. Physically, he had everything Belichick could ever want. He was huge—6-foot-6, 265 pounds at least—and he had the perfect tight end name (Gronkowski!) and the perfect tight end nickname (Gronk!), and he caught every pass thrown his way and he smashed like the Incredible Hulk.

There was one thing Belichick didn't know, though: Just how big was this guy's heart? It was hard to tell; he'd missed his whole junior season in college after having back surgery. And Gronk was . . . well, he was a little bit off. He seemed a bit too happy-go-lucky. Belichick brought Gronk in for an interview. They talked for a time—Belichick wasn't overly impressed—and then he excused himself to go talk with coaches.

When he returned, Rob Gronkowski was asleep on the floor.

"Didn't make a great impression," Belichick would later say.

No, probably not. Gronk would later say he was hungover from the night before. Belichick drafted him anyway. It worked out pretty well, to say the least.

THERE ARE FIVE GRONKS, ACTUALLY: FIVE GRONKOWSKI BROTH- ers, all of them mammoth, all of them elite athletes. They grew up in Buffalo—a Gronk place to grow up—and their father, Gordy Gronkowski, would say that there wasn't a piece of furniture in the house that survived their constant roughhousing.

Each Gronk followed a very Gronky path. The eldest, Gordie, became a slugging designated hitter in the minor leagues. Dan became a bruis- ing pro tight end for Detroit and Denver; Chris, a bruising running back for Dallas; Glenn, a bruising fullback for Buffalo.

You have to use that word "bruising" when talking about Gronks.

And Rob became the Gronkiest Gronk of them all. In his astounding career, he powered and bulled and bashed his way to more than 9,200 receiving yards and 92 touchdowns. His quarterback Tom Brady called him the greatest blocking tight end ever to play. He was the hardest player of his generation to tackle downfield.

How impactful was Gronk? He played eleven seasons, and in that time, his teams won four Super Bowls, lost two Super Bowls, lost three championship games, and merely made the playoffs the other two years. Yes, of course, those were Tom Brady's teams. But where do you think Tom Brady looked when he was in trouble?

Gronk did it all with Gronk style, Gronk panache. He almost fell out of the team bus during a Super Bowl parade because he was trying to high-five everybody. He tried to speak Spanish for an interview with ESPN Deportes and said, *"Yo soy fiesta,"* which means "I am party." He used the Super Bowl trophy as a baseball bat, bunting a ball and leaving a dent in it. Once, Colts defensive back Sergio Brown had been yapping at Gronkowski all game and so finally, on a run play near the end zone, Gronkowski blocked him and kept blocking him and ran him out-of-bounds and knocked him to the ground.

"I took him and threw him out of the club," he said.

Gronk's most mind-boggling play happened in 2014. His Patriots were playing Denver, and the game was in hand. They had the ball on the Broncos' 21. Tom Brady dropped back, faked a pass short, and then threw the ball over the middle to Gronk, who was surrounded by four Broncos. The ball was thrown behind, and Gronkowski somehow—it's still not clear how he did it—contorted his body and reached back with his left hand and pulled the ball in.

"That was unbelievable," Brady said. "How the fuck* did you make that catch?"

And Rob Gronkowski's answer was, well, perfect.

"Before the game," he said, "I dreamed that, like, I'm going to snatch one out of the air."

Brady just laughed and shook his head. What else was there to say?

---

* In *Why We Love Baseball*, I chose to bleep out all the swear words using various methods, such as using comic-strip-style punctuation marks or replacing the expletives with animal sounds such as "quack." That seemed funnier to me and more expressive of the sport. Football is a more in-your-face game, however, and using those same techniques just didn't work as well. There aren't many profanities in here, but like in football itself, there are a few.

NO. 95:

JADEVEON CLOWNEY'S HIT

"Fortunately, Smith's helmet went flying without his head still in it."

—*DETROIT FREE PRESS* COLUMNIST DREW SHARP

—

JANUARY 1, 2013

*B*atman scholars—and I'm referring here to those academics who have spent their lives studying the 1960s *Batman* television show—count eighty-seven different onomatopoeias used to describe the sound of Batman and/or Robin hitting a supervillain or one of a supervillain's henchmen.

That show, which starred Adam West as Batman and Burt Ward as Robin, the Boy Wonder, was gloriously corny. Whenever Batman and Robin would get into the Batmobile, there would be a close-up of them buckling their seat belts ("Safety first, Robin!"). Whenever there was a moral dilemma facing the dynamic duo, Batman always made sure they took the highest road ("Gee, you're right as always, Batman!"). And whenever punches were thrown, the screen would detonate into a cartoon explosion featuring words such as:

BAM!

BANG!

CRASH!

OUCH!

POW!

WHACK!

These are some of the more obvious words they used. And while it's all well and good for a punch to sound like "CRASH!" or "OUCH!" . . . well, there were a hundred twenty episodes of *Batman*, so the writers needed to come up with surprises, words that jolted you out of complacency and made you FEEL that punch. And so, they added "THWACK!" and "BLURP!" and the unimaginably thunderous "FLRBBBBB!"

The writers went overboard on K words,* producing "KLUNK!" and "QUNCKKK!" and "RAKKK!" and a personal favorite, "URKK!" (or with an extra K for particularly ferocious punches: "URKKK!").

However, no matter how many K's you put in a word, no matter how many exclamation points you add to the end, no comic book word can capture the sheer violence and intensity and visual fireworks of University of South Carolina sophomore defensive lineman Jadeveon Clowney smashing into Michigan's Vincent Smith in the Outback Bowl in Tampa on New Year's Day 2013.

Clowney had come into the game with a huge reputation—he was an All-American and there was talk of him being a Heisman Trophy candidate the following year—but he had not done a whole lot during the game. He even got sidelined for a few plays after a collision with Smith.

"Guys, I'm going to show up," he told his teammates. "I'm coming."

With a little more than eight minutes left in the game, Michigan converted on a fake punt to get a first down at their own 41. On the next play, they handed the ball off to Smith. And Clowney, well, he blasted through the line so fast that he just about tackled Michigan quarterback Devin Gardner on the way back to the handoff. Gardner handed the ball off to Smith just in time.

And then . . .

KLUNK!

URKK!

ZZWAPP!

No sound effect can do it. Clowney hit Smith so hard, Smith's helmet

---

* The writers also loved Z words, using fifteen different Z words, assuming you consider "ZAM," "ZAMM" and "ZAMMM!" to be different words. They also used "ZLOTT!" and "ZLOPP!" and "ZZZZZWAP!" and the very excellent "ZGRUPPPP!"

went flying off—and Clowney had not even hit Smith's helmet. He had hit him in the chest. It was the reverberation of the hit that sent the helmet flying.

"It sounded like a car crash," South Carolina receiver Ace Sanders said.

"Like two cars hitting," defensive coordinator Lorenzo Ward said.

But it was more than just the sound, more than just the helmet flying. The ball was jarred loose too. It rocked back and forth and Clowney reached down with his right hand to hold Smith down and with his left hand he plucked the ball off the ground as if to say, *Hmm, what's this item?*

South Carolina promptly took the lead after that and won the game— the hit had changed everything—and afterward someone asked South Carolina coach Steve Spurrier how he kept Clowney from hitting like that in practice against his own team.

"We have a rule," Spurrier said. "Don't clobber teammates."

NO. 94:

"THE DAGGER IS IN!"

"Right now, I'd have to consider ourselves the best ever."

—DERRICK BROOKS

JANUARY 26, 2003

The Tampa Bay Buccaneers defense, from 1997 to 2002, was one of the greatest ever but is rarely talked about that way. The problem might have been that it lacked a great nickname like Pittsburgh's Steel Curtain or Minnesota's Purple People Eaters or Dallas's Doomsday Defense or Seattle's Legion of Boom.

They were just the Tampa defense, you know?

Even more likely, people overlooked that Tampa defense because the linebacker at the center of it was not a fire-breathing Dick Butkus or Lawrence Taylor. Fans didn't call him "Count Dracula" like they did Jack Lambert. His eyes didn't bulge like Mike Singletary's.

No, Derrick Brooks was just a studious and soft-spoken player who was always one step ahead of any offense.

His anticipation worked like a magic trick. While at Florida State, he had a defensive run for the ages. He spearheaded a goal line stand to preserve a shutout against Kansas. The next week, he returned an interception for a touchdown against Duke. The next week, he returned a fumble for a touchdown and blocked a punt against Clemson. The next week, he returned another interception for a touchdown against North Carolina. The next week, he led the team with nine tackles in a shutout of Georgia Tech. And the following week, despite an injured shoulder and playing with the flu, he led the Seminoles to victory over rival Miami.

That was when his outside linebacker coach gave him the weirdest compliment.

"Derrick is like a cockroach," Jim Gladden told the *Orlando Sentinel*. "It's not what he carts off and eats. It's what he falls in and messes up."

I'm not entirely certain I can translate that one, but I think Gladden was saying that Brooks's game was not about unleashing explosive hits or sacking quarterbacks but instead about the way he would get into the machinery of an offense and make it start smoking and splintering and breaking apart.

He would drop back in coverage and—because he spent so many hours in the film room—always seemed to know exactly where the pass was going. And in the running game, he simply did not miss tackles. Brooks seemed invulnerable to feints and jukes.*

His best pro season came in 2002, the year after the Buccaneers rather stunningly fired their coach and Brooks's mentor, Tony Dungy. After a spectacularly chaotic coaching search—"This is a circus, and I don't want to be in the act," Brooks said—and in one of the crazier moves in NFL history, the Bucs *traded* for a head coach. They gave up two first-round picks and two second-round picks for a fiery bulldog named Jon Gruden.

And immediately, Gruden challenged Brooks and his teammates to make big plays.

"If you're so great," he told them, "let's see you score some touchdowns."

Challenge accepted. In 2002, Brooks had one of the great defensive seasons in NFL history. He picked off five passes and returned three for touchdowns.† He also returned a fumble for a touchdown. He and the Buccaneers went on to a 12-4 season and two utterly dominant

---

* In 2004, Atlanta quarterback Michael Vick was the wonder of the NFL as he was all but unstoppable as both a runner and a passer. "No points," Brooks told his teammate repeatedly when the Bucs played his Falcons, and then sure enough the Bucs shut out Atlanta. In that game, Brooks had eleven tackles, two sacks, a forced fumble, and a tipped pass that led to an interception. "That's a Babe Ruth–type shot there," his teammate Simeon Rice said after the game.

† His 218 return yards on interceptions remain a record for linebackers.

playoff victories despite an offense that finished in the bottom ten in points scored.

Then came the moment, Super Bowl XXXVII, the Bucs versus Gruden's former Oakland team. The Raiders didn't stand a chance. Gruden knew the Raiders offense so thoroughly that, during the week, he actually stepped in at quarterback during practice to show exactly what Oakland quarterback Rich Gannon would try to do.

"Some of the same words Coach used in practice, Gannon used in the game," Brooks would say. "We knew exactly what was coming."

Tampa Bay led 34–21 with less than two minutes in the game when Gannon tried to throw a pass over the middle. Brooks stepped in front and headed for the end zone. Nobody stood in his way. It was his fifth defensive touchdown of the season. No player has ever had more.

"There it is!" Tampa Bay radio announcer Gene Deckerhoff shouted as Brooks crossed the goal line. "The dagger is in! We're going to win the Super Bowl!"

NO. 93:

THE HEIN SPECIAL

"The longer you're away from the game, the greater you become. It
thrills me to think how great I'll be when I'm a hundred years old."

—MEL HEIN

———

DECEMBER 17, 1933

B efore we get into the wonders of the Hein Special—the first
meaningful trick play in professional football history—we should
go back a year and talk about the Indoor Game because it changed
everything. In 1932, there was no official championship game. Pro
football was too chaotic to have anything that organized. In 1931,
there were ten teams in the NFL and they all didn't even play the same
number of games. The Green Bay Packers played fourteen, the Chicago
Cardinals played nine, the Frankford Yellow Jackets played eight, the
Providence Steam Roller (that's singular, "Roller") played eleven, and
so on.

But in 1932, a bunch of things happened that began a new future.
The first thing was that the one-loss Chicago Bears and one-loss Ports-
mouth Spartans seemed in an unbreakable tie for the league championship. They had faced each other twice, and both games ended in
scoreless ties. There seemed nothing to separate them.

And so, the teams decided to settle things with a special playoff game
at Wrigley Field a week before Christmas. It was the first NFL Championship Game of sorts. There wasn't *a lot* of excitement about it but
there was some . . . until a titanic snowstorm hit Chicago and temperatures dropped below zero. Suddenly, there wasn't any excitement about
the game.

This was when Bears owner George Halas moved the game indoors into Chicago Stadium, where the Chicago Blackhawks played hockey. This would be the first official NFL game played indoors.*

Lots of rules had to be altered to fit the size of Chicago Stadium. For instance, because the field was only 80 yards long, teams that drove the ball inside their opponent's 10-yard line were then automatically moved back 20 yards. That rule, as you might imagine, didn't last.

But another rule did. Before the Indoor Game, the ball would be placed where the ball was declared dead. But because the field at Chicago Stadium was so narrow, they realized it would be dangerous to start a play right next to the sidelines. So they put hash marks 10 yards from the sidelines, and every time a play ended outside the hash mark, the ball would be moved in, and the next play would begin on the hash mark. That's still the rule in the NFL.

The Bears ended up winning the game 9–0; the winning play was a controversial touchdown pass from Bronko Nagurski to Red Grange.†
More than eleven thousand curious fans had piled into the stadium, and Halas decided that an NFL Championship Game was a good idea. In 1933, the NFL split into two divisions, with the champion of each playing in a title game.

The first NFL Championship featured the Chicago Bears and the New York Giants, and it was a wild game, with six lead changes and two spectacular touchdown passes thrown by Nagurski. People immediately called it the most dramatic professional football game ever played.

But the play that endures—that first trick play—didn't even score a touchdown.

---

* Unrelated fun fact! There had been a circus in Chicago Stadium earlier in the week, a circus with elephants, and the smell was so rancid that at least one player violently vomited while on the sidelines.
† It was controversial because in those days the player had to be at last five yards behind the line of scrimmage to throw a forward pass—and Nagurski very clearly was not five yards behind the line. The touchdown counted anyway, and the rule was changed, probably in direct response to the play.

| | | | | |

THEY CALLED MEL HEIN "OLD INDESTRUCTIBLE." IN THOSE DAYS when players were as disposable as razor blades, he played center and defensive line and linebacker for fifteen years without missing a game.

Hein deeply loved football. While many college football stars did not see pro football as a viable option,* Hein sent out letters to multiple teams in the hopes of playing professionally after an All-American career at Washington State. He wanted to sign with the Giants, but when he didn't hear back, he panicked and signed instead with the Providence Steam Roller.

"What a stupid mistake," the Giants Hall of Fame end Ray Flaherty said to him. "I know for a fact the Giants planned to offer you at least $10 more per game."

Hein promptly called his local postmaster in Pullman, Washington, and asked him to stop the mailed, signed contract from ever getting to Providence. The postmaster had the letter intercepted and Hein signed with the Giants the next day.

Hein was a great player. He revolutionized pass blocking by stepping back toward the quarterback. Nagurski thought him the league's best linebacker. And he was terrific at the shotgun snap. "He could center a ball from 50 yards and hit a needle in its eye," George Halas would say.

And in the first quarter of the championship, he was given a chance for a little immortality. With the ball on the Chicago 45, the Giants called the Hein Special. They shuffled things around so that Hein, though he was the team's center, was at the end of the line, making him an eligible receiver. Hein then snapped the ball to tailback Harry

---

* In 1936, Heisman Trophy winner Jay Berwanger was the first pick in the first NFL draft. He did not like the Chicago Bears' offer and chose instead to take a job with a Chicago rubber company.

Newman, who dropped back to throw. Newman tripped and fell. Chicago's 262-pound tackle George Musso jumped on top of him.

That's when Musso and everybody else realized that Newman did not have the ball.

Newman had taken the snap and then surreptitiously handed the ball *back* to Hein, who then tucked the football under his jersey. Hein started to walk toward the goal line. The plan was for him to keep walking until his blockers could get in front him and escort him all the way into the end zone.

Hein walked unnoticed for twelve yards before having delusions of grandeur. The end zone was *right there*. He just knew that if he took off, he would score a touchdown. So, he took off. Alas, Hein was not the first player—and certainly not the last—to wildly overestimate his own speed. As soon as he started to run, Chicago safety Carl Brumbaugh noticed him and chased him down at the 15-yard line.

The Giants did not score on the drive and eventually lost to the Bears 23–21.

"I guess I thought I was faster than I actually was," Hein would say.

NO. 92:
WHEN PHILADELPHIA BOOED SANTA

"The guy had it coming."
—NFL STAR MATT MILLEN

DECEMBER 15, 1968

L etter of the Day" in the *Philadelphia Inquirer* in December 1968:

> *I am not a football fan, so very seldom do I watch a game on television. However, my five-year-old son and I happened to be watching halftime activities and saw Santa Claus emerge on the field where the Minnesota Vikings and the Philadelphia Eagles had been playing. We were both very upset to notice the fans in the City of Brotherly Love took upon themselves to snowball this cheerful fellow. I must say it was hard to explain to a five-year-old why people were mean to him.*
>
> **DEE LUBANSKI, FRIDLEY, MINN.**

AS THE YEARS HAVE TURNED AND THE STORY HAS BEEN PASSED down from generation to generation, people in Philadelphia fall into two categories when thinking about that cold and miserable December 1968 day when a dreadful Eagles team lost to the Vikings and Eagles fans booed Santa Claus.

The first group will tell you that it has been wildly overplayed and has been used to unfairly paint Philadelphia sports fans as out-of-control loonies who hold nothing sacred. They're sick of the cliché. "Every time someone needs to say something negative about Philadelphia," Bill

Mullen, Eagles director of entertainment that year, griped many times, "they pull out the Santa episode."*

The second group—folks like Matt Millen, who grew up about an hour away and was eleven years old when he went to that game—wear that moment with pride. You'd better believe Philly fans booed Santa! He had it coming.

Philadelphia fans entered that last game of the 1968 season extremely cranky. The team had a 2-11 record. Hilariously, many Eagles fans were angrier about the two wins than about the eleven losses. The Eagles had started the season by losing their first eleven games and seemed certain to get the first pick in the NFL Draft, which they could have used to select the most exciting college running back since, well, since ever, a whirling, spinning, Heisman Trophy–winning blur named O. J. Simpson.

Then, on Thanksgiving Day, the Eagles went to Detroit and shut out the Lions 12–0 in a driving rainstorm.

"[Eagles coach] Joe Kuharich finally won one," the Associated Press reported. "Which could make him a loser."

"We play the season!" Kuharich grumped when told that one more victory would mean losing O.J. "We're concerned with winning and playing a game and that's all."

Sure enough, the Eagles beat New Orleans the next week, thus losing the first and second picks in the draft.† Philadelphia fans were outraged, but the Eagles themselves were pleased, particularly running back Tom Woodeshick, who scored the winning touchdown. "If

---

* You will occasionally see Eagles fans complain that one episode from a half century ago should not define a city or fan base. That is fair except for one thing: It was not one time. Fans had *also* booed Santa a year earlier. And perhaps other times as well. Even by 1968, the *Philadelphia Inquirer* called booing St. Nick "the worst Philadelphia tradition."
† With the third pick, the Eagles selected running back Leroy Keyes out of Purdue. Keyes was nicknamed "Nursey" because, when he was very young, he insisted on being carried around instead of walking himself. Keyes gained a total of 368 yards for the Eagles—or 9,815 fewer yards than Simpson gained for Buffalo.

Simpson came here," Woodeshick told reporters, "I'd get two carries a game."

Eagles fans were surly even before they arrived at Franklin Field on December 15. One fan unveiled a sign that read: "Joe just didn't want next year's coach to have O.J." Another was more direct: "Kuharich stinks." An airplane flew overhead pulling a banner with the words "Joe Must Go!" The weather only added to the mood: An icy wind blew, and the wind chill felt like 15 degrees.

The Eagles had prepared a Christmas show, but bad weather had snowed in their Santa Claus in Atlantic City. Fortunately, a passionate Eagles fan named Frank Olivo came to the game wearing a Santa Claus outfit and the team asked him to fill in. They gave him an equipment bag filled with soggy towels to carry as his sack. His job was to wait for the song "Here Comes Santa Claus" and walk through a pathway lined by cheerleaders.

As he began his walk, the boos came crashing down, and when he reached the end zone, he was hit with what Olivo's cousin would call a "tsunami of snowballs." Olivo was not entirely surprised nor bothered. He was never upset about the booing or snowballs. Olivo was an Eagles fan through and through, and he might have booed himself if given the chance. When one fan threw a snowball at him and missed, Olivo remembered yelling out, "You're not getting anything for Christmas."

Years later, the Eagles PR director Jim Gallagher would be quoted in *The Great Philadelphia Fan Book*: "He was the worst Santa I've ever seen. Bad suit. Scraggly beard. I'm not sure whether he was drunk, but he appeared to be."

Olivo did take offense to *that*; he told ESPN's Liz Merrill that he was certainly not drunk, *and* he'd paid $100 for that suit, which was always a hit with his family. It was a nice suit.

NO. 91:
LINDA JEFFERSON
CAN'T BE STOPPED

"I run out of fear. I want to get out of the way."

—LINDA JEFFERSON

FEBRUARY 18, 1973

When Linda Jefferson was sixteen years old, she wrote this in her journal: "I believe that I can be among the best athletes in the world."

The trouble was that this was 1970, and Jefferson had absolutely no idea how a young woman could become one of the best athletes in the world. She dominated the neighborhood touch football games on the streets of South Toledo.* She ran track and played basketball at Libbey High School. She felt faster than anyone.

But what did it mean? This was before Title IX, before women could get college scholarships to play sports. This was before women's sports were ever shown on television except, maybe, for a few tennis highlights. This was when women's basketball was often played six on six, with only three players allowed to score and the three others allowed only to play defense. It is striking that even five years later, in 1975, a women's college basketball game between Miami and Cincinnati was halted and disbanded because it was time for the men to warm up for their game.

Linda Jefferson knew, just knew, she was destined to be an elite athlete.

She just had no idea how it could happen.

---

* "As I got older, the boys started holding and squeezing me instead of tapping," Linda Jefferson told the *Louisville Courier*. "I knew it was time to get out."

It happened in the strangest way. When she was seventeen years old and still in high school, a woman named Sheila Browne watched Jefferson fly around the bases in a softball game. Browne just happened to be a center on the Toledo Troopers, an all-woman team in the Women's Professional Football League (later the National Women's Football League). Browne brought her out to a practice, where she immediately ran by everybody. She was nervous about playing football mainly because her mother, Sally, had forbidden it. Sally called the sport barbarian. But once Linda started running away from defenders, sending them to the ground with her moves, she couldn't give it up. She played secretly for a while, but she was too good for it to stay a secret for long. Finally, she stood up and told her mother that she loved the sport too much to give it up.

"Just don't let them hit you," Sally finally said.

"Momma," Linda replied, "they can't catch me."

WITH LINDA JEFFERSON, YOU CAN PRETTY MUCH PICK ANY GAME and it would be a highlight. To say she dominated women's professional football is to wildly understate things.

"She's got moves like O. J. Simpson," said Sally Orwig, a star cornerback for the Detroit Demons.

"She'll crisscross the field until you can't stand up anymore," Detroit's coach Tom Brown said.

The New York Times began a 1974 story this way:

> Question: The hardest-running, highest-scoring professional
> football player is:
> (A)   O. J. Simpson
> (B)   Larry Csonka
> (C)   Mercury Morris
> (D)   A 21-year-old Toledo woman?

Answer: A 21-year-old Toledo woman named Linda Jefferson,
who in two years as halfback for the Toledo Troopers
has rushed 173 times for 2,174 yards (a 12.5 average) and
has scored 43 touchdowns (every fourth time she carries
the ball).

The numbers are simply mind-blowing. In her seven years with the Troopers, Jefferson scored 140 touchdowns, ran for more than 8,000 yards, and averaged more than 13 yards per carry. In 1975, *WomenSport*—a magazine founded by Billie Jean King—named her the Female Athlete of the Year. This led in 1976 to her being invited to *The Superstars*, an ABC show that matched up athletes in a variety of competitions (bowling, tennis, the obstacle course, etc.). Jefferson finished fourth overall—she won the 60-yard dash and the softball toss—beating out, among others, legendary athletes Martina Navratilova and Althea Gibson. She won $2,533 dollars. It was, by far, her biggest payday as an athlete.

"We play football because we love football," Linda told a reporter. "There certainly isn't any money in it."

If you had to pick her greatest game, the game against the Dallas Bluebonnets at Texas Stadium is a pretty good option.

"Dallas players earned $25 for the game, plus a share of the profits," the Associated Press reported. "Toledo team members played for 'fun and expenses.'"

This was the first professional women's football game played in the Southwest—there were 2,842 in attendance—and Jefferson was electrifying. In the first quarter, according to Stephen Guinan's fine book, *We Are the Troopers*, she was supposed to take a handoff and sweep left but instead collided with quarterback Lee Hollar and the ball popped free. Jefferson then ran back, scooped up the ball, and ran 92 yards for a touchdown.

Before she was done, she added a 42-yard touchdown run, a 15-yard touchdown run, and a 13-yard touchdown run. She took a screen pass and turned that into a 53-yard touchdown. She also had 2 long touchdowns nullified by penalties. In all, she ran the ball ten times for 209 yards. Texas Stadium was demolished in 2010. Linda Jefferson was the only professional player to ever score 5 touchdowns there.

NO. 90:

ANTHONY MUÑOZ

"Mister, I know you would have loved playing for Lombardi."

—BART STARR TO ANTHONY MUÑOZ

—

APRIL 10, 1980

One remarkable part of football history is how one thing leads to another. The great Packers coach Vince Lombardi, rather famously, did not have favorites among his players. "He treats us all the same," Henry Jordan said. "Like dogs." But there was one guy Lombardi truly and rather openly admired: offensive lineman Forrest Gregg.

"This man," Lombardi used to say, "is a real football player."

It's no mystery why Lombardi loved him so. Forrest Gregg never complained or took credit for anything. He seemed impervious to pain. He never missed a game, not ever; he played in 188 straight, an NFL record at the time. And he was always working to improve. Even at the end of his career, he would spend hours and hours on the most basic things, like perfecting his blocking stance.

How much did Lombardi love Gregg? In 1975, when Cleveland Browns owner Art Modell was looking for a head coach, he got an unexpected call from Marie Lombardi, Vince's widow. She made it searingly clear that Vince would have ordered him to hire Forrest Gregg.

Modell promptly hired Forrest Gregg.

Five years later, Paul Brown hired Gregg to be the new coach of the Cincinnati Bengals. The Bengals were terrible, particularly on defense, and Gregg knew that the most important decision he would make as coach was choosing who to take with the third pick in the draft. The obvious choice was Penn State defensive end Bruce Clark, since the Bengals had given up the most points in the NFL.

But Gregg was an offensive lineman through and through, and he kept going back to two offensive tackles, teammates at USC, Anthony Muñoz and Brad Budde.*

Gregg liked them both, but he was more intrigued by Muñoz. Some were calling him the greatest offensive lineman ever in college football. He was 6-foot-6, 280 pounds, a giant in his day, and he was fast enough that some scouts thought he could play tight end. All things being equal, he was the best talent in the draft by acclamation.

But all things were not equal: Muñoz had had three knee surgeries while in college. He insisted that he was healthy, but teams across the league were hesitant. Gregg was hesitant too. He had to be sure.

On April 10, a couple of weeks before the draft, an extraordinary encounter took place. Gregg went out to California to meet with Muñoz. They talked for a while, but Gregg was never much for talking. He said, "Let's go to the field." Gregg ran Muñoz through a few drills and then said, "OK, I'm going to rush you now. Let's see what you've got."

Here was the clash of generations, the greatest tackle of the 1960s up against a young player who would become the greatest tackle of all time. It was like Joe Louis trying out the young Muhammad Ali in the ring or Sandy Koufax pitching to a twenty-year-old Shohei Ohtani or Michael Jordan playing one-on-one against high school LeBron James.

Understand, Forrest Gregg was already forty-six—by this point he'd been in the Pro Football Hall of Fame for three years—but he was still a rock of a man, and he probably knew more about blocking than anyone on earth. First, Gregg tried to run around Muñoz. No chance. Muñoz was a dancer; he had the best movement Gregg had ever seen

---

* Brad was the son of Ed Budde, an all-time-great Kansas City Chiefs offensive lineman. When Brad was selected in the first round by Kansas City, they became the first and only father-son pairing to be first-round picks by the same team.

from any offensive lineman. Then Gregg tried bull-rushing Muñoz, coming straight on. Again, no chance; Muñoz didn't budge. Not even a millimeter. It was like running into the base of a mountain.

Then Gregg went for the final exam. He faked left as if he were going to slip inside Muñoz, then broke outside. Muñoz put out one arm and knocked the great Forrest Gregg to the ground.

While flat on his back, Lombardi's ideal player smiled to himself.

"I said to myself," Gregg would say, "'We've *got* to have this guy.'"

ANTHONY MUÑOZ WAS AN ARTIST PLAYING A POSITION THAT was decidedly unartistic. Offensive tackle is a grueling, no-glory position where you smash into giants (and Giants) and try—without holding, clipping, punching, spearing, tripping, kicking, chopping, crack-backing, or any other sort of roughness deemed unnecessary—to keep your man away from the football and the person carrying it.

"Anything can be great," Fast Eddie Felson says in *The Hustler*. "I don't care. Bricklaying can be great. If a guy knows. If he knows what he's doing and why and if he can make it come off."

That's the quote that always came to mind with Anthony Muñoz. Because he knew. Yes, of course, he was a fantastic athlete—he was actually a big-league pitching prospect in college.* But there were plenty of fantastic athletes in pro football. What made Muñoz so great was the very thing that Forrest Gregg saw in him that first time: He knew the answer to every question.

If pass rushers came right at him, that was easy: He just held his ground. If they tried to run around him, he would use their momen-

---

* After his football-playing days, Muñoz played shortstop in Cincinnati's elite softball league and he would routinely make dazzling defensive plays that left the crowd breathless.

tum and guide them past the quarterback. Rushers couldn't fake him out because he seemed to know where they were going before they did.

As NFL tight end and broadcaster Bob Trumpy said: "He gave linemen no place to go."

You shouldn't reduce a glorious career like Muñoz's to one series, but let's revisit a regular-season game between the Bengals and Bills in 1988. Muñoz was locked up against Bruce Smith, one of the best defensive linemen ever. The two battled for three quarters to something of a draw; Smith won some battles and Muñoz won some, and the Bengals led by a touchdown in the fourth quarter.

"There are a lot of crazy things going on here," Bengals quarterback Boomer Esiason told his offensive line. "But it's time for us to show who we are."

Then the Bengals, running behind Muñoz, just jammed the ball right through Buffalo's defense. They went on a fifteen-play, 65-yard drive that lasted nine minutes and twenty-four seconds and ended when running back Ickey Woods crashed in from the 1. The Bills were frantic throughout, screaming at one another: "We've got to stop them." But they couldn't.

"The holes were so big," Woods would say, "I couldn't even believe it."

Of course, this wasn't Muñoz alone, but one of his great skills—the one he took the most pride in, actually—was his ability to raise the game of players around him. When someone asked Bruce Smith to offer a scouting report for Muñoz, Smith shrugged helplessly.

"What's amazing about Muñoz," he said, "is that he does everything right."

NO. 89:
THE BUTT FUMBLE

"It's mind-boggling. Are your eyes closed? I really can't relate to that."

—HALL OF FAMER JOE NAMATH ON THE BUTT FUMBLE

—

NOVEMBER 22, 2012

Everything about the Butt Fumble is perfect, except offensive lineman Brandon Moore was totally wrong for his part. Moore is everything that is solid and dependable and unwavering about football. Making him the butt of the Butt Fumble is like hitting Daniel Day-Lewis in the face with a shaving cream pie or putting Meryl Streep in a Three Stooges short or pressing Robert Caro to write a scholarly book about the Kardashians. It's all sorts of wrong.

On that day in East Rutherford, New Jersey, Moore was making his hundred-thirty-second consecutive start for the New York Jets, the longest streak for any offensive lineman in the NFL. And he hadn't even come into the league as an offensive lineman. He had been an all-conference defensive tackle at Illinois. Nobody drafted him and he showed up at the Jets camp, and they told him he was too slow to be an NFL defensive lineman. So, he became an offensive lineman.

Then the Jets cut him anyway and he returned home to Gary, Indiana, and became a substitute teacher, hoping to get a callback. And they did call him back. Then they cut him again. Then they brought him back a third time, and he became the team's starting guard and stayed there for ten years.

"He's one of the toughest guys I've ever been around," his third coach, Rex Ryan, said.

No, Brandon Moore absolutely didn't deserve to be involved in the Butt Fumble.

But as Clint Eastwood says in *Unforgiven*: "Deserve's got nothin' to do with it."

THE BUTT FUMBLE IS THE SECOND-FUNNIEST PLAY IN FOOT-ball history. There are so many competitors. Many will point to the time Vikings defensive lineman Jim Marshall recovered a fumble against San Francisco and ran the wrong way 66 yards for what he thought was a touchdown but was actually a safety.* Some will favor Dan Orlovsky's stroll during his first start for the Lions, when he took the shotgun snap from the 1-yard line, retreated to the back of the end zone, and then just ran out of the back of the end zone for a safety. "Poor guy," broadcaster Ron Pitts said. "I don't think he even realized it."

There was the time Louisiana Tech had the ball on the Mississippi State 7, second down, and botched the snap. Everybody chased after the ball, kicking and pushing it back *86 yards* back to the Louisiana Tech 7. That made it third and 93.

There was the fake punt that the Colts tried against New England in 2014, when for mystifying reasons they lined up just two players in the middle of the field—the other nine were all on the right side—and then snapped the ball, allowing, like, five Patriots to just smash poor Colt Anderson. "I've never seen anything more bizarre than that," NBC's Cris Collinsworth said.

There are so many others.

But the Butt Fumble stands apart because of its exquisite choreography. . . . The Marx Brothers never had such timing. The Jets were trailing New England on Thanksgiving night. Jets quarterback Mark Sanchez took the snap and turned left to hand off the ball.

---

* On the plane ride home from the game, which the Vikings ended up winning, Marshall's teammates kept telling him to go to the cockpit and fly the plane home. "That way," Marshall explained, "we'd end up in Hawaii instead of Minnesota."

Unfortunately, Lex Hilliard, the fullback who was supposed to take that handoff, went right instead.

Sanchez did a comical double take and then took off running. The trouble with that was that he didn't seem quite sure where to run, so he just sort of ran into a mass of defenders waiting to crush him. That's when he made the executive decision to slide rather than get crunched.

And he slid directly into the backside of Brandon Moore, who was busy trying to block a 325-pound neutron bomb named Vince Wilfork. Sanchez smashed face-first into Moore's behind—"Are your eyes closed?" Jets great Joe Namath would wonder—and was knocked hard to the ground.

It goes without saying that he fumbled the ball. It goes without saying that ball was promptly scooped up by the Patriots' Steve Gregory, who ran it back for a touchdown.

Gregory kept the football but wanted to be sure that it wouldn't get lost with other mementos of his NFL career.

He wrote on it: "Butt fumble."

It's fair to say that Brandon Moore never found any humor in the play. You can't blame him. Moore was an unwitting participant. But he had to be there because Brandon Moore was that kind of player. He was always there, every game, every play, even on nights like these—especially on nights like these. That's what made him special in the first place.

NO. 88:

RED RIGHT 88

"If it isn't there, throw the ball into Lake Erie."

—SAM RUTIGLIANO TO BRIAN SIPE

—

JANUARY 4, 1981

We have been avoiding this for a few happier chapters, but it's time to talk about the cold, hard center of football: heartbreak. I was thirteen years old when the Cleveland Browns—my Cleveland Browns—called the play "Red Right 88" on a gray day when, as was usually true in Cleveland Januarys, an icy wind swept in from Lake Erie.

If you are a football fan with some mileage on you, you surely have your own Red Right 88. You have a play, a moment, that dug its way into your stomach and still flaps around in there. No number of Super Bowl victories can make the Helmet Catch go away. Time barely dulls the agony of Wide Right or the Hail Mary or Montana to Taylor or Kick Six.

Football, as the Dread Pirate Roberts would tell you, *is* pain, and anyone who tells you otherwise is selling something.

The 1980 Cleveland Browns were the brightest light of my childhood. They were something you never expected to see in Cleveland, among the rust and slush and potholes and mud and cold winds that made you walk backward: Those Browns were *glamorous*. They had a wisecracking coach named Sam Rutigliano. They had two running backs named Pruitt, Mike and Greg (unrelated), the former a bruiser with thighs the size of oak trees, the latter a nifty sprite who wore tear-away jerseys so that defenders were left with a souvenir after he pulled away.

They had a wizard, Ozzie Newsome, a tight end who specialized in contorting his body and making gravity-defying catches.

Most of all, they had my hero, the quarterback Brian Sipe. He was too small and too slow, and his arm was spaghetti—Sipe's passes fluttered even on still afternoons—but he was somehow the best quarterback in the world that year. His superpower was this James Bond–level confidence:* He always seemed sure that when he threw the ball, no matter how many defenders were covering his man, it would turn out well. Things mostly turned out well in 1980. Sipe would be named the NFL's most valuable player.

Together, they were called the "Kardiac Kids" because of their habit of winning games in the final moments. All fall and into winter, when you turned on the radio in Cleveland, you were almost certain to come upon the song "The Kardiac Kids" by Messenger.

That's the Cleveland Browns

When they're Siped up, you can't shut them down

Take your tranquilizers, pop your beer can lids

It's the Kardiac Kids

Those Browns so filled my heart, there was no room for anything or anyone else. I woke up thinking about them, and I went to bed thinking about them, and at night I dreamed about them. When they made the playoffs, I spent every day for two weeks preparing myself mentally, emotionally, and spiritually for their playoff game against the Raiders.

I still wasn't prepared.

That game was played on the most Cleveland day imaginable. The kickoff temperature was 1 degree—the coldest NFL game since the Ice

---

* He was also a staggeringly handsome fellow. As a young fan, I often wondered what this movie star was doing playing football in Cleveland when he undoubtedly could have been walking among starlets on a beach somewhere.

Bowl in Green Bay—but in Cleveland you never looked at the temperature. You looked at the windchill. And that was –36.

The field was frozen. It was so cold that if you took your hands out of your pocket for even a few seconds, they would go numb. Predictably, Browns kicker Don Cockroft missed an extra point and failed on three field goal attempts, one when holder Paul McDonald couldn't handle a snap. McDonald was wearing gloves. He had never worn gloves when holding before.

All of this led to the big finish: The Browns trailed Oakland 14–12 with less than a minute left, but they had the ball at the Oakland 13. This was how they did things. They won in the end. I was too young to pop any beer can lids, but I'd seen this act so many times before, I felt entirely certain—certain in a way I would never feel again about anything—that the Browns would win this game. Brian Sipe would make it so.

Rutigliano—not trusting Cockroft to make even a 30-yard field goal—called the play: Red Right 88. Well, the full name was "Red Slot Right, Halfback Stay, 88." But it is remembered only as Red Right 88. It was a pass play. It was meant to go to sure-handed Dave Logan, who was crossing the field from left to right. The last thing Rutigliano said to Sipe was: "If it isn't there, throw the ball into Lake Erie."

Rutigliano's final warning was sensible enough, but there was one problem: Brian Sipe *always* thought it was there. That's what made him Brian Sipe. He always thought a receiver was open, or at least open enough. Sipe dropped back nine yards and, for whatever reason, turned his attention away from Logan and focused on Ozzie Newsome. When the Raiders' 6-foot-7 monster, Ted Hendricks, closed in, Sipe made the snap decision to throw to Newsome . . . because of course he did.

The Wizard was not open. He couldn't get his footing on the sheet of ice in the back of the end zone. Sipe's throw wriggled and twisted in the wind and landed in the hands of Oakland's Mike Davis, who secured it and fell to the ground with the interception that ended the game and the season and all my dreams and my childhood.

NO. 87:

MIRACLE AT THE (NEW) MEADOWLANDS

"Why didn't you kick it out-of-bounds? Why didn't you kick it out-of-bounds? WHY DIDN'T YOU KICK IT OUT-OF-BOUNDS?"

—GIANTS COACH TOM COUGHLIN TO PUNTER MATT DODGE

—

DECEMBER 19, 2010

You know how the poet Robert Frost wrote about those two roads that diverged in a yellow wood. Well, Matt Dodge didn't want to be a football player. As a freshman at West Carteret High on the North Carolina coast, he signed up to play soccer. When he was dropped off a couple of minutes late for his first practice, the unimpressed soccer coach threw him off the team, and he was left with the other road.

He had no idea that the other road led to New York football infamy.

Ah, but we never know where the road will lead, do we? Matt Dodge never really fell in love with football. His true love was weight lifting. "The mindset I have is a bodybuilder mindset," he told the *Raleigh News and Observer*.

But it just so happened he could, in his own words, "kick stuff really hard," so he became a seventh-round pick of the New York Giants. They selected him to replace the venerable Jeff Feagles, who had punted 1,713 times, still the NFL record.

Dodge did kick stuff really hard. He nailed two 60-plus-yard punts against the Eagles the first time his Giants played them, punted a 69-yarder against the Cowboys (the second-longest punt in the NFL that year), and finished in the top ten in the league in average punt yardage.

And he was having perhaps his best day the second time that season the Giants played the Eagles on that December day in 2010. Everybody on the Giants was having a great day. They led 31–10 with eight minutes left. This game was essentially for the division title, and all was going well for New York.

Then it wasn't. The Eagles quarterback then was the mercurial Michael Vick, who had the ability to transform into the most dangerous player in football at any point. And so he did. He threw two touchdown passes and ran in a third to tie the game with 1:16 left.

The Giants offense quickly stalled, and Dodge had to go out to punt one more time with fourteen seconds left. The Eagles sent their most dynamic returner, DeSean Jackson, back to field the punt.

"Kick the ball out-of-bounds," Giants coach Tom Coughlin told him.

"He wasn't the only one," Dodge said. "My teammates told me to kick it out-of-bounds. Everybody in the stands told me to kick it out-of-bounds. The hot dog guy told me to kick it out-of-bounds."

Dodge took the snap from his long-snap specialist, Zak DeOssie* and tried to kick the ball out-of-bounds. But when the snap came in a little high, it threw off his rhythm a bit. When he kicked, he felt a thud. The ball had hit the inside of his foot. Dodge watched in horror as the ball fluttered and twitched and did not have the aerodynamics or distance to get out-of-bounds.

Two words came to mind: *Oh. No.*

Jackson could not believe his fortune. "I'm just thinking to myself, 'They're not going to kick it to me.'"

Jackson dropped the ball, probably out of shock, and then picked it up and took a few steps back to the 30-yard line to assess the situation. Then he just stopped, like he wanted to take a photograph of the oncoming Giants.

---

* Long snapping was a DeOssie family business. His father, Steve DeOssie, was one of the first full-time long snappers. Bill Belichick credits him with being the player who changed the whole punting game.

"I'm looking right at him," Dodge would say. "It was like the parting of the Red Sea."

Yep, the first seven Giants who had raced down to tackle him had left open this beautiful gap between them. Jackson ran through them and had only four Giants to beat.

Then it was three: Bear Pascoe went straight at Jackson, a losing strategy if there ever was one. Jackson made a move and Pascoe went flying by. "He put a little shimmy on me," Bear said.

The Giants' Danny Ware tried to get in on the play, but he took a bad angle and never got close. That left two players. Zak DeOssie, that Giants long snapper, had the best shot. He had a good angle. But when he closed in, well, some of you might remember back when Atari put out the first home football video game. In that game, offensive linemen would block so hard, they would actually make defenders disappear from the screen.

That is what Philadelphia's Jason Avant did. Avant blocked DeOssie so hard, he *deleted* him—briefly knocking himself unconscious in the process.

That left Dodge. And . . .

"Believe it or not, he juked me," Dodge would say, "because I'm paid to punt, not to tackle."

DeSean Jackson took the ball to the end zone—actually, he ran alongside the end zone first to make entirely sure that the clock ran out—and the Eagles beat the Giants, and Coughlin went out to scream at Dodge. ("Why didn't you kick the ball out-of-bounds?" he asked repeatedly.) People came down hard on Dodge. He even got some death threats. He was cut the next year and never punted again in the NFL.

But as the years passed, he began to look back at the miracle differently: Because of that play, people still remember him. They still want to talk to him. It has opened countless doors.

"It's one of those things," he told Fox Sports. "God works in mysterious ways."

NO. 86:

DITKA!

Bill Swerski: "OK, Ditka versus God in a golf match.
Now, he's a good golfer. Who you got?"

Bears fan 1: "Ditka."

Bears fan 2: "Ditka."

Bears fan 3: "Ditka."

—THE ORIGINAL "BILL SWERSKI'S SUPER FANS"
SKIT ON *SATURDAY NIGHT LIVE*, 1991

—

NOVEMBER 24, 1963

The most Ditka play of them all happened two days after the assassination of John F. Kennedy. It boggles the mind now that the NFL actually played games two days after the assassination. Commissioner Pete Rozelle would publicly call it the worst decision of his career. Privately, though, he wasn't so sure. Rozelle had been college buddies with Kennedy's press secretary Pierre Salinger. He had even known Kennedy a little bit.

Both of them thoroughly believed that JFK would have wanted the games to go on.

In the moment, the NFL took a fierce beating for his decision. Several NFL owners were against playing. The networks announced they wouldn't even broadcast the games. The American Football League postponed its games. Then, on Sunday morning, before any game kicked off, Jack Ruby shot Lee Harvey Oswald on national television, and America was shaken to its core.

Having football games on after that seemed so wrong to so many.

"In the civilized world, it was a day of mourning," Red Smith wrote in the *New York Herald Tribune*. "In the National Football League, it was the 11th Sunday of the business year, a quarter-million-dollar day in Yankee Stadium."

"Did Pete live to regret his decision? I'd say yes due to all the negative attention," Joe Browne, Rozelle's longtime friend and an NFL employee for a half century, told WBAL radio in Baltimore. "But that being said, did he think he made the wrong decision? I'd say no. And he told me that on several occasions."

See, in many ways, playing those games did provide exactly what Salinger and Rozelle had hoped: It brought a little normalcy to the nation. More than sixty-two thousand fans were in New York to watch St. Louis beat the Giants. More than sixty thousand were in Philadelphia as Washington beat the Eagles. In Cleveland, fifty-five thousand were there to see the Browns intercept four Don Meredith passes in a victory over the Cowboys.

And in Pittsburgh, one of the Chicago Bears' great legends was launched.

MIKE DYCZKO—THE MAN WHO WOULD COME TO LIVE IN THE pantheon of Chicago's greatest figures with Dick Butkus and Michael Jordan and Ernie Banks and Walter Payton and Bobby Hull—was not actually from Chicago. He, like so many of football's greatest players and characters, was born and raised in the coal-mining heart of Western Pennsylvania. Ditka—the family name was changed when he was young so that people could pronounce it—was, from the start, the fiercest competitor. His high school baseball coach, Press Maravich—the father of basketball legend Pete Maravich—was asked what Ditka was like back then.

"Did you ever see a lion jump through a hoop of flames?" Maravich said. "That's how Mike was."

When the Bears drafted him in 1961, tight end wasn't even a position.

His new coach, George Halas, referred to him as a "closed end." They did not draft Ditka to catch passes. "We are counting on his blocking to give our running game a lift," Halas said.

But the Bears soon found that Ditka was unlike any blocking end before him because he was a dangerous receiver. In his rookie season, he caught fifty-six passes for 1,076 yards and 12 touchdowns. That made him just the tenth player in pro football history—and the first tight end—to have more than 1,000 yards receiving and 10 touchdown catches in a season.

And he played with the sort of ferocity that spoke to Chicago. Years later, of course, Ditka would become coach of the '85 Bears, perhaps the most beloved team in Chicago sports history, but it was as a player that he first won the city's heart. And on that Sunday after JFK's assassination, he made the play that, more than any other, created his legend.

The game was in Ditka's Pittsburgh hometown, at what the *Chicago Tribune* called "Dingy, antiquated Forbes Field." The field was torn up and muddy, and the game was mostly drudgery. Then in the fourth quarter, with the Bears trailing 17–14, Chicago quarterback Billy Wade asked Ditka if he could go long. He said no, not in those conditions.

"But," Ditka added, "if you hit me with a 10-yard or 12-yard hook, I'll try to run with it."

Wade dropped back, looked around, and found Ditka on that 12-yard-hook play. The pass was a little high, but Ditka reached up and pulled it in. Steelers safety Clendon Thomas seemed to be in position to make the tackle, but Ditka made a hard move to his left and Thomas whiffed. Linebacker John Reger looked to chase Ditka down from behind, but by then Ditka was up to full speed and Reger's dive left him smashing his face mask into the turf.

Ditka saw Steelers defensive back Glenn Glass standing in his way, so he just lowered his head and ran him over. While he was doing that, rookie linebacker Bob Rowley grabbed his leg; Ditka yanked his leg free and kept running.

Another Steelers defensive back, Willie Daniel, grabbed Ditka around the waist. Ditka kept on running and pulled from Daniel's grasp. When Ditka's old college teammate Dick Haley* was knocked to the ground, Ditka was free, and he ran as fast as he could.

Which was . . . not very fast.

"He seemed to be running in slow motion," the Associated Press wrote.

"Give me a break, man," Ditka would say. "I was tired."

Who could blame him? He had smashed through six tackles. Clendon Thomas, the man who missed the first one, finally chased Ditka down at the 15-yard line. Writers at the time called it the greatest run they'd ever seen. Even now, on grainy black-and-white film, the run still electrifies.

"You know what's funny?" Ditka said afterward. "I was looking to lateral the ball the whole time."

---

* Dick Haley did not have an especially memorable NFL career as a player, but he is a part of NFL history in another way. After he retired as a player, he became Pittsburgh's director of player personnel, and he helped build the four-time Super Bowl Champions. In 1974, Haley was largely responsible for the greatest NFL Draft in NFL history. That year, the Steelers drafted FOUR Hall of Famers—receiver Lynn Swann, linebacker Jack Lambert, receiver John Stallworth, and center Mike Webster.

NO. 85:

WE ARE THE BEARS' SHUFFLIN' CREW

"Look, if George Halas was coaching this team, you know what he'd do with the 'Super Bowl Shuffle'? He'd take a copy of it, call a team meeting, then put it on the floor and stomp all over it."

—MIKE DITKA

—

DECEMBER 3, 1985

How about a little more Chicago? Because the brassiest, cheekiest, most audaciously arrogant move in professional football history happened on a cold Tuesday morning in Chicago.

The night before, the Bears got smoked by Dan Marino and the Miami Dolphins. It was the Bears' first loss of the season, and it was a doozy. Marino threw three touchdown passes, running back Ron Davenport ran for two more, and the proud and swaggering Bears' defense was run off the field. The game was a disaster in every imaginable way. At halftime, with the Bears down 31–10, coach Mike Ditka and defensive coordinator Buddy Ryan had to be pulled apart before they started punching each other.*

The next morning, just a few hours after the plane landed in Chicago, those same Chicago Bears went into a concert venue called Park West and recorded the video of a song they had recorded earlier in the season. The song was called "The Super Bowl Shuffle."

---

* Ditka and Ryan truly despised each other. Ditka loathed how much credit Ryan took for the defense's success: "He took a lot of bows, and I let him." Ryan, meanwhile, thought Ditka was entirely overmatched as a coach. "I should be so lucky to have a Buddy Ryan around," he once said. "It would be nice to have someone around to make me look like I know what I'm doing."

We are the Bears' Shufflin' Crew

Shufflin' on down, doin' it for you . . .

We're not here to start no trouble

We're just here to do the Super Bowl Shuffle

How much gall does it take to get destroyed on *Monday Night Football* for all of America to see and then wake up Tuesday morning and start singing and dancing* about going to the Super Bowl? Understand, the Bears had NEVER been to the Super Bowl. They had never been close to the Super Bowl. One year earlier, they had made it to their first-ever conference championship game, and they got crushed by San Francisco.

Then, that was the story of the '85 Bears.

"We're going to the Super Bowl," linebacker Otis Wilson told reporters moments after the Dolphins' loss. Then, if anyone was still unclear, he went on: "And we're going to win it."

No, not everybody on the team was thrilled about "The Super Bowl Shuffle." Defensive lineman Steve McMichael was particularly irked. "How often do things work out for you when you brag about doing them before the fact?" McMichael would write years later in *Amazing Tales from the Chicago Bears Sideline*. "Hardly ever. I thought the sumbitches had jinxed us."

But mostly, those Bears just didn't care what anyone else thought. They were a reflection of Mike Ditka, and he didn't care. "The guys are having fun," he said. "I'm supposed to stop them?" They were a reflection of Buddy Ryan, their ferocious defensive coordinator, and he didn't care. Ryan had fought in the Korean War and included this quote in his defensive playbook: "Quarterbacks are overpaid, overrated pompous bastards and must be punished."

---

* We do use the verb "dancing" pretty loosely here.

They were a reflection of middle linebacker Mike Singletary, the "Samurai," who saw all with those bulging eyes that grew huge just before the play, like he was a cartoon character who had spotted an oncoming train.

They were a reflection of their quarterback Jim McMahon, a punky would-be rebel who dived headfirst for extra yards and constantly defied authority. The week after Commissioner Pete Rozelle fined him for wearing an Adidas headband, he wore a headband that read "Rozelle" instead.

They were a reflection of their 340-pound rookie defensive lineman, William "Refrigerator" Perry, a lovable soul who became a national sensation when Ditka lined him in the backfield as a running back in order to embarrass other teams.

They were a reflection of their already legendary running back, Walter Payton, who trained by running up giant hills and who ran for more yards than any player before him.

Maybe most of all, they were a reflection of their city, the Second City, the Windy City, the City of Big Shoulders. There had not been a great football team in Chicago—a truly great team—since Ditka himself was running over defenders like they were traffic cones. Desperation was as much a part of the city's constitution as deep-dish pizza. The '85 Bears were an answer to prayers. They didn't just want to win. They wanted to rule the world.

And they did rule, just as they promised. In the playoffs, they obliterated the Giants 21–0.

Then they shut out the Los Angeles Rams.

And then, finally, they humiliated New England 46–10 in the Super Bowl. The game wasn't even as close as the score. The Patriots, at some point, seemed interested only in surviving the game.

"We got our butts beat," a somewhat shell-shocked Patriots coach Raymond Berry said.

All these years later, the 1985 Bears endure . . . and you know a big reason why? It's that dumb song. "The Super Bowl Shuffle" went to No. 41 on the charts and sold more than 500,000 copies, even though it got little radio airplay. This was also in the heyday of MTV and music videos, and the astonishingly awkward video of the Bears dancing stays fresh in the mind. Believe it or not, at the 1987 Grammy Awards, the nominees for Best Rhythm & Blues Vocal Performance by a Duo or Group were:

- Prince & the Revolution for "Kiss"
- Sade for *Promise*
- Run-D.M.C. for *Raising Hell*
- Ashford & Simpson for *Real Love*
- Cameo for "Word Up!"
- And, yes, the Chicago Bears' Shufflin' Crew for "The Super Bowl Shuffle."

Prince, thankfully, won. But the Shuffle endures, much to the eternal chagrin of Steve McMichael. "I do appearances to this day," he wrote, "and people come up to me and say, 'Weren't you in the "Super Bowl Shuffle?"' I've got a Super Bowl ring on, and the thing they remember is that 'Super Bowl Shuffle.' I loathe it."

NO. 84:

DEVINE INTERVENTION

"I didn't realize that I would be such a heavy heavy."

—DAN DEVINE

——

NOVEMBER 8, 1975

Angelo Pizzo did not want to write the movie that ended up becoming *Rudy*. One, he'd already done the sports-movie thing. He had become a breakout writing star for a movie about a small-town Indiana basketball team beating the odds. That was *Hoosiers*.* So he didn't want to get typecast as someone who could write only small-town-underdog sports movies.

Two, he just didn't see the movie's potential. The story was fine. But he just didn't think that any studio would buy a film about Rudy Ruettiger walking on at Notre Dame.

That leads to the third thing: Pizzo grew up in Bloomington, Indiana. He *hated* Notre Dame.

Ah, but it happened anyway. Pizzo teamed up once again with college frat buddy David Anspaugh, this time to tell the story of Rudy Ruettiger, a glorious overachiever who grew up in Joliet, Illinois, as part of a family who lived and died Notre Dame football. Rudy would tell anyone who would listen—a number that grew smaller and smaller as the years went along—that he would go to Notre Dame and he would play on the football team. It made no sense to anybody else. He was small, slow, and a terrible student (largely because of his undiagnosed dyslexia) and, as such, did not seem to be Notre Dame football material.

---

* Hilariously, the studio despised the name *Hoosiers* and kept demanding that Pizzo and director David Anspaugh change it. Do you know what they wanted to call the movie? *One Last Shot.* Thank goodness Pizzo and Anspaugh held their ground.

Or as Pizzo wrote the line for Fortune, Rudy's mentor in the movie: "You're five feet nothing. One hundred and nothing. And you've got hardly a speck of athletic ability!"

Rudy made it to the Notre Dame football team despite all of that. He went to Holy Cross College for two years to get his grades up. He made the team as a walk-on when his hero Ara Parseghian* was still coaching. He endured practice after practice of getting bashed around by Notre Dame players who outweighed him by more than a hundred pounds.

"I was just a lost puppy out there," the real Rudy told a reporter in 1975. "[Offensive tackle] Steve Neece was the first guy to hit me, and he really laid me out. Everyone yelled, 'Get up, Rudy!' And I've been getting up ever since."

This part of the story was, relatively speaking, easy for Pizzo and Anspaugh to tell. Here was Rudy refusing to give up. Here was Rudy overcoming the odds. Here were a couple of gorgeous scenes of Notre Dame.† It all made movie sense.

But ... they needed a big finish. In real life, the crescendo came when Rudy was allowed to dress for the Georgia Tech game his senior year and then actually made it into the game, sacked the quarterback on the final play, and was carried off the field by his teammates.

The finish itself was glorious. Pizzo's storytelling problem was: It came too easy.

In movies, nothing can come that easy.

"When I'm translating a true story," Pizzo explained, "if I don't get to the letter of the truth, my goal is to get to the spirit of the truth."

And that's how Dan Devine became the bad guy in *Rudy*.

---

* In the movie, Parseghian is lovingly played by Jason Miller, who was best known for playing Father Damien in *The Exorcist* and for winning a Pulitzer Prize for his play *That Championship Season*.
† For the longest time, Notre Dame refused to let Anspaugh and company film *Rudy* on the campus. They had a standing policy. The Notre Dame people were perfectly content to have the celebratory *Knute Rockne, All American*—with Pat O'Brien and Ronald Reagan—be the only movie ever filmed on campus.

| | | | | |

DAN DEVINE KNEW HE WAS GOING TO BE THE BAD GUY—OR THE "heavy," as Pizzo described it. Devine was a hero in Rudy's real story. He had come to Notre Dame to replace Coach Parseghian, who had retired before Rudy's senior year. Devine was a more distant figure than Parseghian—as the movie shows, he often coached from a mobile tower high above the practice field—but he truly loved Rudy. While Parseghian was only vaguely aware of Rudy's presence ("Is that kid OK?" he would occasionally ask after Rudy had taken an especially hard hit), Devine would single Rudy out for praise because of his effort.

"Coach Devine noticed," Ruettiger wrote in his book *Rudy: My Story*. "There were a couple of times during practice when he gathered everyone around for a pep talk and brought up my name. 'I wish you guys had more heart, like Rudy.' . . . That embarrassed me. I was just doing my job."

In real life, Devine never considered not letting Rudy dress for the Georgia Tech game. He was the one who wanted to be sure that Rudy not only dressed but played. At one point, Devine was so desperate to put Rudy in the game, he considered using him on offense.

The trouble for the movie was: That didn't create enough drama. You can't have a big finish without a big lead-up. "It's not enough for the plot to go forward," screenwriter Blake Snyder wrote in *Save the Cat!* "It must go forward faster, and with more complexity, to the climax."

And so, Pizzo approached Devine and said: "This movie will only be a success if you agree to be the heavy."

Devine responded: "Anything for Rudy."

And like that, Devine became the bad guy of the story. In the movie, he is played by marvelously flinty Chelcie Ross, who also played the heavy in *Hoosiers*.* Ross plays it to the hilt. His Devine is distant and cold and

---

* In his diverse career, playing jerky sports people became Ross's specialty. He played Devine in *Rudy*, he played the unruly fan who tries to take over as coach in *Hoosiers*, he

very anti-Rudy. He refuses to let Rudy dress for the Georgia Tech game, prompting Rudy to briefly quit the team. In the movie, Rudy gets to dress only because his teammates march into Devine's office, one by one, and drape their jerseys on his desk in solidarity with Rudy. It is, unquestionably, a fantastic and touching movie scene. And it is made up.

Once he is dressed, Devine is adamant that Rudy does not play. This time it is only the crowd chanting, "Rudy! Rudy!" that makes him relent. Then, and only then, does Rudy go in, get his sack, and get carried off the field as stirring music plays and then the screen fades to black.

And the important thing to say is: It works. Pizzo's instincts were pitch-perfect. The ending creates chills. *Rudy* has become a movie classic. *Esquire* and *USA Today*, among others, called it the greatest football movie ever made. The American Film Institute named *Rudy* the fifty-fourth most inspirational movie ever made.

But what about Dan Devine? In the end, he did not take his character's hard turn well. Pizzo had sent him the script, but he didn't spend any time looking at it. Instead, he showed up at the premiere in St. Louis with his family. When his grandkids saw how their grandfather was portrayed, they cried.

Writer Vahe Gregorian was with Devine that day and said he spent the entire movie just being agitated. "Dan spent a lot of time grumbling, 'That never happened,'" he said.

Rudy expressed regret that Devine was hurt by the portrayal. Pizzo did too, but they believe the movie wouldn't have been as powerful otherwise. Dan Devine would stay friends with Rudy for the rest of his life. But he never did grow comfortable with the way he was portrayed in the movie.

"I didn't realize that I would be such a heavy heavy," he said.

---

played the religious spitball pitcher in *Major League*, AND he played a grumpy baseball scout in *Trouble with the Curve*. Ross is actually a sweet guy, and he was a three-sport star in high school.

NO. 83:

EMMITT IN MOTION

"I may win, and I may lose, but I will never be defeated."

—EMMITT SMITH

—

DECEMBER 21, 1992

Football fans don't have the obsessive attachment to statistics that baseball fans do. And so, few can tell you that Emmitt Smith had 18,355 career rushing yards. Baseball fans can tell you that Pete Rose had 4,256 hits. They can tell you that Cy Young had 511 wins. They can tell you Henry Aaron hit 755 home runs.*

But Emmitt's 18,355 yards? Almost nobody can summon that number off the top of their heads. And that's a shame too because it's well worth remembering. Emmitt's rushing record will never be broken.

Look at that number again. That's *eighteen* 1,000-yard seasons. Or perhaps an even more incomprehensible twelve 1,500-yard seasons. That's more yards than Earl Campbell and Terrell Davis had, combined. It's more yards than Larry Csonka plus Gale Sayers plus Lenny Moore. As I write this, no active running back has even 10,000 yards. The remarkable Derrick Henry has been running over defenders for eight years now; he's an extraordinary combination of power and speed.

Derrick Henry is barely halfway to Emmitt Smith's rushing record.

No, that record will never be broken, and yet, somehow, Emmitt Smith's particular greatness seems to be fading from memory. The legendary Cowboys executive Gil Brandt did not list Smith among his top

---

* Aaron's 755 home runs, as the baseball fans among you will know, are not the home run record; Barry Bonds broke it. And yet it's Aaron's 755 and Babe Ruth's 714 and even Willie Mays's 660 that endure forever in the memory of baseball fans.

ten running backs. While that's extreme, few people seem to remember him with awe the way they do with Jim Brown or Walter Payton or Smith's dazzling contemporary Barry Sanders.

I think there are two reasons why Emmitt Smith gets overlooked so often in conversations about the greatest running backs ever. One reason is that Emmitt's brilliance was made up of a thousand little things and so it was easy to miss the big picture. There are those who will say he was a product of a great offensive line, but the truth is, nobody ever set up blockers better. There are those who will say he benefited from having a Hall of Fame quarterback (Troy Aikman) and that's undoubtedly true, but Emmitt was a fantastic pass receiver and perhaps the best ever at picking up the blitz. He was the ultimate teammate. There are those who will say he put up big numbers by lasting a long time, but that's because he was the most indestructible running back ever.

The other reason is that—let's face it—Emmitt's brilliance was kind of boring. He set up his blockers, found his holes, fell forward to get every inch. He prepared like nobody else. He rushed for 164 touchdowns, more than anybody ever, but 114 of them were five yards or less.

Sure, Emmitt broke tackles and made moves and had his share of long runs. But did he leave people breathless? No, not often.

Well, there was this one time. Dallas was playing in Atlanta on a Monday night in 1992. It was late in the third quarter. Smith took the handoff and started to run up the middle, but he saw it clogged up. His instincts in such moments were unmatched.

Smith bounced to his right and began running outside. He then found himself running right at free safety Scott Case, one of the harder hitters in the game. Case thrust his shoulder into Smith, and at precisely that moment, Falcons' linebacker Darion Conner crashed into Smith's back. That combination propelled Smith into the waiting arms of Jessie Tuggle, the surest tackler in football. In 1992, Tuggle led the NFL in tackles for the third straight year.

Tuggle wrapped up Smith and began pushing him back. Atlanta's Jeff Donaldson and three other Falcons joined in on the fun to finish Smith off. "Every Falcon you could possibly imagine was there," Smith would say.

Only then, instead of going down, Smith simply let those Falcons move him into an open space, at which point he disengaged and ran free down the sideline. It was incredible. Near the end zone, Atlanta's Deion Sanders shoved him hard out-of-bounds, but Emmitt crossed the goal line anyway because Emmitt *always* crossed the goal line.

"Emmitt Smith," Al Michaels said up in the booth, "doing his best Barry Sanders impression."

Sigh. Even after his most thrilling run, Emmitt Smith was still trying to live up to Barry Sanders. So it goes. It was one of the most absurd runs in NFL history. My favorite part is that after the play, Dallas's Hall of Fame wide receiver Michael Irvin ran over to say, "That was the greatest play I've ever seen."

To which Emmitt, ever the perfect back, said, "You shouldn't have seen it. You should have been blocking Deion."

NO. 82:

ATWATER'S BEDTIME STORY

"Daddy! Tell us the Okoye story!"

—PARIS ATWATER

—

SEPTEMBER 17, 1990

When the boys were young, if they had been good and brushed their teeth and washed up and put on their pajamas without complaining or fighting, Steve Atwater would sit down with the three of them on the bed and begin:

"Once upon a time," he would say, "we were in Cover 2."

The boys would tremble with anticipation. This was their favorite story. It's no surprise that they would all go on to play football. Paris, just two then, would play in high school with his father coaching. Di Andre was four; he would play football at Princeton. Stephen Jr. was the eldest—he was six—and he would play football at Georgetown and, after that, become an NFL agent.

Sometimes, one of the boys would ask: "What's Cover 2?" And then Dad would go to the floor, and he would draw a Cover 2 defense on the carpet using his finger. The boys loved that, and they would cheer and scream until Mom, Letha, walked in and told everyone to calm down.

"It was late at night," Steve Atwater continued. He was one heck of a football player, Steve Atwater. He's in the Hall of Fame. He played safety, mostly for the Denver Broncos, and he became known for how hard he hit. He came upon that skill naturally: When he was in high school, he played quarterback, and he threw a lot of interceptions.

"A *lot* of interceptions," he reiterated.

He would get so mad about the interceptions that he would furiously chase after the defensive player and unload with everything he had, and soon he realized he liked hitting people more than he liked throwing interceptions.

Back to story time. Steve told the kids that it was a Monday night, and the Denver Broncos were playing the hated Kansas City Chiefs. ("Boo!" the kids would shout.) Atwater looked and saw that the running back lined up in the backfield was Christian Okoye, the Nigerian Nightmare.

If you are old enough, you are smiling now. Christian Okoye! He was 6-foot-1 and 260 pounds* and he wore shoulder pads roughly the size of Buicks. He did grow up in Nigeria and knew absolutely nothing about football when he came to America as a track sensation. He was an Olympic-level star in the discus and a college star in the shot put and hammer throw and long jump—imagine a 260-pound man flying through the air, and that will give you some idea of what a freakish athlete Okoye was.

It was inevitable that *someone* would ask him to play football. That someone turned out to be Jim Milhon, an associate professor of physical education at Azusa Pacific University. Milhon would say that the first time Okoye took a handoff (he was already twenty-four years old), he looked at the ball and said: "Very interesting but very impractical."

Still, Okoye took to football so quickly that the Chiefs drafted him in the second round in 1987, and two years later, he led the NFL in rushing. "Okoye," linebacker David Wyman would say, "was a frickin' monster."

And back to story time.

"I start backpedaling," Steve would say. "Then I saw them hand the ball off to Christian Okoye! The Nigerian Nightmare!" (The kids would shudder.) "And he comes running up the middle. And I start running toward him. And then . . ."

---

* Chiefs teammate Deron Cherry insisted that when Okoye stepped on the scale in full uniform, he weighed 300 pounds.

The kids readied themselves.

"And then . . ."

The kids bit their blankets.

"And then . . ."

The kids sat up in bed.

"BOOYAH!" Steve shouted as he grabbed his sons.

"BOOYAH!" the kids shouted as he jumped around in bed.

Booyah. The hit that Steve Atwater put on Christian Okoye still rings. Atwater came crashing in, leading with his shoulder, and the two men collided, and the sound was like a meteor hitting earth. Then, as NFL Hall of Famer Len Dawson said, "for the first time in his life, Christian Okoye went backwards."

"We could hear the hit from the sideline," Broncos legend John Elway would say.

"One of the best hits I've ever seen," said Bill Cowher, who was a Chiefs assistant then.

The hit became so famous that many would later believe that it essentially ended Okoye's career. This wasn't right. He ran for 1,000 yards the next year and made the Pro Bowl. In all, Okoye took all of it with good spirit—"He's such a nice guy," Atwater told me—but he was always just a little annoyed that the hit became such a thing.

"We played them twice a year, you know," Okoye would say. "They never show the hits I put on him."

Atwater smiled when asked about the hits he took from Okoye. Sure, they happened. But Steve Atwater wasn't about to tell those stories to his sons.

NO. 81:

THE 100-YARD PLAY

"My hobby is looking in the mirror. I'm impressed.
I'm impressed with what I see."

—MILT STEGALL

———

JULY 20, 2006

Milt Stegall was already a Canadian legend when the 100-yard play happened. He was a legend because of his play on the field—he would retire with the most receiving yards and touchdown catches in the Canadian Football League—but even more, he was a legend because, well, Milt Stegall just was a legend.

"I am the best-looking guy in Canada," he told the nation.

"I can make $10 jeans look like a million dollars," he told reporters.

"It's hard looking this pretty on TV," he told a television audience.

He told the *Leader Post* in Regina, Saskatchewan, that there are only six sure things in life. They are, in order:

1. **Death.**
2. **Taxes.**
3. **Trouble.**
4. **Milt Stegall is always going to look good.**
5. **Milt Stegall is always going to be on time.**
6. **Milt Stegall is always going to be in tip-top shape.**

What a beauty.

"Yeah," Stegall told me. "I had a pretty good time up there in Canada."

He didn't want to go to Canada. Stegall grew up in Cincinnati and dreamed only of playing in the NFL. And he did play in the NFL for a

short while, for his hometown Bengals, but after he got released, his
agent called and said a team in Canada had made him an offer.

"Which team?" he asked.

"Winnipeg," his agent said.

"What's a Winnipeg?" Stegall asked.

He remembers getting off the plane in Winnipeg, getting to the facil-
ity, being given a uniform and a helmet, and then being put into his
first game for the Winnipeg Blue Bombers against the Calgary Stam-
peders. He almost immediately caught his first touchdown pass.

That began not only the greatest receiving career in Canadian Football League history—Stegall would catch 147 touchdown passes, a CFL
record, and he is a member of the Canadian Football Hall of Fame—
but a love affair.

"It was the greatest time ever," Stegall says. "I really didn't enjoy my
time in the NFL. You would go out there knowing that every day might
be your last. But in Canada, man, it was so great. I lived in a house with
some fans. I didn't have any bills.

"I'd be surrounded by all these great guys who were so much fun.
There were no egos. And the fans were the best. They'd come up to me
on the street and just go, 'Hey, Milt Stegall! I love you.' There was this
lady who would bake cookies for every practice."

He loved every minute of it. But, yeah, he loved one moment most of
all, the play he still considers to be the greatest in all of football history. It happened in 2006, closer to the end of Stegall's career than to
the beginning, and Winnipeg trailed Edmonton 22–19 with four seconds left. The Blue Bombers had the ball on their own 10-yard line. You
perhaps know that in Canada the football field is 110 yards long—
midfield is the 55-yard line—so Winnipeg was literally 100 yards away
from the touchdown they needed.

There is no play you can design to go 100 yards. Nobody can throw
the ball anywhere far enough to even threaten a touchdown. So, all
Winnipeg quarterback Kevin Glenn could do was take the snap and,

with the blitz in his face, quickly throw the ball about 30 yards down-field to a streaking Milt Stegall.

There were two Edmonton defenders running with him.

And then, suddenly, there were none. Edmonton's Malcolm Frank went for the tackle, and he whiffed. In the process, he ran into his teammate Keyuo Craver. And they both fell down.

"It was like the Keystone Kops," Stegall says. "That was just bad defense. It's like I just happened to turn invisible."

Stegall ran the final 60 or so yards with no one even chasing him except for his teammate Chris Braswell. He scored after the clock expired. It is the only 100-yard last-second touchdown in football history, and it was the perfect crescendo for the career of Milt Stegall.

"When Chris hit me in the end zone, it's like he woke me up from a dream," Stegall says. "I thought, 'This can't be happening.' . . . Look, I'm going to be honest. I didn't run a great route. And I wasn't even thinking about winning the game. I was thinking, 'OK, this is pretty much over.' I don't care how optimistic you are. It's hard to think you have a chance when you are 100 yards away from pay dirt."

He laughs. "But sometimes," he says, "if you stay positive, things work out better than you could have ever dreamed."

NO. 80:

SAMMY BAUGH

"Sammy Baugh is the greatest forward passer football has ever seen."
—WILFRID SMITH

—

DECEMBER 12, 1937

*C*hicago Tribune sportswriter Wilfrid Smith wrote those words about Sammy Baugh being the greatest forward passer ever after Baugh's *sixth* NFL start. You would think that "greatest ever" might have been just a bit premature for a twenty-three-year-old rookie quarterback.

But Smith was only writing what everybody *already* knew to be true.

From the start, Slingin' Sammy Baugh was the greatest ever.

SAMMY BAUGH ESSENTIALLY INVENTED THE QUARTERBACK PO- sition. Before him, there was almost no passing. The football in those days was fat, hard to grip, inconvenient to throw. Teams essentially only threw the ball out of desperation or trickery. Baugh changed everything.

It's funny, his famous nickname, "Slingin' Sammy Baugh"—he didn't get that as a football player. He got the nickname going back to his childhood in Texas, because of his rifle arm as a third baseman. Hall of Fame baseball player Rogers Hornsby said Baugh had the best infield arm he ever saw.

But Baugh's obsession was football. When he was twelve, he started throwing footballs through a tire hanging in his backyard. That's a cliché now, but only because Sammy Baugh invented it. That year, the Green Bay Packers led the NFL with eight touchdown passes. Yes, *eight*. And we don't even know for sure who threw those eight because teams back then didn't have quarterbacks, and nobody bothered to keep track of who threw touchdown passes.

By the time Baugh retired, he had just about every NFL passing record—and some of those records would last for two decades. But it was more than the numbers, more than the passing. Baugh created the whole quarterback persona that would lead to Unitas and Namath and Staubach and Marino and Montana and Manning and Brady and Mahomes. His grace under pressure, his toughness in the pocket, his passing accuracy (he led the NFL in completion percentage eight times), his leadership on and off the field—the man was just the essence of quarterback cool.

How cool was he? Well, put it this way: When actor Robert Duvall was preparing for his now legendary role as a retired Texas Ranger in *Lonesome Dove*, he found himself struggling to get to the heart of the character.

A friend said, "Hey, I want you to meet somebody."

He introduced Duvall to Sammy Baugh.

"We talked for hours about football and his life," Duvall would say. "So that's where I got my gestures and everything. Watching Sammy Baugh."

THE CHAMPIONSHIP GAME OF 1937 MATCHING GEORGE HALAS'S Chicago Bears and George Preston Marshall's Washington Redskins— a nickname Marshall had personally chosen*—was played on a bitterly cold day at Chicago's Wrigley Field.

---

* In those days, pro football owners often gave their teams the same name as the baseball team. There were football teams through the years called the Brooklyn Dodgers, the Pittsburgh Pirates, the Cincinnati Reds, the Cleveland Indians, and, most famously, the New York Giants, usually called the New York Football Giants to differentiate them from the baseball team. Well, when Marshall founded his team in Boston in 1932, the National League baseball team in town was the Braves. So Marshall named his team the Braves too. The next year, on July 5, Marshall announced that he was changing the name

The Bears were the class of the NFL that year, with the legendary Bronko Nagurski still smashing away on both offense and defense. He was joined by Hall of Fame tough guys Joe Stydahar and Danny Fortmann. Halas gave all of them very specific orders for how he wanted them to defend Washington's pass-happy rookie quarterback.

"I want you to hit that son of a bitch until blood is coming out of his ears."

The Bears did indeed hit Baugh until he bled. The field was frozen solid—the players wore sneakers instead of cleats*—and Baugh was slammed into the hard ground repeatedly. Once on defense (everybody played both ways in those days), Baugh made the mistake of trying to take Nagurski head-on. The next thing he knew, he was being helped off the field by a trainer. "He plumb ran over me!" was the only thing Baugh could think to say.

Later still, Baugh was crushed by four Bears and got up with his hand bleeding and a shooting pain in his left hip. Shortly after that, the Bears—sensing weakness—twisted his leg after a play. Baugh could barely walk back to the sideline. The Bears led at halftime 14–7.

Baugh went into the locker room exhausted and battered and generally unexcited about returning to the frigid temperature to take more beatings.

But, you know, he was Sammy Baugh.

His third quarter still echoes through the years.

---

to the Redskins to avoid confusion. "Redskins and Braves are synonymous," the *Boston Globe* wrote in a short editorial approving the name. In 1937, the team moved to Washington.

* This was a leftover from the 1934 NFL Championship Game between the Bears and Giants. Chicago led by a touchdown going into halftime. In the locker room, the Giants end Ray Flaherty—the same Ray Flaherty who would coach Washington in the '37 Championship—suggested that the team might be better off wearing sneakers on the frozen field. The team sent a trainer to Manhattan College to grab every basketball sneaker he could find. The shoes made it to the stadium at the start of the fourth quarter. New York's players, who were getting much better traction with the sneakers, outscored Chicago 27–0 in the fourth quarter to win the title. The game has gone down in history as the "Sneakers Game."

"Baugh appeared, limping, his face bruised and bleeding," Jimmy Powers wrote in the *New York Daily News* the next day, "but his lips spread in an amiable grin. In the space of 12 heart-thumping minutes, Baugh proceeded to give an unbelievable exhibition. A Hollywood movie director would hesitate to write it into his script for fear of stretching the credulity of his audience."

In those twelve minutes, Baugh threw three remarkable touchdown passes. The first was a 55-yard pass to Wayne Millner, who was streaking over the middle. The pass was, in the words of one reporter, a "20-yard cobra strike," perfectly leading Millner, who sprinted the rest of the way for a touchdown.

The Washington defense held and Baugh and Millner connected again for a 78-yard touchdown pass. Once again, Baugh's throw hit Millner in stride, leaving Nagurski no chance to run Millner down from behind. That tied the game.

The Washington defense held again, and the final touchdown pass was some sleight-of-hand magic; Baugh got the ball and jumped in the air to make an apparent jump throw right to Millner. But it was a fake. The defense raced over, leaving Chug Justice (so named for the way he chugged along) wide-open on the left side. As soon as Baugh landed, he fired the ball across the field to Justice, who chugged unbothered the final 20 yards for what would be the winning touchdown.

Three touchdown passes in a single quarter? It was unheard-of. Impossible. The Cleveland Rams had thrown three touchdown passes *all season*.

"So accurate were [his passes] that a blind man could have caught them," Arthur Daley of the *New York Times* wrote.

"The greatest one-man exhibition in football history," the United Press wrote.

The Bears kept pummeling Baugh—Chicago's Dick Plasman actually punched him in the face at one point—but it did no good. Washington won the game. When Baugh limped off the field, he received a standing ovation and raucous cheers from Bears fans.

"You're a fine fella and a great quarterback," Nagurski told him as he offered a handshake.

When reporters raced over to Baugh to get a comment after the game, he grinned.

"Boy, I'll sure be glad to get back to Texas," he said. "I'd freeze to death up here."

NO. 79:

SWANN SONG

"I've always seen myself as put to music."

—LYNN SWANN

—

JANUARY 18, 1976

ynn Swann was not supposed to play in Super Bowl X. Two weeks
earlier, during a savage AFC Championship Game between Pittsburgh and Oakland, Swann was battered repeatedly by the Raiders'
bone-grinding defensive backs Jack Tatum and George Atkinson. On
what he counted as the fourth particularly vicious hit, this one delivered by Atkinson, Swann was knocked unconscious and taken to a
nearby hospital.

"There is a certain criminal element in every aspect of society," Steelers coach Chuck Noll had raged early in the season. "Apparently, we
have it in the NFL too."

All during Super Bowl week, doctors tried to dissuade Swann from
playing. Noll kept him out of practice. The Steelers' Super Bowl opponent, the Cowboys, tried to play mind games with him.

"I'm not going to hurt anyone intentionally," Dallas's Cliff Harris
said. "But getting hit again must be in the back of Swann's mind."

Yes, people were always underestimating Lynn Swann's toughness.
Part of it was that he just didn't look or act like a tough football player.
He certainly didn't look or act like anyone else on the ferocious Pitts-
burgh Steelers. This was the team of Mean Joe Greene, of the hard-
nosed Vietnam veteran Rocky Bleier, of the fanged linebacker Jack
Lambert,[*] and other such ruffians.

---

[*] Lambert was widely viewed as the most vicious player in the NFL. He had a huge gap
where his front teeth once were, and it made him look fanged and everybody called him

But there was a delicateness to Swann. He had grown up studying ballet and tap dancing and that was the spirit he brought to football.

"All the hard work in dance translates very well to football," he told Fred Rogers and America's children when he appeared on the kids' show *Mister Rogers' Neighborhood.*

Nobody else talked like that. Then again, nobody else played football with quite his grace, quite his finesse, quite his fluidity. Each Lynn Swann catch was like a song. The toughness was hidden beneath. Swann determined late in the week that he would play, and then he showed up at the Orange Bowl in Miami for the game and promptly took an hour nap on the locker room floor.

Then came the game. Swann caught only four passes. But with Lynn Swann—as the actor William Hurt once said about the size of an acting role—"quantity is not the point." Three of those four catches live forever.

The most important and perhaps least spectacular of the three was the last: a 64-yard lightning bolt from Terry Bradshaw after Swann raced behind Dallas defensive back Mark Washington. That was the touchdown that put away the game for Pittsburgh.

"It's just tough to cover a guy like Swann," Washington said glumly afterward.

The most graceful catch was probably the first one Swann made. In the first quarter, the Steelers had the ball at midfield and Bradshaw rifled a long throw down the right sideline. Swann looked to be out of position as Washington appeared to have him sealed off. Instead, Swann leaped up impossibly high off one foot—"That's called a jeté," Swann explained to Mister Rogers's television audience—and reached up and pulled the ball in. He then got both feet in bounds, displaying the tap-dancing expertise he had developed as a child.

"Count Dracula." On the field, he loved that persona. Off the field, however, he was quiet and a devoted bird-watcher.

Then there was the greatest catch of them all. It happened with a little less than three minutes left in the first half. Bradshaw dropped back and again fired the ball deep. Washington had ideal coverage. He leaped up with Swann—not quite as high as Swann, of course, but he timed the jump beautifully—and tipped the ball away.

Then Swann, as he was falling, maintained his balance and focus, followed the ball and reached out his left hand, pulled the ball toward him, and cradled it.

One game. Three all-time catches. And he did it in a Super Bowl after the Cowboys had spent all week trying to intimidate him.

"What do you have to say to Cliff Harris and the Cowboys?" a reporter asked.

"They can talk all day," he said. "My conversation is six points."

NO. 78:

SARACEN SAVES THE DAY

"Clear eyes. Full hearts. Can't lose."

—COACH ERIC TAYLOR

OCTOBER 3, 2006

*A*n admission: I didn't start watching the television series Friday Night Lights until I was almost finished with this book. I've read (more than once!) Buzz Bissinger's seminal book about the 1988 Permian High football team in Odessa, Texas. I watched the Friday Night Lights movie starring Billy Bob Thornton. I was engrossed in the true stories of Boobie Miles and Mike Winchell and Brian Chavez and all those kids—now fathers and even grandfathers—who played football under the intense light that shines on Texas high school football.

The television show? Nah. Well, it's fictional, and I've never thought football played very well as a fictional sport. Baseball? Sure. The Natural. Major League. Field of Dreams. Bull Durham. On and on. But football? Not so much. There're The Longest Yard and a couple of other decent stories but generally the power of football is that it's real. So I passed on the TV show until more than a decade after it went off the air.

That, as it turns out, was a big mistake. The show is great and we've now binged almost all of it.

After watching a few episodes, I realized (at almost the exact same time that my editor realized it) that Why We Love Football needed a Friday Night Lights chapter. Alas, I'm not at all qualified to write it. So I went to the only person I know who is qualified to write it, my friend Alan Sepinwall, Rolling Stone's television critic. Alan literally reviewed every single one of the seventy-six FNL episodes. I asked him to pick the single football moment that best captures this show and how it explains why we love football.

| | | | | |

MATT SARACEN WAS NOT SUPPOSED TO BE IN THE GAME. MATT
Saracen was never supposed to be in any games, really.

The old saying is that the backup quarterback is the most popular
guy in town. That never applied to Matt, not with him going to high
school in one of the most football-crazed towns in the most football-
crazed state in the union. No, in Dillon, Texas, all anyone could talk
about was Jason Street, the starting quarterback for their beloved Dillon Panthers. Street was like a god: tall, handsome, charismatic, lovable, and a deadly assassin with a football in his hands. Street was
destined to be the next Peyton Manning. He was so idolized that, going
into his senior season, the school gave the head coaching job to his personal mentor, Panthers offensive coordinator Eric Taylor, even though
many around town had serious doubts.

Everybody seemed to expect the opening game of the season to be an
easy victory lap for Street in front of the home fans, the ravenous college scouts, and members of Jason's extended family who flew in from
out of state to watch him play. Coach Taylor warned all week that the
Westerby Chaps weren't pushovers—the Chaps were fast and ran a lot
of tricky counterplays—but nobody wanted to hear that. Surely any
team with an offense built around Street, bruising fullback Tim Riggins, and slippery tailback Brian "Smash" Williams would dominate
the opposition all year, right?

Unfortunately, the overconfident Panthers had no answer for those
counters, nor for a furious Westerby pass rush. The Panthers were
down by 10 with six minutes left. This was supposed to be Jason Street
time, the heroic opportunity he'd been groomed for since birth.

Instead, Street picked the worst moment of his young life to throw a
wobbly pass. A Westerby player intercepted the ball and was in the
clear; the only thing between him and the game-clinching touchdown was Jason Street, who crashed into the defender and forced a

game-saving fumble. But he came in at a bad angle, went down, and did not—could not—get back up. A stunned silence filled the stadium. Members of the Dillon marching band nervously crossed their fingers in the air. Street's horrified mother ran out onto the field.

And a doctor told the EMTs that he believed this was a spinal cord fracture.

It was the nightmare scenario: the kind of thing that leaves you wondering why anyone would place their body and life at risk to play such a violent game. Street was indeed paralyzed. He would never play football again.

The game went on. Three minutes still remained on the clock. Suddenly all eyes turned to poor, terrified sophomore third-string quarterback Matt Saracen.*

He was, in the most obvious ways, the opposite of Jason Street: small, skinny, inarticulate. While Street had been raised to play football by loving parents in a stable home, Saracen's mother had walked out when he was little. His soldier father was overseas. Matt had been left to care for his aging grandmother. He seemed perpetually surprised to be on the football team at all, and he played so little that in a mortifying attempt to flirt with Coach Taylor's daughter Julie, the best he could offer was: "I hold extra points sometimes."

Now he was at the center of a football town's hopes and dreams. Things began as you might expect. On first down, Saracen got the play backward, tried handing the ball off to a player who wasn't there, and was crushed by a defender. On second down, he threw the ball off the helmet of one of his own linemen.

Coach Taylor called time-out. Taylor didn't always impress with his play calling or time management. But he knew how to motivate players.

---

* Who was the second-string quarterback? Why didn't he enter the game instead of Saracen? Like the unnamed right fielder in Abbott and Costello's "Who's on First?" routine, we don't know and are better off not asking.

And he instinctively knew that what Saracen needed was to tune out the pressure overwhelming him. "You look and see where the defense is and you see where our guys are," Taylor said, resorting to the most basic QB advice possible. "Then you throw it to our guys."

And Saracen did. On third and very long, he hit Smash Williams with a shovel pass, and the running back sliced through the defense for a first down. With less than a minute to go, Saracen pitched the ball to Smash, who leaped into the end zone. Then Tim Riggins—Street's best friend—recovered the onside kick. Dillon drove downfield desperately and, with seven seconds left, had time for one final play.

And in this moment, Matt Saracen—who could barely stand upright just a moment earlier—took the snap, eluded defenders like he was Eli Manning in the Super Bowl, and uncorked as pretty a deep pass as had ever been thrown within the Dillon town limits, including those by Jason Street himself. It fell perfectly to receiver Tony Golia, who had gotten behind the Westerby defense, and he scored as the clock ran out. The fans roared, and Saracen was enveloped by approving team-mates, who wouldn't have known his name a few hours earlier. Then Smash led the Panthers and Chaps in a prayer for Jason Street, because even this celebration couldn't ignore the terrible thing that had happened on the way to this improbable ending.

And there was everybody feeling every emotion—triumphant, devastated, hopeful, despondent—because this is what football, both real and imagined, means.

NO. 77:

THE BLUEGRASS MIRACLE

"It's just like a dream."

—LSU RECEIVER DEVERY HENDERSON

"I'll never get over it."

—KENTUCKY LINEBACKER RONNIE RILEY

—

NOVEMBER 9, 2002

Football, like all sports, comes down to perspective. So much of the joy and sorrow revolves around where you're from, how you grew up, where you're sitting, what you believe in.

Take a Saturday afternoon in Lexington, Kentucky. Louisiana State comes into the game ranked No. 16 in the country and features one of college football's best defenses. Kentucky comes into the game in the midst of a surprisingly happy season and features one of the best offenses in the country. The excitement builds.

Through three quarters, LSU seems to have the game in hand. They lead 24–14, and with their terrific defense, that seems insurmountable. But then Kentucky, led by their remarkable 300-pound quarterback, Jared Lorenzen—known lovingly as the "Hefty Lefty" and the "Pillsbury Throwboy"—begins a stirring comeback. He throws two touchdown passes, both to receiver Aaron Boone, and then in the final minutes pushes Kentucky on what looks like the game-winning drive.

On second and 1 from the LSU 13 and only seconds remaining, Lorenzen reminds everybody in the huddle: "If we get the first down here, do not call time-out until the clock is all the way down close to zero."

Lorenzen gets the first down. But then one of the Kentucky linemen— nobody will ever say who it is—calls Kentucky's last time-out with fifteen seconds left. It's one of those errors that shouldn't mean any-thing; Kentucky's Taylor makes the 29-yard field goal and the Wildcats have the lead with only eleven seconds left.

What can a team do with 11 seconds anyway?

Ah, but you already know, don't you? LSU moves the ball to their own 25 with two seconds left. Their quarterback Marcus Randall certainly does not have the arm to throw the ball the necessary 75 yards for a Hail Mary. The game is over.

This is when the Kentucky players dump Gatorade on their coach Guy Morriss to celebrate victory.

LSU coach Nick Saban and his offensive coordinator, Jimbo Fisher, agree on their play: "Dash Right 93 Berlin."

A soaked Morriss and his coaches agree on their defense—named "Victory"—which only demands that players knock the ball down.

LSU quarterback Marcus Randall rolls out to his right and throws the ball as far as he can. The ball spirals 60 yards in the air—Randall will later say it is the farthest he's ever thrown a football—but still not nearly far enough.

With the ball still in flight, scores of Kentucky fans storm the field to celebrate. Some climb the goalpost.

On the other side of the field, the ball comes down. Kentucky defen-sive back Quentus Cumby tries to catch it and the ball bounces off his hands and up in the air. Linebacker Morris Lane tries to knock the ball to the ground, but he misses. Defensive back Earven Flowers has his shot, and the ball deflects off his hands too.

Then the ball hops into the arms of LSU receiver Devery Henderson.

"I don't know," Henderson will say. "I just kind of looked up and the ball was in my hands. We run the play in practice, but it doesn't work like that."

No. Gravity doesn't work like that. Logic doesn't work like that. Hen-derson grabs the ball and sprints for his end zone and victory while Kentucky fans celebrate in the other.

So what is this thing? Is it the Bluegrass Miracle?

"Hail Tigers!" is the headline in the Baton Rouge paper.

Or is it, as Lorenzen tells reporters afterward, a part of a long-standing bit of voodoo that has long tormented the Wildcats?

"CAT-atstrophe" is the headline in Louisville.

This is football. It is ecstasy and it is pain, and it all depends on which end zone you happen to be standing in when fate calls.

NO. 76:

WHITNEY'S ANTHEM

"It was hope. We needed hope, you know?"

—WHITNEY HOUSTON

—

JANUARY 27, 1991

The night before Super Bowl XXV in Tampa, Al Michaels and his ABC broadcasting partners, Frank Gifford and Dan Dierdorf, were summoned to an unexpected meeting. They got into a hotel conference room and were greeted by members of the Secret Service and a SWAT team.

And they were instructed on how to act should they be taken hostage.

"I mean, hostages?" Michaels would say. "Us? Broadcasters taken hostage?"

This was the panicked scene before that Super Bowl between the Buffalo Bills and New York Giants, a decade before 9/11, long before Americans had grown used to taking off their shoes at airport security and emptying their pockets at games and accepting that real danger lurked.

Ten days before the game, a coalition of nations led by America began a military campaign to force Iraq to withdraw from neighboring Kuwait. It was the United States' first major military campaign since the Vietnam War. The threat of terrorism felt more real than it had in many years.

Things were especially tense around the Super Bowl. People had long imagined the Super Bowl at the center of a dangerous crisis. In the mid-1970s, not one but two different movies—*Two-Minute Warning* with Charlton Heston and *Black Sunday* with Robert Shaw—had built their plots around Super Bowl terrorist attacks.

"Black Sunday," the movie poster warned. "It could be tomorrow!"

Now the threats felt very real. The Goodyear Blimp was grounded. Military aircraft hovered over the stadium. Metal detectors and bomb-sniffing dogs were at every entrance. Concrete barriers were built and placed around the stadium to direct people away from open spaces. People were warned to leave their beepers at home.*

The Commissioner's Super Bowl Party, always one of the biggest events of Super Bowl Week, was canceled.

The commissioner himself, Paul Tagliabue, came to the game in a bulletproof flak jacket.

"We'd never seen anything like that," Michaels says. "Now it's normal. But back then it all felt stressful. I remember it was a gloomy day. And there was a strange feeling in the crowd because of what was going on in the world. I mean, we were at war."

Moments before the game, Gifford's voice rang through the stadium: "And now to honor America—especially the brave men and women serving our nation in the Persian Gulf and throughout the world—please join in the singing of our national anthem."

Cheering began. Cheering and flag-waving and more cheering.

Gifford said that there would be a flyover of F-16 jets. More cheering. He said that the anthem would be performed by the Florida Orchestra. More flag-waving.

Then Gifford said: "And sung by Grammy Award winner Whitney Houston."

She was twenty-seven years old then and at the height of her super-powers. The Super Bowl national anthem had not always been a star attraction. Leslie Easterbrook, who had played Rhonda Lee on the television show *Laverne & Shirley*, sang it one year. So did Cheryl Ladd, who had replaced Farrah Fawcett on *Charlie's Angels*. An a cappella group

---

* For the kids out there, in olden times such as 1991, very few people had cell phones. Instead, people carried around beepers, those marvels of technology that would allow callers to "beep" them with a return phone number. The person beeped would then have to find a pay phone to return the call. I can explain the concept of "pay phones" later.

from Colgate University sang it one year and seventy-year-old big band singer Helen O'Connell sang it another. In 1978, a student at Southeastern Louisiana University, Phyllis Kelly, was chosen to sing.

Even by 1991, though, the Super Bowl was the biggest thing in America, and every part of it had to be big. No one was bigger than Whitney Houston.* She wore a white track outfit and raised her arms to the crowd. And then she began.

It would later come out that the song was prerecorded. The Super Bowl production people did not think it possible for Houston to sing it live with the roar of the crowd coming at her. Houston sang into a dead microphone while her recording played.

"O say can you see . . ." she began in that unparalleled voice of hers. She had chosen a slower rhythm. It would later be revealed there were some Super Bowl officials who thought it was TOO slow and asked her to rerecord it, which she thankfully did not do. The pace was exactly right for the moment.

All around the stadium, people waved their flags and sang along as she worked through the early part of the song. And then she hit the crescendo—"And the rocket's red glare!"—and everyone seemed to be lifted a foot off the ground. As she moved for the big finish—"O say does that star-spangled banner yet wave?"—people were crying and singing at the tops of their voices.

In bars across America, patrons chanted, "USA! USA!"

In less than two minutes—one minute and fifty-six seconds to be exact[†] —she had transfixed and inspired the nation. She didn't know it then, of course. She went up to a luxury box and watched the game.

---

[*] After Houston, pretty much ALL the pop super divas had to sing the anthem—Beyoncé, Cher, Mariah Carey, Jennifer Hudson, Lady Gaga, etc.

[†] Paul Zimmerman, *Sports Illustrated*'s legendary football writer, used to meticulously time the national anthem before every game. He said the slowest he ever recorded was by Pearl Bailey before a World Series game in 1978. She extended the song to two minutes and twenty-eight seconds.

"It wasn't until a day or two later," she said, "that I realized the whole country was in an uproar." Radio stations across America were asking for a copy of the song to play for their listeners. Three days later, the Associated Press wrote a story that ran across the country under headlines like "Houston's 'Star-Spangled Banner' a Smash Hit."

Soon after that, the song was released as a single—with proceeds going to the Red Cross. It rose to No. 20 on the charts. This is the only time a recording of the national anthem has been a top-twenty hit. Pro football has long intertwined itself with American patriotism, sometimes with cringeworthy results. But this was a time when a voice rose to the circumstances and gave the country exactly what it needed.

"In the stadium, I could see the fear, the hope, the intensity, the prayers going up, you know?" Houston would say about that day. "And I just felt like: This is the moment."

NO. 75:

THE ART OF DEVIN HESTER

"I'd like to say that the best art on a football
field happens during kickoff returns."

—WRITER KEVIN SAMPSELL

—

FEBRUARY 4, 2007

Kick returns are chaos. How can they be anything but chaos? On one side, you have a kicker plus ten kamikazes tearing down the field as fast as they can on a seek-and-destroy mission. On the other side, you have a returner plus ten would-be blockers hoping to get in somebody's way without committing one of the countless felonies and misdemeanors that officials frown upon. It's a jumble, a mess, a gallery of yellow flags and injured players and deafening collisions.

This is what made Devin Hester so wonderful.

He didn't just bring order to the chaos. He made it all look so easy.

The easy part makes no sense at all. When you look back on Hester's record 20 punt- and kickoff-return touchdowns—6 more than anyone else—you would expect to see an abundance of jaw-dropping cuts, broken tackles, and hypnotizing dance moves. That's how everyone else tries to return kicks.

But not Hester. What boggles the mind, as you watch his many touchdown returns one after another after another, is how rarely he was even touched. How few moves he had to make. Oh, sure, now and again, when absolutely necessary, he'd show you a Gale Sayers lateral cut or a Billy "White Shoes" Johnson feint or he'd gracefully leap over a player sprawled on the ground.

But most of the time, he did something even more remarkable: He'd just run into the clear. One move. One miss. He was gone. He'd turn a twenty-two-car pileup into open highway. You know how in movies sometimes they will show a couple dancing for the first time and the power of their emerging love makes everyone else on the dance floor disappear? That's how it was with Hester. Somehow, through speed and vision and an inexpressible genius, he'd make everyone else just disappear.

The Indianapolis Colts knew all about Devin Hester's sorcery going into Super Bowl XLI against the Bears. Hester had led the NFL both in punt-return touchdowns and kickoff-return touchdowns in 2006 as a rookie. Before the game, Colts special teams coach Russ Purnell admitted that he hadn't really been sleeping.

"The Colts," *Indianapolis Star* columnist Bob Kravitz wrote, "would be insane to kick or punt to Devin Hester."

And then, to start the game, they kicked off to Devin Hester anyway.

"As men," Colts' safety Antoine Bethea told NFL Films, "guys said, 'You're not going to do that against us. We're going to kick him the ball.'"

Kicker Adam Vinatieri did kick the ball to his right in an effort to box in Hester. That sort of strategy worked against mortals. But Hester drifted to his left, caught the kickoff, and started for the other side of the field. He made one cut left to avoid rookie linebacker Tyjuan Hagler. He made one cut right to avoid Marlin Jackson.

And he was free.

Free, for 80 yards, Hester alone on the stage. The last 20 yards, he looked at the jumbotron and watched himself run. "I didn't see anybody there," Hester would say, "and I thought, 'I can't believe this. This is exactly what I had envisioned.'"

It's the only opening-kickoff touchdown return in Super Bowl history.

"After that, on the sideline," Bethea said, "everyone was like 'Don't kick it to that man.'"

NO. 74:

RUN, LINDSAY!

"I broke my chair. I came right through a chair.
A metal steel chair with about a five-inch cushion."

—LARRY MUNSON

——

NOVEMBER 8, 1980

College football broadcasters have all the fun. In Texas, Wally Pryor would often interrupt his radio calls of Longhorns' college football games with fun emergency updates of what was happening at Slippery Rock University's games, even though nobody in the whole state of Texas listening had ever even heard of Slippery Rock University.

Bob Ufer used to honk a horn after every Michigan touchdown—a horn, he said, that had been on George Patton's jeep during World War II.

In North Carolina, whenever the Tar Heels found themselves in dire circumstances, Woody Durham would implore fans to "go where you go and do what you do" to bring them luck.

When games kicked off at Tennessee, John Ward shouted, "It's football time in Tennessee!" When Iowa made a brilliant play, Jim Zabel said, "Hug and kiss those radios, folks!" In Alabama, Eli Gold became so beloved—"Touchdown Alabama!" is his trademark call—that he was inducted into the Alabama Sports Hall of Fame—an unlikely outcome, he said, for a "Jewish kid from Brooklyn with zero athletic talent."

Perhaps no sports broadcasters are more beloved than college football broadcasters.

And none were more beloved than Georgia broadcaster Larry Munson.

I am not and never have been a Georgia fan. But Larry Munson fills my heart anyway. He was the radio voice of the Bulldogs from 1966 to 2018. For forty-two years he spoke directly and entirely to Georgia fans. The Bulldogs were "we." The opponents were "the other guys." The odds were always against our heroes. Hope was all but gone. The end was nigh.

And when the good guys somehow won anyway, well, Munson's call of Kevin Butler's 60-yard field goal attempt to beat Clemson in 1984 is pretty representative:

"The clock is at seventeen seconds. So, we'll try to kick one 100,000 miles. We're holding it on our own 49 and a half. Gonna try to kick it 60 yards and a half—and Butler kicked a long one, a long one. OH MY GOD! OH MY GOD! [Long pause.] The stadium is worse than bonkers! Eleven seconds. I can't believe what he did! This is ungodly!"

Worse than bonkers. For a time, I worked in Georgia and with friends used to recite our favorite Munson lines. There was Herschel Walker's first touchdown when he ran over at least three Tennessee players: "My God, a freshman!"

There was the time in 1982 when Auburn was threatening late and Munson beseeched the defense to hold ("I know I'm asking a lot, you guys," he pleaded, "but hunker it down one more time!"), and they did hold to secure a Sugar Bowl bid:

"Look at the sugar falling out of the sky!" he shouted.

There was the time in '81 when Georgia beat Tennessee in the final minute. "We just stepped on their face with a hobnail boot and broke their nose!" he said.

Most of all, though, there was "Run, Lindsay." This was 1980, Georgia versus Florida, a stormy rivalry that *Florida Times-Union* sports editor Bill Kastelz called the "World's Largest Outdoor Cocktail Party." Georgia was No. 2 in the country and thinking national championship but trailed Florida by a point with less than two minutes left. The Bulldogs were on their own 7-yard line and facing third down and 11. These were the Bulldogs of Vince Dooley, which meant they threw the ball only in case of emergencies and often not even then. Georgia quarterback Buck Belue had completed six passes all day. His season per-game average was seven.

Now, though, it was an emergency situation and Belue dropped into the end zone and was chased to his right. He wasn't trying for a big play; he just wanted a first down. He flung the ball over the middle to a receiver named Lindsay Scott. Scott caught the ball, looked around, and thought, *Why is nobody here?*

Nobody was there. Two Florida defenders tried to close in, but Scott pulled away from them. He outran two more Florida defenders and went 93 yards for the score and Georgia went on to win the national championship and the rest, well, the rest is Larry Munson.

"And he's got 45, 50, and he's got 45, 40—run, Lindsay!—25, 20, 15, 10, 5, Lindsay Scott! Lindsay Scott! Lindsay Scott! [Pause.] Well, I can't believe it. Ninety-two yards and Lindsay really got in a footrace, and I broke my chair. I went right through a chair, a metal steel chair, with about a five-inch cushion. I broke it. The booth came apart! The stadium? Well, the stadium fell down. They'll have to rebuild it now.

"This is incredible! You know this game has always been called the 'World's Greatest Cocktail Party.' Do you know what is going to happen here tonight? And up at St. Simons? And Jekyll Island? And all those places where all those dog people have got those condominiums for four days? Man, is there going to be some property destroyed tonight!"

NO. 73:

THE TIP

"Don't you ever talk about me!"

—RICHARD SHERMAN

—

JANUARY 19, 2014

When Richard Sherman played Pop Warner football in Compton, California, his brother and best friend, Branton, loved to wind him up by saying that he heard opposing players talking smack about him.

"That guy there says you can't play," Branton would say.

"Yeah?" Richard shouted.

"I heard that guy talking about how he was going to crush you today," Branton would say.

"Yeah?" Richard shouted.

Richard Sherman would get so angry, so impossibly angry, he couldn't even describe the feeling. "Yeah?" he'd say. "I'll score *10* touchdowns and show him."

Yep. He would score 10 touchdowns. One or 2 or 8 wouldn't be nearly enough.

ON THE LAST PLAY THAT MATTERED IN THE 2013 NFC CHAMPIonship Game between San Francisco and Seattle, the 49ers had the ball at the Seahawks' 18. Seattle led by 6. There were thirty seconds left. A San Francisco touchdown would win it.

As 49ers quarterback Colin Kaepernick prepared for the snap, he glanced right and saw Michael Crabtree covered by only one man. Crabtree was an athletic marvel, a receiver who should have been able to win against one-on-one coverage pretty much every time. Kaepernick knew his target.

"I had a one-on-one matchup with Crabtree," he would say. "I'll take that anytime."

Ah, but that wasn't an ordinary man lined up against Crabtree. It was a trash-talking, ball-hawking,* coverage-locking, always mocking, receiver-stalking All-Pro cornerback named Richard Sherman. And there is nothing in the world that Sherman wanted more in that moment—more than riches, more than jewels—than to have Colin Kaepernick throw the ball his way.

"They hadn't come at me all day long," he would say. He hated how quarterbacks avoided him week after week. He would *plead* with them. "Give me a chance!" he'd shout during press conferences.

Of course, the one thing he hated more than quarterbacks avoiding him was quarterbacks challenging him. "What are you doing throwing at the best?" he'd taunt.

"Throw it my way," he'd hope.

"Don't you dare throw it my way," Sherman warned.

Kaepernick dropped back and looked for Crabtree all the way. He threw the ball high, hoping that Crabtree would rise higher and make the catch. But it was Sherman who rose. He thought that he had an interception. "I already had the celebration in my head," he would write in the Players' Tribune.

But as Sherman rose up, he felt a push in his back. That moved him out of position. Suddenly, it looked like Crabtree might make the catch after all.

---

* "Ball hawk"—meaning a player particularly skilled at intercepting the ball—is an expression that goes back in football to at least the early 1920s. It has also been used in basketball, and even in baseball to describe a particularly good outfielder, but it is a most evocative image in football, where you can imagine great ball hawks (from Emlen Tunnell to Paul Krause to Richard Sherman) being actual hawks swooping in to steal away the football.

Instead, Sherman contorted his body and reached back with his left hand, tipping the ball back toward the field. His teammate Malcolm Smith was there; he cradled the ball and fell to the ground. The Seahawks were going to the Super Bowl.

The instant the game was over, sideline reporter Erin Andrews raced over to Sherman, and the two embraced.

Their on-camera exchange is now football history.

> **Andrews:** "Richard, let me ask you: The final play, take me through it."
>
> **Sherman [fuming]:** "I'm the best corner in the game! When you try me with a sorry receiver like Crabtree, that's the result you're gonna get! [Looking into camera.] Don't you ever talk about me!"
>
> **Andrews:** "Who was talking about you?"
>
> **Sherman:** "Crabtree! Don't you open your mouth about the best! Or I'm gonna shut it for you real quick. LOB!"
> [Which stands for "Legions of Boom," the Seattle defense's self-designed nickname.]

Sherman then stormed off before Andrews could ask another question.

He never really clarified what he meant, never specified what Crabtree had or had not said. There was no need. His outburst was all anyone could talk about for a while. Some thought it classless, others thought it refreshingly authentic, but Sherman himself shrugged. He might have preferred scoring 10 touchdowns. But the tip worked too.

NO. 72:

GARO'S GAFFE

"I was throwing to somebody, yes.
I don't remember the guy's number."

—GARO YEPREMIAN

—

JANUARY 14, 1973

Remember a few chapters ago when I wrote that the Butt Fumble was the second-funniest play in football history?* Well, here is your payoff:

Garo's Gaffe is *the* funniest football play ever.

The play happened in Super Bowl VII, Miami versus Washington. That was the Dolphins' perfect season, the year they went 17-0, the very pinnacle of football flawlessness. They led Washington 14–0 with 2:38 left, and coach Don Shula sent out kicker Garo Yepremian to kick a 42-yard field goal that would put the game on ice.

What can you say about Garo Yepremian? He was 5-foot-8, 148 pounds, balding, left-footed, optimistic, and utterly lovable. The first American football game he ever saw was one he played in. His onetime Lions teammate Alex Karras insisted he would run on the field shouting, "I keek a touchdown!"

Garo grew up on Cyprus as a soccer and tennis player.† You know how he became a kicker? His older brother, Krikor, was the captain of the

---

* I'm assuming here that you are reading this book in order, which you very well might not be doing. There is no right or wrong way to read this book, so if you just happened to turn to this chapter or if you are reading all the even-numbered chapters first or whatever, the only thing you need to know is that a few chapters ago, I wrote that the Butt Fumble was the second-funniest play ever. There's nothing else to catch up on.
† Yepremian also played the piano and spoke four languages.

1963 Indiana University soccer team, and he saw a football game and was stupefied by how Americans kicked. Everybody kicked straight on. It was ridiculous to him. There wasn't a single soccer-style kicker in professional football then.*

Krikor thought, *Hey, my younger brother kicks better than these guys do.*

So he sent for his younger brother, Garo. Garo couldn't play college football because he had not graduated from high school, but they let him kick a few at Butler University, and in one of those practices, he made eighteen of nineteen field goals from 55 yards out.

Understand, at that time, the NFL record for longest field goal was 56 yards.

And like that, he became an NFL kicker. Several teams tried to sign him. During his tryout with Detroit, the Lions had several of their biggest linemen come out and try to block Garo's kicks.

"They don't scare me," Yepremian said. "I'm too quick. They won't be able to find me."

The Lions signed him, and he was an immediate sensation. In one game against Minnesota, he kicked what was then a record six field goals.† Then he went to the Dolphins and was even better. In 1972, that season, Yepremian kicked 50-plus-yard field goals against Minnesota and Buffalo, providing the winning margin in both games.

OK, so Yepremian went out there to ice the game. He kicked the ball . . . and it was blocked by Washington's Bill Brundige. It started bouncing around. And Garo instinctively went to chase after it. The ball bounced up into his hands as if it recognized him.

And then, well, I guess you could say Garo tried to throw it. But that

---

* The first to kick field goals soccer-style in the NFL was Hungarian native Pete Gogolak in 1964 and then his brother, Charlie. Until they came around, everybody kicked toe first, so much so that the most famous kicker of them all, Lou Groza, was actually nicknamed "the Toe."

† In 2007, a kicker named Rob Bironas made *eight* field goals for the Tennessee Titans in their 38–36 victory over the Houston Texans.

verb "throw" doesn't really do justice to what happened because (1) he didn't actually have a grip on the ball, (2) the ball didn't go anywhere, and (3) there wasn't anyone around to catch it even if he had thrown it.

What happened instead is that the ball popped straight up in the air about a foot, like a wet bottle rocket, and then Garo tried to catch it again but instead punched it up even higher in the air volleyball-style. At this point, Washington's Mike Bass ran over, plucked the ball out of the air, and ran 49 yards for a touchdown.

How funny is that play? Well, Don Shula—who hardly struck anybody as a connoisseur of great comedy—said that he never tired of watching the play.

And it happened to *his team*.

There are a couple of other reasons, beyond the obvious ones, why this play is the funniest ever. The first reason is the Dolphins won the game. If they had somehow lost the game, it wouldn't be funny. It would be tragic. If the Dolphins had lost, the ever-delightful Garo—"Whether it's snowing, raining or cloudy, to me it's always a gorgeous day," he likes to say—would have been the forever villain and that would have been awful.

But the Dolphins won the game and went undefeated, and Garo became something of a hero.

"Teammates," he says, "are kind of jealous that I get so much attention."

The other reason I think it's the funniest ever is that Garo's Gaffe is the most memorable of the Dolphins' perfect season. Without it, that season lacks life, lacks color. Those Dolphins were great but in the most boring and leaden way imaginable. Their defense was literally called the "No-Name Defense." They won by being solid and sterile, making no mistakes, taking no unnecessary chances, winning close games. Before Garo, that Super Bowl was well on its way to becoming the most boring one ever.

Then Garo's kick got blocked, he chased after it, he tried to throw, that went poorly, and the Gaffe has made people laugh for fifty years. It will make people laugh for the next fifty years too. It's timeless. And it's also a marvelously choreographed representation of Stephen Hawking's famous line: "One of the basic rules of the universe is that nothing is perfect."*

---

* When speaking of perfection, it's worth mentioning that had Garo's Gaffe not happened, the Dolphins would have won the game 17–0 to finish their season at 17-0.

NO. 71:

THE WINNING TOUCHDOWN

"Everybody was on the same team."

—LIZ PORTER

—

OCTOBER 18, 2002

Sometimes, you get lucky. Just before Halloween in 2002, an email arrived in my inbox from Ohio about a high school football game in a rural community called McDermott, a hundred miles east of Cincinnati. I wrote about the game, even though I was in Kansas City at the time, because it seemed a story worth telling.

In the next weeks and months, that game would make it around the country. *Sports Illustrated*'s back-page columnist Rick Reilly wrote a story about it titled "Play of the Year." All the morning news shows featured it. The people in the story would have brief but memorable brushes with fame. They were honored at bowl games and award banquets. They received gifts. A song was written about the game. Screenplays were written. That game became the centerpiece of a thousand sermons in churches and synagogues across the country.

I didn't write the story expecting any of that. All I remember was reading that email and crying happily.

The story goes like so:

At Northwest High School, in a small Ohio town called McDermott, there was a student named Jake Porter. Everybody loved Jake because he was always so positive, always so optimistic, always so full of life. Jake had a genetic disease called Chromosomal Fragile X syndrome, which made learning difficult. Each day, he would practice writing his name.

Sometimes, when he would get frustrated trying to write his name, his teacher would say, "Jake, you have to write your name. What if people want your autograph?"

Jake liked that. He was on the football team and track team and basketball team at Northwest. His teammates helped him a lot, helped him tie his shoes and put on his pads. He helped them too. Once, at the end of a basketball tournament, he watched another team cut down the nets in celebration, and he wanted to know why Northwest wasn't allowed to cut down the nets after a victory.

They explained to him that some games are more important than others.

Jake wouldn't believe that. All games are important, he said.

That was something to think about.

At the end of the season, the Northwest football coach Dave Frantz came up with an idea: He wanted Jake to actually play in the game. Well, Northwest's last game against the season was against Waverly, a team having its best season in years, and Dave was honest enough with himself to know that the game wouldn't be close. So he came up with the idea that Jake would come into the game late, they would hand him the ball, and he'd take a knee. It seemed a great way to reward him for coming to practice every day, for all his hard work, and for his perpetually sunny point of view. All the guys on the team wanted it to happen.

Dave called up Waverly's new coach, Derek Dewitt, and told him the plan. Derek, a tough football player from Los Angeles who had brought a new attitude to Waverly football, indicated that would be fine.

The day of the game came. Nobody at all was surprised that Waverly took a 42–0 lead. With a few seconds left, Dave Frantz called time-out. He was ready to put Jake into the game. Only then, Dewitt called him out to the middle of the field. Nobody knew what was happening. Jake's mother, Liz, was working the concession stand and she wondered if someone had gotten hurt. The others watched as the two coaches talked, each one shaking his head as if they were having some sort of disagreement.

And then Dave Frantz returned to the sidelines, called Jake over, and said, "You're in the game!" They had named the play "84 Iso." Jake knew he was going to get the ball and he was going to take a knee.

Then came the snap. The ball was handed to Jake. He did not go all the way down to one knee but instead just sort of curtsied. He was ready to give the ball back to the official or anyone else, but nobody came to get the ball. Instead, Jake looked up and saw his teammates lined up.

They were pointing to the end zone.

Then he looked over at the Waverly players.

They also were pointing to the end zone.

"Run, Jake!" they yelled, and he started to run, 50 yards in all, escorted by his teammates and by his opponents—though, at this point, what difference was there? "There weren't two teams out there," Liz Porter would tell me. "Everybody was on the same team."

When Jake scored the touchdown, he raised his arm in triumph. "It was like the Rose Bowl," Derek Dewitt would say. The reason he had been shaking his head was that he had told Dave Frantz that he wanted to let Jake score, his whole team wanted to let Jake score. Dave had protested, but Derek insisted.

"Look, I'm no hero. Jake is the hero," he would say later when the attention grew around him and everybody wanted to interview him and get inside his head. He received so much mail, so many calls, even a few critical ones saying he'd broken a principle of sport by letting Jake score.

"I feel sorry for those people," he said. "There's so much hate in the world. . . . But this, well, this was bigger than hate."

In the stands, people broke down in happy tears. Kids pretended to be Jake Porter. He loved it. For weeks after, he too did interview after interview, and he never grew tired of it. He also signed more than a few autographs. Then he rejoined the basketball team, went back to his classes, and would spend a couple hours every day helping out the custodian.

"It didn't change him," his mother said. "He's still just Jake."

When I wrote the story the first time, all those years ago, I ended it this way:

"To this day, Jake Porter is sure he scored the winning touchdown in that game against Waverly. And you know what? He did."

NO. 70:

WALTER PAYTON

"You have to believe in love. It's the way of life."

—WALTER PAYTON

—

NOVEMBER 13, 1977

No single play can capture the essence of Walter Jerry Payton, the man everyone called "Sweetness." He was the most complete player, surely, who ever lived. He could play running back, quarterback, receiver, tight end, kicker, punter, safety, and just about any other position.

Eleven Walter Paytons undoubtedly would beat eleven clones of anybody else.

What does it mean to be that complete a player? Well, just listen to what Jim Brown said about him as a runner:

"He fought for every inch. He twisted and turned and knocked guys over, went around them and accelerated.... First time I saw him, I said: 'Oh my goodness, what kind of animal is this? What kind of guy is this? All those moves. All that strength and tenacity.' That was it. I didn't have to see any more."

What about Walter Payton as a blocker? In September of 1985, in a game against the Vikings, quarterback Jim McMahon wanted to try a quick screen pass. Unfortunately, the Vikings had called the perfect defense: Linebacker Dennis Johnson blasted right up the middle on a blitz and was, in the words of Bears coach Mike Ditka, "about to kill McMahon."

Only then Walter Payton swooped in and blasted Johnson with a block, knocked him out of the television picture even though Johnson outweighed him by 35 pounds. McMahon promptly threw a bomb to speedster Willie Gault and the Bears won the game.

"McMahon Magic!" the newspaper headlines roared. But everybody on the Bears knew who had created the magic.

He was a great receiver. He was the team's emergency quarterback. He was the team's emergency kicker and punter too (though he was called out for only one emergency punt). And he was all heart—so much heart that if he weighed 200 pounds, 180 of those were his heart.

In 1977, the Bears played the Vikings and Payton could barely stand up before the game. He had a 104-degree fever. "It wasn't the flu," Payton would say later. "It was kryptonite."

"He was laying on the floor in the locker room, covered up in towels, shivering and shaking," Bill McGrane, the Bears' director of communications, told NFL Films.

Payton then went out and set the then NFL rushing record, carrying the ball forty times for 275 yards* and the Bears' only touchdown.

"I can't say anything more about him that hasn't been said before," Minnesota coach Bud Grant said after the game. "I wish I were better at words. Then maybe I could."

In the *Chicago Tribune*, Don Pierson wrote it this way: "Walter Payton proved Sunday the Bears are not a one-man team. They are a one-superman team."

No, you can't find one play to capture Walter Payton. But the run against Kansas City that same year comes closest. It was a dreary day in Chicago. Both teams had losing records. The Bears had not made the playoffs in a decade. The Chiefs had just fired their coach. More than seven thousand people who bought tickets to the game didn't show.

In the third quarter, the Chiefs led 17–0. The Bears had the ball at the Kansas City 22-yard line and quarterback Bob Avellini handed the ball off to Payton on a simple sweep to the right side. Kansas City safety

---

* The Minnesota Vikings' Adrian Peterson set the current record in 2007 when he rushed for 296 yards in a game against the San Diego Chargers. Incredibly, he had only 43 yards at halftime of that game. Yes, that's right: He ran for 253 yards in the second half.

Tim Gray blocked his path, so Payton stopped quickly and reversed his field (leaving behind Hall of Fame linebacker Willie Lanier). He ran back to his left and into the arms of rookie linebacker Tom Howard.

Payton ran through his arm tackle with ease.

Defensive tackle Cliff Frazier was next, and Payton ran through him too. Then came defensive end Whitney Paul; Payton somehow cut away from his tackle attempt. And that led directly into Hall of Fame cornerback Emmitt Thomas. Payton lowered his shoulder and busted through Thomas.

Then it was Pro Bowl safety Gary Barbaro in front of him, and Payton lowered his shoulder again and bulled through him too, leaving Barbaro on the ground.

And then Payton ran free as four Chiefs players chased him. It was finally Howard, the player who had missed the first tackle, who dragged Payton down at the 4. It was only an 18-yard run. It didn't score a touchdown. And yet it was everything.

Payton scored the touchdown two plays later, and the Bears won the game, and, impossibly, Payton actually carried those Bears to the playoffs.

"My God," Willie Lanier would say after the game. "The man is incredible."

NO. 69:

DEION TO THE HOUSE

*"I'm not here to sell out to you guys.
I'm here to sell out the stadium."*

—DEION SANDERS

—

SEPTEMBER 10, 1989

There are great athletes. There are towering entertainers. And every now and again, once or twice a generation, maybe, you get someone who is both, someone who craves more than touchdowns or home runs or points, someone who also must leave the crowd breathless, or else, honestly, what's the point?

Deion Sanders stood back at the 35-yard line and waited for the punt. He lifted his arms high, asking the crowd to roar louder.

"Were you feeling butterflies?" Atlanta columnist Mark Bradley asked Deion after the game.

"Butterflies?" he asked back. "No, I had *buzzards* flying around in there."

This was Deion Sanders's first NFL game, playing for the Falcons versus the Rams. It wasn't just his first NFL game as a player. It was the first NFL game he'd ever seen live. He had arrived in Atlanta two days earlier after a long holdout for more money.* He signed for more than $4 million. During his first practice, the lights went out in the stadium.

"The Falcons paid Deion so much money," Falcons center Jamie Dukes shouted out, "they can't even pay the light bill."

Dale Hatcher's punt was high and long, sending Sanders back to the

---

* Sanders told one reporter that if he had been drafted by Detroit, "I woulda asked for so much money, they would have had to put me on layaway."

32-yard line. The crowd wasn't huge that day in Atlanta—the Falcons had not been good since . . . well, if I'm being honest, they'd never been all that good. They'd made the playoffs only three times and they lost all three playoff games. Going into the 1989 season, the Falcons had had seven consecutive losing seasons. Nothing was going on with the Falcons. They had no identity.

Deion planned to change all that.

The ball came down and Sanders promptly fumbled it . . . or, as he later put it, "I dropped the durned ball!" Hey, he hadn't played football for a while. He'd spent the summer playing minor-league baseball, working his way all the way up to center field for the New York Yankees. Five days earlier, he'd gotten three hits, including a home run against the Seattle Mariners. Being Deion was a full-time gig.

After he dropped the ball, he seemed like a sitting duck for Rams safety James Washington, who had come galloping in. Deion reached down, picked up the ball, and quickly cut left. Washington went flying by.

"Punt returning is instinct," Deion would say. "And I could always trust my instincts."

He went right and Los Angeles's Anthony Newman rammed into him, sending him backward five yards. Then two more Rams—Frank Stams and Brett Faryniarz—closed in.

He got away from all of them.

How did he get away from all of them? How does James Bond get away from all the people shooting at him? How does Luke Skywalker escape all the stormtroopers' blasts? How did Houdini get out of the inescapable *Mirror* handcuffs? Sometimes there are no answers.

The best move was yet to come. Deion ran right and into the sights of the Rams' Mike Wilcher, a fine linebacker for several years. That's when Deion Sanders made this move, this Gale Sayers–Barry Sanders–Crazylegs Hirsch move. It's like he disappeared and reappeared; it's like he shrunk like Ant-Man and went back to full size. All Mike Wilcher could do was go sliding by. He is still seeing that move in his night-mares.

After that, it was easy. At the 25-yard line, the Rams' running back Buford McGee closed in and Sanders looked back as if to say: *Hi! Are you here to escort me into the end zone?* He high-stepped the rest of the way. The cheers in the crowd that day would follow Deion Sanders through-out his electrifying Hall of Fame career.

"The thrill is here!" Deion Sanders had told Atlanta on the day he was drafted.

The thrill, indeed, had arrived.

NO. 68:

HASSELBECK'S CALL

"We want the ball, and we're going to score."

—MATT HASSELBECK

——

JANUARY 4, 2004

For a time, people called quarterback Matt Hasselbeck "Mr. August." He didn't love the nickname for pretty obvious reasons: The NFL regular season doesn't usually start until the next month. But being "Mr. August" seemed his fate, as he found himself the backup quarterback in Green Bay behind the most indestructible quarterback ever, Brett Favre, who started a record 297 straight games.

That left only the August preseason game for Hasselbeck. He played well in those games—thus the "Mr. August" nickname—but he wanted more.

"If I had an arm like John Elway or Brett Favre, that would be great," he told reporters. "I don't think having a great arm is what makes a great quarterback."

Hasselbeck was convinced that, instead, it is confidence and verve and the ability to lead that makes a great quarterback. And he proved it in 2003, after the Seattle Seahawks had traded for him. That year, he made the Pro Bowl and he led the Seahawks to the playoffs for just the second time in fourteen years. His arm had not gotten any better, but he made up for it with that blazing confidence.

"When Matt's having fun and smiling and being confident, when he's that way, he's unbelievable," his teammate Trent Dilfer said.

"You have to let your emotions drive you a little bit," Hasselbeck said.

In the playoffs, Seattle was matched up against Green Bay, and Hasselbeck got into a magnificent duel with the guy who had banished him to August football, Brett Favre. The game went back and forth, both quarterbacks throwing for 300-plus yards. Hasselbeck was magnificent, especially when you consider he was dealing with a shoulder injury and an ankle injury. If anything, Hasselbeck was outplaying the master.

The game went into overtime. Hasselbeck, as one of the team's captains, went out to call the coin toss. "I'd like to call heads," he said.

The coin landed on heads.

And then Hasselbeck—without thinking much about it—uttered one of the most famous guarantees in pro football history.

"We want the ball and we're going to score!" Hasselbeck said.

Famous. Infamous. You make the call.

"I believed we would score with all my heart," Hasselbeck would later say.

How could you blame Matt Hasselbeck, a sixth-round pick, a lifelong overachiever, Mr. August, for letting his passion loose? *We want the ball and we're going to score!*

On third and 11, Hasselbeck took a three-step drop. Safety Marques Anderson blitzed, and Hasselbeck was forced to throw the ball earlier than he wanted. He hoped—prayed, even—that receiver Alex Bannister would be on the other side.

Alex Bannister was not on the other side.

But Green Bay safety Al Harris was.

"I was just praying that he would throw the ball," Harris said.

Harris stepped in front of Bannister, picked off the pass, and ran untouched 52 yards for the game-winning touchdown. One of the more poignant parts of the play happened at the 10-yard line, where a desperate Hasselbeck dived hopelessly at Harris's legs. He was about 10 feet away from making contact; there was no chance, but he had to try.

After the game, Hasselbeck needed treatment on his injured shoulder and ankle, and his face was bruised. A reporter asked him which part hurt worst. He smiled glumly.

"Right now," he said, "my feelings."

NO. 67:

THE MINNEAPOLIS MIRACLE

"It's a storybook ending. And it never ends that way."

—STEFON DIGGS

—

JANUARY 14, 2018

This miracle had a gloriously spiritual name: "Seven Heaven." The play wasn't anything special. Three Minnesota Vikings receivers—Kyle Rudolph, Aldrick Robinson, and Stefon Diggs—lined up to the right side. The first two ran sideline patterns. The third, Stefon Diggs, ran deep. They had run the play countless times, and often Diggs wasn't even the target. His job was clearing out the safeties to open things up underneath.

This time, though, Diggs was the *only* target. The Vikings didn't have time for short patterns. There were just 10 seconds left in the game, and New Orleans led by one, and Vikings fans were feeling that all-too-familiar agony that had marked the franchise's history.

The Minnesota story, it seemed, always ended in heartbreak.

Four times the Vikings had been in the Super Bowl. Four times they lost. They once had the Dallas Cowboys down and out in a playoff game and lost on a Hail Mary. In 1998, they had the highest-scoring offense in NFL history but lost their ride to the Super Bowl when a kicker who had not missed a field goal all year missed a field goal.

And this game had played out like a compilation of Vikings nightmares. They led 17–0 at halftime. The rest was a blur—a long Saints drive, an interception, a blocked punt, a huge New Orleans comeback.

The Vikings took the lead back with just 1:29 left on the clock. But that was when New Orleans quarterback Drew Brees stole the Vikings' heart. He threw nine consecutive passes on the final drive, and he completed enough of them—including a 13-yard pass to Willie Snead on fourth and 10—to push the Saints into field goal range. Will Lutz made the go-ahead field goal with twenty-five seconds left.

You can imagine that pretty much all 66,612 people there had the same word pop into their heads at the same time.

*Again!**

The Vikings were on their own 39-yard line with those 10 seconds left; Minnesota had no time-outs; there weren't many options left. Quarterback Case Keenum called the play: Seven Heaven. The faint hope was that Keenum could throw a long pass to Diggs. Maybe he would catch it; maybe he could step out-of-bounds to stop the clock; maybe they'd be close enough to kick the field goal.

Keenum dropped back to the 29, waited a beat, and then fired the long pass to Diggs, who had somehow worked his way open. As the ball approached Diggs, two things became clear:

1. **Diggs really did have a good chance of catching it.**
2. **New Orleans safety Marcus Williams was going to tackle Diggs in bounds, essentially ending the game.**

Then the strange thing that makes football miracles happened. Diggs did indeed catch the ball. But Williams dropped his head as he went in for the hit and . . . he missed. Totally missed.

"Get out-of-bounds! Get out-of-bounds!" Vikings coach Mike Zimmer yelled, but Diggs saw the end zone. It was, he would say, the most beautiful sight he'd ever seen. Diggs briefly stumbled, put his hand on the ground to steady himself, and then ran the final 31 yards for a touchdown.

---

* Actually, I can think of another word or two that might have popped into Vikings fans minds.

He then spread his arms out wide as if to say to that euphoric crowd soaring in seventh heaven: *ARE . . . YOU . . . NOT . . . ENTERTAINED?*

"Are you kidding me?" Vikings radio announcer Paul Allen shouted while his partner, Pete Bercich, screamed, "Oh, my God!" and "No way!" and "GRAHEHHHG!" or some other unspellable word like that.

"It's a Minneapolis Miracle," Allen added.

NO. 66:
THE HEISMAN POSE

"One of my players wouldn't do that."

—MICHIGAN COACH GARY MOELLER

—

NOVEMBER 23, 1991

In full disclosure, I cannot begin to describe how much it hurts me to put Desmond Howard's Heisman pose in this book. Growing up in Cleveland, I was inundated with Ohio State football; the Buckeyes were all around us. While their tyrannical coach Woody Hayes was like a grumpy uncle, his replacement, Earle Bruce, like a friendly but inept cousin.

That is not fair to Bruce, who won a lot of games for the Buckeyes.

But the guy couldn't beat Michigan. And that was all that mattered.

Funny, I never really fell in love with Ohio State football. I did, however, fall in hate with Michigan football.

Why? Who can explain what stays with us from childhood? I vividly remember how I would go with my father to his Sunday bowling league, and I would idolize all the factory workers and construction guys and muscle-bound men who seemed to spend their days folding refrigerators with their bare hands and their evening rolling thundering strikes. They drank their coffee tar back, they smoked their cigarettes unfiltered, and they all hated Michigan.

Ever since, like an Easter Christian or Yom Kippur Jew, I show up as an Ohio State fan once a year: the day they play Michigan. On that day I am devout.

I cannot tell you how it hurts me to put Desmond Howard's Heisman pose in this book.

But what else can I do? In the late 1980s, that school up north—as

Hayes himself insisted we refer to Michigan—had taken hold of the Michigan–Ohio State rivalry. They came into the 1991 game No. 4 in America, and they were trying to beat the Buckeyes for the fourth straight year. Woody Hayes, undoubtedly, was ripping his Ohio State cap to shreds in the afterlife.

There was talk going into the game of Ohio State playing spoiler. The talk ended just after kickoff. Michigan took the lead early and the Buckeyes were never really close.

Then, with Michigan up 17–3, the Buckeyes' Tim Williams hit a high, booming punt that sent Desmond Howard back to the 7-yard line. There are three things to say here:

1. **Williams wasn't supposed to kick a booming punt to the 7-yard line. He was supposed to kick the ball out-of-bounds because, to quote Ohio State coach John Cooper, "that Howard kid is fucking killing us."**
2. **Howard grew up in Cleveland.**
3. **He initially wanted to call a fair catch because Ohio State players were coming at him so fast. "But then I remembered," he said, "this is Ohio State."**

Howard slipped past Ohio State's Brent Johnson. He sprinted by a diving Jim Borchers. He outran three Ohio State players who seemed to have a good angle on him. And that was that. Nobody else came close. Howard raised his arm and signaled "No. 1" as he covered the final 10 yards.

When he crossed the goal line, he made the Heisman pose. He didn't look remotely like the trophy. He raised up his left leg; the trophy has both legs firmly on the ground. He put out his left arm when the trophy has the right arm out.

But everybody got the point.

Two weeks later, he won the Heisman.

"I told my parents that if I scored against Ohio State, I'd do something special," Howard said after the game. Originally, he planned a backflip. But at the last minute, he chickened out—imagine how embarrassing a blown backflip would have been—and the Heisman pose became a part of football lore. Players have been striking the pose ever since.

After the game, when asked about the pose, Michigan's ultraconservative coach Gary Moeller refused to believe Howard had actually struck the pose. Moeller abhorred self-promoting acts, and Howard had always celebrated his touchdowns by modestly flipping the ball to the official. "I don't believe it until I see it," he told reporters. When he did see it, he was not happy. "It's not in the best interest of the team," he said.

But he added: "If I was voting for the Heisman, I'd write his name down there ten times."

NO. 65:

65 TOSS POWER TRAP

"Sixty-five Toss Power Trap! It might pop wide open, Rats!"

—HANK STRAM

JANUARY 11, 1970

Our story of the 65 Toss Power Trap begins with an overcoat salesman in Philadelphia. The salesman was good at his job, but he did not love it. He'd had loftier ambitions. The man had been an Olympic-level swimmer, he had fought at Normandy, and, after the war, he had performed on Broadway with the famous Ritz Brothers.

But, he determined, at some point a man had to be practical.

So, Ed Sabol sold overcoats.

He couldn't entirely let go of his larger dreams, though. When Ed got married, someone gave him a sixteen-millimeter Bell & Howell movie camera as a gift. He decided to make movies. His first cinematic feature was a film about whales. It had style and music but it did lack something.

"What it lacked," his son, Steve, would say, "was actual whales."

Mostly, though, Ed Sabol focused on less exotic topics, most revolving around Steve. Now presenting: *Steve Sabol Getting a Haircut!* Don't miss: *Steve Sabol Riding a Pony!* Don't walk, run to see: *Steve Sabol Has a Birthday Party!*

Ed's favorite things to film, though, were Steve Sabol's youth football games in Moorestown, New Jersey, just outside of Philadelphia. Ed filmed every one of Steve's games from the fourth grade through high school. Then he would carefully edit, cutting and pasting; he'd work in slow motion, and he would enhance the action with inspiring music (he was partial to John Philip Sousa marches).

Ed then put out ginger cookies and invited everyone in the neighborhood to see the premieres.

When Steve went off to college, Ed Sabol did something that made perfect sense to him and absolutely no sense at all to anybody else: He went to NFL commissioner Pete Rozelle and bid $5,000 for the rights to film the 1962 NFL Championship Game. That might not sound like a lot of money, but it was double what a company called TelRa Productions had paid in '61.

"What experience do you have producing football movies?" Rozelle asked Ed.

"I've filmed my son's high school games," Ed Sabol said.

Rozelle liked Ed and sold him the rights. Why not? Nobody else wanted them.

Within three years, Ed Sabol was running a new company called NFL Films.

WHILE ED SABOL WAS BACK HOME TRYING TO FIGURE OUT HOW to film an NFL Championship Game, Steve Sabol was at Colorado College trying to make himself into a legend. Why Colorado College? He went there for the most Steve Sabol of reasons: because Dutch Clark, the first great running back in NFL history, had gone to Colorado College.

Some people grow into their stardom. Steve Sabol didn't have time to wait for all that. Like his father's whale movie without whales, Steve decided to become a football star without actually being all that good at football. "When I got to Colorado the coach looked at me as if to say, 'How did you get here?'" Steve said.

He gave himself a nickname, Sudden Death Sabol,* and a backstory: He was no longer a Philadelphia kid who played his football at the

---

* Sabol also called himself the "Prince of Pigskin Pageantry."

illustrious Haverford School; no, he was now a brilliant young running back from Possum Trot, Mississippi. He sent out press releases about himself, made T-shirts about himself along with brochures and buttons, and because he also produced the game programs, he included an ad that read:

> The Possum Trot Chamber of Commerce wishes a successful season to our favorite son, Sudden Death Sabol.

He was so relentless—"The only thing I've ever really feared is going unnoticed," he told me—that at one point *Sports Illustrated* ran a four-page spread on him headlined: "The Fearless Tot from Possum Trot."

He didn't know where all this manic energy would take him. And then one day in his senior year, his father called. Ed Sabol said, "I can tell from your grades that you have been basically doing two things at college. One is playing football. The other is going to the movies."

For another father talking to a son in college, that conversation might have taken an unpleasant turn. But this was Ed Sabol, so . . .

"It just so happens," he continued, "that makes you uniquely qualified to come work with me at NFL Films."

TOGETHER, ED AND STEVE SABOL WOULD CHANGE THE VERY character of professional football. Before them, mud was something players slipped on, snow and ice and cold just meant the teams couldn't throw, Lombardi was just an Italian name, the Raiders were just a football team, and the 65 Toss Power Trap was mumbo jumbo.

When they were done, all those were wrapped up in the mythology of the game.

"My father," Steve said, "wanted to make the memories even better than the moments themselves."

To make the memories better than the moments. Well, how do you do that? The Sabols did it with brilliant filmmaking, with soul-searing original music, with the Voice of God, John Facenda, reciting Steve's words.

"It starts with a whistle and ends with a gun."

"Lombardi. A certain magic still lingers in the very name."

"Do you feel the force of the wind? The slash of the rain? Go face and fight them. Be savage again."

Before the Sabols, pro football lacked a place in American folklore. It lacked the poetry of baseball, the soul of college football, the raw fury of boxing, the thunder of horse racing. When the Sabols were done, football had all of those and a singular spot at the top of American sports.

"Life is good," Steve said. "Football is better."

NOW, FINALLY, WE GET TO 65 TOSS POWER TRAP. THIS WAS FROM Super Bowl IV. The 1970 NFL champion Minnesota Vikings were favored by 2 touchdowns over the AFL champion Kansas City Chiefs. "They told us," Chiefs Hall of Famer Bobby Bell would say, "that it wasn't even worth it for us to show up."

Still, the Sabols made the decision to put a microphone on the Chiefs coach Hank Stram for the NFL Films Super Bowl movie.

And what followed was movie magic.

"You did good. You did good. You marked it good!" Stram shouted at an official.

"This stuff in front is like stealing."

"Just keep matriculating the ball down the field, boys!" he said.

At one point he had a marvelous discussion with an official:

> **Stram:** "How can all of you miss a play like that?"
> **Official:** "What play, Coach?"
> **Stram:** "The ball arrived before we made contact . . ."
> **Official:** "Oh, I thought you meant the play where you are standing on the field illegally."
> **Stram:** "No . . . What?"

It went on and on like this. Stram was like a Borscht Belt comic spewing jokes and complaints and cheers. If you watch that Super Bowl film closely, you will sometimes see the camera shake ever so slightly. That's Steve Sabol laughing.

"He wasn't normally like that," Chiefs Hall of Fame quarterback Len Dawson said of Stram. "We didn't know he was mic'd up, so we kept wondering why he was talking so much, why he was so joyous on the sideline. But, you know, Hank was a showman."

With the Chiefs up 9–0 and driving late in the first half, Stram had a brainstorm.

"Look for 65 Toss Power Trap. What does it look like?" he asked an assistant coach, who quickly asked a coach up in the booth. The coach in the booth thought it looked fine. So Stram sent wide receiver Gloster Richardson in with the play.

"Sixty-five Toss Power Trap," he then said to everybody. "It might pop wide open, Rats."

Stram called his coaches "Rats."

On the play, Dawson turned so that it looked like he was setting up a sweep play. Instead, running back Mike Garrett cut inside and took the ball. Chiefs guard Mo Moorman took out the Vikings' star right end, Jim Marshall. That opened up the huge hole, and Garrett scored the 5-yard touchdown that gave the Chiefs a 16–0 lead.

"It's in there!" Stram shouted. Then he turned to his coaches. "Was that there, boys? Was that there, Rats? Yes, sir, Rats! The Mentor! Sixty-five Toss Power Trap! I told you that baby was there."

Yes, in his joy, Stram called himself the "Mentor."

The Chiefs went on to win 23–7. Even now, when I hear those seemingly incongruent words "Sixty-five . . . Toss . . . Power . . . Trap," I am transported to that time, that place. Ed and Steve Sabol got it exactly right. The memory is even greater than the moment.

NO. 64:

"I PLAY WHEN I WANT TO PLAY"

"If I can't get to it, nobody can."

—RANDY MOSS

—

SEPTEMBER 19, 2010

How does one sum up the thrill and wonder and baffling genius of Randy Moss? Maybe this is the best way: In 2001, against the New York Giants, Moss had one of the great individual performances in the history of *Monday Night Football*. He caught ten passes for 171 yards and 3 touchdowns.

And it was virtuoso Moss, complete with a one-handed catch, an absurd leaping grab over a defender, a 15-yard penalty for dancing and strutting into the end zone, an end-around run that gave the Vikings a huge first down, a brief benching for some reason or another, and a simple catch over the middle that he turned into an electrifying 57-yard touchdown by outrunning the entire Giants defense.

Randy Moss contained multitudes.

When the game was over, Minneapolis's iconic sportswriter Sid Hartman went up to him and asked how he felt about the prevailing opinion that he did not always give his all.

Moss said this: "I play when I want to play. Do I play to my top performance, my ability every time? Maybe not. I just keep doing what I do and that is playing football. When I make my mind up, I am going out there to tear somebody's head off. When I go out there and play football, man, it's not anybody telling me to play or how I should play. I play when I want to play. Case closed."

He said more. But he had also said enough. From that moment on, seven words would follow him everywhere he went.

"I play when I want to play."

"Is Randy Moss the biggest waste of $75 million in professional sports?" the *Los Angeles Times* asked.

"Moss is well on his way to becoming the most despised athlete in America," the *Buffalo News*'s Jerry Sullivan posited.

"What do you do when your franchise player says he'll play only when he feels like it?" Les Carpenter wrote.

"Randy has his reasons," Scott Ostler wrote of the quote. "Religious reasons. Moss occasionally takes Sunday off to worship himself."

"If I was Randy," Brett Favre said, "I would feel bad about what I said."

My favorite overreaction to the quote came when St. Paul columnist Bob Sansevere found various people named Randy Moss across the country and asked each what they thought of football Randy Moss. It's fair to say that none of them were overly impressed. My favorite was retired Air Force fighter pilot Randy Moss in Niceville, Florida, who said: "Making the kind of money he makes, he should be giving 110 percent. When I was flying fighters, if I didn't give 110 percent, I'd be dead right now."

It's possible—likely, even—that Moss's quote was misunderstood. As football writer Michael MacCambridge said, "Not everything Randy said was easily translatable into middle-aged white fan language." But Moss himself never really seemed too interested in clearing things up, and the quote did seem an easy way to get at Moss's mercurial game. He was 6-foot-4, 210 pounds; he could jump to the sky; he had Spider-Man hands; and when he accelerated—really accelerated—well, the only thing I can compare it with is Usain Bolt in the 100-meter dash at the Beijing Olympics. Obviously, Moss could not run with Bolt—no one could—but the jolt of watching them take off was the same.

Some weeks, Moss would be the greatest wide receiver the game has ever known.

Some weeks, he'd be entirely absent.

The Randy Moss moment I've chosen happened when he was

thirty-three and, no longer an athletic phenomenon, could no longer touch the sun. He made clear coming into the game that he was unhappy—he did not feel appreciated by the New England Patriots and would soon be traded. But this day, the Patriots were playing the Jets, which meant he was lined up against one of the game's best cover corners, Darrelle Revis. Late in the first half, Moss took off at the snap and sprinted right by. Revis pulled his hamstring trying to catch up.

Tom Brady's throw was on-target. Moss could have made a conventional catch. Instead, he reached out with one hand and plucked the ball out of the air for the touchdown. His left hand never touched the ball.

After that, Moss caught just eight more passes in the season, got waived, retired, tried a comeback, made a few more catches, and then retired again for good.

"I never knew so many people wanted me to fail," he said at his Hall of Fame induction. "Why? Is it because of the man He made me to be or the talent He blessed me with?"

I don't think most people wanted Randy Moss to fail. I think they just wanted to understand him better. But he didn't want to be understood, and maybe it's better that way. I prefer to remember that Jets play, Moss running by the defender and catching the ball with one hand to prove a point. What point? When Randy Moss was right, he could do anything.

NO. 63:

TOM DEMPSEY'S KICK

Soldier: "Football, sir?"

George Washington: "Yes. It is a sport where you throw a ball with your hands."

Soldier: "So in football, there is no kicking?"

George Washington: "There's a little kicking."

—*SATURDAY NIGHT LIVE* SKIT "WASHINGTON'S DREAM," 2023

—

NOVEMBER 8, 1970

In the earliest days of football, kicking was a huge part of the game. The game in those days was a messy mix of other games that involved way too many people, way too few rules, and a heaping helping of violence. There was no forward pass and so kicking was the main way to score back then, not unlike rugby.

Slowly, very slowly, football evolved away from kicking. In 1904, for the first time, a touchdown was determined to be worth more points than a field goal. Eight years after that, a touchdown was determined to be worth twice as much as a field goal. By the early 1930s, it was common in newspaper stories to see teams having to "settle for a field goal."

After that, the game's best kickers were hulking men who played other positions and happened to show a knack for kicking. The most famous kicker of the 1950s—Lou "the Toe" Groza, an Army veteran who had served on Okinawa—was an offensive lineman. Bob Waterfield was the Rams' star quarterback and he moonlighted as a kicker who led the league in field goals made three times. Gino Cappelletti was a star receiver and defensive back in addition to being the best kicker in the early days of the American Football League.

Almost everybody kicked straight on in those days too, and, as such, long field goals were rare. In the 1960s, teams tried just over four hundred field goals from at least 50 yards away. They made just 15 percent of them.* Fred Cox, one of the early specialists, was the Minnesota Vikings' regular kicker for fifteen years. He made a total of two 50-yard field goals in his entire career. Pete Gogolak kicked for the Giants and Bills for eleven years. He made just one.

So, yes, 50-yard field goals were like lottery tickets. Sure, you'd try them now and again out of desperation or reckless hope, and who knows? Maybe you'd pick a winner. But mostly, a 50-yard field goal was a foolish waste of time.

So, then, what would you call a 63-yard field goal?

TOM DEMPSEY DIDN'T LOOK LIKE A KICKER BECAUSE HE HAD never intended to be one. He was 260-plus pounds, making him, probably, the heaviest regular field goal kicker ever. He played offensive and defensive line at Palomar College. He knew there was no professional future in it.

"One day," he said, "I decided I wanted to kick a football."

Nobody quite knew how that would work. See, Dempsey had been born without toes on his right foot. But he developed a powerful kicking style—"A little hop, stop, and get on the toes of my left foot and drive the ball with my whole body" was how he described it—and after kicking some long field goals for a semiprofessional team in Lowell, Massachusetts, he signed to kick for the lowly New Orleans Saints.

The Saints were convinced that Dempsey was the guy to break Bert

---

* To give you an idea about how much the game has changed: From 2014 to 2023, teams attempted 1,717 field goals from 50 yards out and made 65 percent of them.

Rechichar's NFL record for the longest field goal. Way back in 1953, Rechichar had kicked a 56-yarder on the first field goal he ever attempted, and nobody had topped it. The Saints sent Dempsey out six different times in 1969 to break the record. Dempsey missed all six times. But he was undaunted.

"I can make one from 60," he assured the press. "Not every time. But I can make one."

The Saints, predictably, started the 1970 season poorly. They won just one of their first seven games and they fired their coach, Tom Fears. They were then matched up against a playoff-bound Lions team. Detroit was a 10-point favorite even though the game was in New Orleans. The Lions played sluggishly all game, but they made a late drive. Detroit's Errol Mann kicked an 18-yard field goal with eleven seconds left to give the Lions a 1-point lead.

The Saints scrambled but all they could do was get the ball to their own 45-yard line with two seconds left. In those days, the goalpost was in front of the end zone, not in the back like now, but even so the idea of a 63-yard field goal was ludicrous. Don Criqui, calling the game on television, told the viewers to expect a long desperation pass. He was as surprised as anyone when, instead, the Saints sent Tom Dempsey out.

Dempsey stood behind the ball. Wearing a specially designed shoe to fit his right foot,* he waited for the snap. From where he was standing, Dempsey later said, he could barely even see the goalpost. He took a deep breath and then, at the snap, he took his little hop, stopped, got on the toes of his left foot, and kicked the ball as hard as he could.

Don Criqui's call echoes through the years: "I don't believe this. . . .

---

* The shoe cost $200—a fact I learned from many class trips to the Pro Football Hall of Fame in nearby Canton, Ohio. In those days, the Hall of Fame was pretty sparse and not the interactive sort of place to entertain a class of preteen Cleveland boys, but they did have a special exhibit for Tom Dempsey, and the cost of his shoes has stayed lodged in my brain. I'm not sure what those shoes would cost now.

It's good! I don't believe it! The field goal kick was good from 63 yards away! It's incredible! Tulane Stadium has gone wild!"

Even after it was over, nobody could believe it.

"We got beaten by a miracle. What else can you say?" coach Joe Schmidt said.

"A miracle," Lions linebacker Mike Lucci said.

"A miracle," Lions linebacker Wayne Walker echoed. "Bobby Thomson's home run. Nothing compares to it."

When Dempsey was asked how he did it, he smiled and said he just put all his weight behind the ball. "It also helps to weigh 275 pounds," he added.

NO. 62:

THE MAD SCRAMBLER

"I didn't know who was down there.
All I saw were about three purple jerseys.
Besides, I was getting tired."

—FRAN TARKENTON

—

OCTOBER 30, 1966

The play had no business working. Then, that was what people always said after Fran Tarkenton pulled off another one of his grand illusions. None of it should have worked. He ran around, fast as he could, a real-life gingerbread man, and you couldn't catch him, something he would happily remind defensive players now and again.

He once frustrated Mean Joe Greene to the breaking point, and when Greene finally caught that son of a gun, he made sure to put a little extra into the hit. "Hah! What do you think of that?" Mean Joe said.

At which point Tarkenton pointed to where they were—about five yards out-of-bounds.

Mean Joe was tossed from the game.

None of it should have worked. At 6 foot, 190 pounds, Tarkenton was not big enough or strong enough to be a great quarterback. He did not have a particularly strong arm. He did not throw with pinpoint accuracy. He was fast and elusive, but he spent as much time running backward as he did forward.

And yet he completed more passes for more yards and more touchdowns than any quarterback before him. He led the Vikings to three Super Bowls. He was, as his Hall of Fame teammate Carl Eller said, a football genius. But there was something else, something harder to capture. Legendary Georgia Tech coach Bobby Dodd—whose teams could never beat Tarkenton when he played at Georgia—used to say: "If you think you're lucky, you are."

Tarkenton thought himself lucky.

On third and 25 in a 1966 game between Tarkenton's Vikings and the San Francisco 49ers, he dropped back. He wanted to throw the ball to receiver Paul Flatley over the middle. But after settling in the pocket, he didn't think Flatley was open. There was nobody else in the pattern, so Tarkenton decided to do what he did: run around until somebody decided to get open.

"The old-timers have never accepted me as a good quarterback because I've run out of the pocket too often," Tarkenton said. "All that does is amuse me."

The 49ers' big Roland Lakes—6-foot-4, 280 pounds—was the first to try to tackle Tarkenton. To get away from him, Tarkenton ran backward 25 yards.

Once he got way back there, he was met by linebacker Bob Harrison. He led Harrison into a massive block the way the Road Runner would have led Wile E. Coyote into the side of a mountain.

Lakes did not give up. He stumbled toward Tarkenton, who had stopped to throw the ball. But when Lakes got there, Tarkenton took off again, leaving Lakes to grasp at air and fall away. He was still 20 yards behind the line.

Then defensive tackle Charlie Krueger closed in, but Tarkenton had seen three Vikings jerseys somewhere down there, and he decided to just take his chances and throw on the run downfield. Unfortunately for him, while there *were* three purple jerseys, there were two white 49er jerseys in front of them.

The play had no business working. The throw should have been intercepted by Pro Bowl defensive back Bernie Casey. Then it should have been intercepted by Hall of Fame defensive back Jimmy Johnson. In fact, Johnson had two chances to intercept it. He bobbled the ball when it first hit his hands and then had a second chance with the ball still in the air.

He didn't catch it either time and the ball fell into the arms of Minnesota's Preston Carpenter for a touchdown.

"I knew I was going to catch that ball," Carpenter would say. "I was waiting for it. I knew they'd tip it up in the air."

How could he possibly have known they'd tip it up in the air? There's no logical answer except to say: That was Fran Tarkenton.

NO. 61:

TECMO BO

"Bo Jackson is probably the best video
game athlete of all time."

—TIGER WOODS

—

NOVEMBER 30, 1987

I still see the lot of us surrounding a glowing television, all in our
young twenties, all scraping by on Krystal burgers and stolen Quin-
cy's yeast rolls and cheap beer and the vague hope that an unopened
bill was eternally not yet due. This was the early 1990s, and we were all
reporters and editors at the *Augusta Chronicle*, the newspaper in Augusta, Georgia. But perhaps you will see something of yourself here.

Two things kept us going in those days despite the pitiful pay and
constantly screaming bosses and stifling humidity.

The first was the chance, however remote, that something better
would come along.

The second was *Tecmo Super Bowl* . . . and more specifically Tecmo Bo
Jackson.[*]

ESPN has called *Tecmo Super Bowl* the greatest sports video game of
all time . . . and for those of us who lived through the revolution, that
only understates its grandeur. That game was our sun and moon; we
played the game every waking moment. Even now I see football players
from that time through the *Tecmo* prism. Jerry Rice was unstoppable;
Lawrence Taylor couldn't be blocked; Dan Marino completed virtually every pass; David Fulcher hit like a cartoon anvil. The Eagles

---

[*] Bo Jackson is the only player to have moments in both *Why We Love Baseball* and *Why
We Love Football*. Deion Sanders *almost* had moments in both. On October 11, 1992, he
played in an Atlanta Falcons game and then flew to Pittsburgh for the Atlanta Braves
playoff game against the Pirates. But the Braves did not play him.

QB—which is how Randall Cunningham was listed because he was not a member of the NFL Players Association—was blazing fast.

Here, I'll just offer a name that will mean nothing to most of you but will make every *Tecmo Bowl* geek out there smile just a little bit.

Cap Boso.*

That's a free little delight just for you obsessives.

Tecmo Super Bowl† was created by two Japanese men, Shinichiro Tomie and Akihiko Shimoji. A Minnesota television reporter named Lou Raguse—another *Tecmo Bowl* fanatic—actually chased them down and interviewed them, and the story is utterly delightful.

It turns out neither man knew anything about the NFL. Well, they learned as they went. Tomie was the game designer and he learned football by reading Japan's magazine *Touchdown Pro* and watching whatever highlights he could find on Japanese satellite television. By piecing together some of the clues that Tomie left behind, I believe this is what happened:

He saw Bo Jackson's epic 91-yard run against the Seahawks on a Monday night in 1987. That was Bo's fifth NFL game, and while he'd had a few interesting moments in the first four, well, the Raiders had lost all four and everybody was still waiting for the explosion. Bo had America's attention. He had won the Heisman Trophy at Auburn and then he went to play baseball for the Kansas City Royals, where he was doing supernatural things.

This was the night he detonated football fans' imaginations. In all he ran for 221 yards and scored 3 touchdowns. "I can do the same things that Bo can do," Raiders tight end Todd Christiansen said. "But I can only do them in my sleep."

---

* For those who did not live and die with *Tecmo Bowl*, Cap Boso was a hardworking but seldom used tight end for the Chicago Bears. And the *Tecmo Bowl* people gave him the lowest speed rating in the game but they did bless him with good hands, so every now and again, on a key play, my friends and I would have the quarterback throw the ball to him and then we'd all shout in unison: "CAP BOSO!"

† *Tecmo Super Bowl* was, technically, a sequel to the original *Tecmo Bowl*. But, you know, we all just called it *Tecmo Bowl*.

And on a night of titanic Bo moments—on that same night, he plowed over Seattle's tough-guy linebacker Brian Bosworth—perhaps the best came in the second quarter, the Raiders on their own 9. Quarterback Marc Wilson handed the ball to Jackson on a simple sweep left. And then Bo was gone. That's it. Just gone. I'm not sure anyone or anything has ever moved so fast. He was a blur. He was moving so fast and with such force that after he scored, he just ran into the tunnel that led to the Seahawks' locker room.

"It's not that easy to stop after running that far with 230 pounds," Bo said.

I feel sure that Tomie saw that play . . . and then realized that he would have to make the Tecmo version of Bo Jackson something that lived up to it.

"Unfortunately, he is not well-known in Japan," he told Raguse through an interpreter. "But he is always someone of high popularity to me. When I first saw him play on television, it was quite a big impact. This raised the question 'How do I represent that big impact through a game?'"

Answer: He and Shimoji made Tecmo Bo Jackson into the most awesome sports video character of them all.

"I remember playing *Tecmo Bowl* with Bo," star running back Priest Holmes would say. "That's all I wanted to do. Defenders would grab him, and he would just shake them off and go. He was unstoppable."

Unstoppable. You might have seen the *Family Guy* episode featuring a video of Tecmo Bo running 99 yards, then U-turning just before the goal line and heading all the way back into his own end zone, then turning back around again and going the 99 yards once more for a touchdown.

We did stuff like that all the time with Bo. We used to fight over who got to be the Raiders.* I think it was like that all across America.

"As an opponent," Tomie told Raguse, "his speed is a terror."

---

* The funny part is, the Raiders, in all other respects, were not a fun team to play with. Their quarterback was a wildly inaccurate Jay Schroeder, who would get every other pass knocked down at the line. And the defense was hopeless, with the exception of defensive end Howie Long, whom you would need to make every tackle, even those way downfield.

NO. 60:

PEYTON MANNING

"I don't get into monkeys and vindication."

—PEYTON MANNING

JANUARY 21, 2007

So let me pop in here with a thought: A very famous football guy is furious that I put Peyton Manning among my top ten players of all time. I hope you have picked up by now that within this book I have strategically placed the ten greatest players in football history at chapter numbers that end in zero. So here, in addition to the moment itself, I'm ranking Peyton Manning the sixth-greatest player in football history.

This football guy thinks this ridiculous. He has no problem with Manning—"Great player," he says—but he insists that you must put Joe Montana ahead of him. Montana, he says, was a winner. Manning was . . . well, he was a great numbers guy, but his record as a winner is spottier. And, look, I get it. Joe Montana was a winner. He was a fantastic quarterback.

But the idea that Peyton Manning wasn't a winner is an idea that needs to be stomped out.

LET ME TELL YOU MY FAVORITE PEYTON MANNING STATISTIC: HE led four teams to the Super Bowl. And those four teams had four different coaches.

Nobody else has a record quite like that. Here are the quarterbacks who have appeared in at least four Super Bowls and the number of head coaches they had in those years:

- Tom Brady, ten Super Bowls, two coaches (Bill Belichick, Bruce Arians)
- John Elway, five Super Bowls, two coaches (Dan Reeves, Mike Shanahan)

- Terry Bradshaw, four Super Bowls, one coach (Chuck Noll)
- Jim Kelly, four Super Bowls, one coach (Marv Levy)
- Joe Montana, four Super Bowls, two coaches (Bill Walsh, George Seifert)
- Roger Staubach, four Super Bowls, one coach (Tom Landry)

What you see there is stability. In many ways, the greatest teams—going back to Paul Brown and Otto Graham, Vince Lombardi and Bart Starr, Don Shula and Bob Griese—featured a coach and a quarterback who were in sync tactically and emotionally.

Peyton Manning never had that. Playing for just two teams, he never had the same coach for more than seven years. And look at his four Super Bowl coaches. His best, surely, was Tony Dungy, who was successful in Tampa Bay before he came to Indianapolis but got fired anyway because Bucs owner Malcolm Glazer was convinced that he lacked the gravitas to take the team to the Super Bowl. They won the Super Bowl together. After Dungy retired with the Colts, Jim Caldwell took over. Peyton went to a Super Bowl with him too. Without Peyton Manning, Caldwell went 38-42 and was fired twice. In Denver, Manning's first Super Bowl coach was John Fox, who went to the Bears for three pretty disastrous seasons. Finally, there was Gary Kubiak, who had come off a losing record in eight seasons with Houston.

This is not meant to knock any of them but to say that Peyton Manning took a lot of hits in his years as a quarterback. People seemed to question his heart and his ability to win big games. It didn't help to be constantly matched up against (and compared with) Tom Brady, the ultimate winner. And to be fair, it also didn't help that he had some rough times in big games, particularly early in his career, and never quite had that awe-inspiring Super Bowl performance. In those four Super Bowls, he threw just three touchdown passes and five interceptions.

But I think this wildly misses the larger picture.

After Manning turned twenty-seven, his teams never had a losing record. And he carried more than a few pretty flawed teams. The 2004 Colts were twenty-ninth in the NFL in total defense. They went 12-4. The 2006 Colts were twenty-third in points allowed. They won the Super Bowl. The 2009 Colts were dead last in the NFL in rushing yards. They went 14-2. The 2013 Broncos had trouble stopping the run and stopping the pass. Manning put up a season for the ages and they went 13-3 and to the Super Bowl.

"If you take him out of the game," Ravens linebacker Ray Lewis said, "no disrespect to anybody else on the Colts, but you make them a very below-average ball club."

In twelve seasons after turning twenty-seven, Manning led his teams to a 144-41 record and to those four Super Bowls. He posted a 101.2 passer rating and won the MVP Award five times. Again, that's with four different coaches. Tom Brady himself said, "He set the standard for how to play the quarterback position."

And the knock was that he couldn't win.

It's one of the strangest criticisms in the history of pro football.

IN EARLY 2007, AT THE HEIGHT OF THE "MANNING CAN'T WIN the Big Game" noise, Manning's Colts played Tom Brady's Patriots in the AFC Championship Game. Four years earlier, the Patriots had bludgeoned the Colts in the championship game; Bill Belichick's defense had Manning running from ghosts. Peyton threw four interceptions and was sacked four times that day. It's hard to imagine a bigger beatdown.

On this day, in the first half, Manning again looked entirely shaken. He threw a pick-six and was sacked twice and picked up a delay of game. The Patriots led 21–6 at halftime.

The Same Ol' Peyton crowd was crowing. People had all sorts of theories about why Manning couldn't win the big games. He was too intense.* He was not intense enough. He was too cerebral. He was too distracted. He did too many commercials. He cared too much. He didn't care enough. The baseball writer Bill James likes to call theories like these, ahem, "bullshit." People instinctively come up with reasons why things happen and become convinced that those reasons make sense. Peyton Manning can never win because X.

Then Manning went on to have a second half for the ages.

In the second half, he completed fourteen of twenty-three passes for 225 yards, he threw a touchdown pass, he ran for a touchdown, and in the final two minutes he drove the Colts 80 yards against one of the best defenses of the decade, and the Colts scored the winning touchdown to go to the Super Bowl.

"I don't get into monkeys and vindication," Manning said when asked if he felt like he had finally gotten the monkey off his back and shut up the critics. It was a wise answer. He hadn't shut them up, not entirely, and he never would. The critics would be there to his last game, a Super Bowl victory that he didn't play well enough in to get their credit.

It always seemed to me that the critics missed the main thing with Peyton Manning. You look at his career. He was a seven-time All-Pro (NFL record). He won five MVP Awards (NFL record). When he was thirty-seven years old and coming off what appeared to be a career-ending neck injury, he threw for 5,477 yards (NFL record) and 55 touchdowns (NFL record). He was named NFL Player of the Week thirty-seven times, second only to Brady. His teams went to the playoffs fifteen times in his seventeen years.

They wanted to talk about how Manning didn't win the big game. They failed to understand: For Peyton Manning, every game was a big game.

---

* A favorite Peyton Manning story: Once during a Friday practice, a receiver dropped a pass. But, I mean, it was a Friday pass. Who cares, right? Manning cared. He ran over to the receiver and screamed: "WE DO NOT DROP PASSES ON FRIDAYS!"

NO. 59:

ERNIE DAVIS WINS THE HEISMAN

"Some people say I'm unlucky. I don't believe it."

—ERNIE DAVIS

DECEMBER 6, 1961

The first Heisman Trophy was not yet called the Heisman Trophy. John Heisman was against the whole idea of it. Heisman was a pioneering coach[*]—nobody lobbied harder to make the forward pass legal—and by the mid-1930s, he had become athletic director of the Downtown Athletic Club (DAC) in New York.

The DAC wanted to give an award to the most outstanding football player in America. Heisman thought this was one of the worst ideas he'd ever heard. Football, he said—as Bill Pennington quoted him in the book *The Heisman*—was meant "to exemplify the grandeur of a thousand men." The idea of singling out an individual over the team was anathema to Heisman.

The DAC decided to go ahead with the award anyway.

In 1935, the club named its first winner, the University of Chicago's Jay Berwanger, and gave him an award called the "DAC Trophy." Berwanger would use his DAC Trophy as a doorstop.

The following October, John Heisman died at age sixty-six. Days later, the DAC announced that they were renaming the award the "Heisman Trophy" in his honor (and because he was no longer around to protest). Within a few years, the Heisman became perhaps the most revered individual trophy in American sports. Sportswriters

---

[*] He was also a successful college baseball coach and a less successful college basketball coach. He was also an actor and a minor-league baseball team president.

were asked to vote for not only the most outstanding college football player but for the player whose "performance epitomizes great ability combined with diligence, perseverance and hard work."

Year after year, the voters were able to find true heroes to give the award to, such as Iowa's Nile Kinnick (who became a naval aviator and died while serving in World War II) and Princeton's Dick Kazmaier (who became the director of the American Red Cross) and Pete Dawkins (who became a Rhodes scholar and a brigadier general).

And until 1961, all of the Heisman Trophy winners were white. Only one African American player, Syracuse's Jim Brown in 1956, had come close. He finished a distant fifth to Notre Dame's Paul Hornung. Brown got the most votes from the Eastern sportswriters. "But he stands no chance with one third of the vote contributed by the South, where Brown won't pick up a single tally," wrote John Cunavelis in the *Vermont Sunday News*.

That was not exactly right. No, Brown did not do well in the South, but he did better there than he did in the Southwest or West. The feeling was simply: If Jim Brown can't win the Heisman Trophy, no Black player can win the Heisman Trophy.

And then came Ernie Davis.

PEOPLE HAVE LONG STRUGGLED TO FIND THE WORDS TO DE-scribe the strength and kindness and decency of Ernie Davis. Maybe Jim Brown came closest.

"I thought of him as a certain kind of spiritual individual," Brown told *Sports Illustrated*'s Bill Nack. "He had the ability to rise above things. . . . Ernie Davis transcended racism. That was his essence. That was his greatness."

Davis was the straightest of arrows, the quintessential Heisman Trophy candidate. He didn't smoke. He didn't drink. He didn't swear. His roommate at Syracuse was future Hall of Famer John Mackey, who said that every night, before bed, Davis would get on his knees and pray.

"The perfect kid," Syracuse coach Ben Schwartzwalder called him.

He averaged 6.6 yards per carry in his three years at Syracuse—an even higher per-carry average than Jim Brown—and he scored 33 touchdowns, and it seemed like there was nobody on the field strong enough to bring him down and no one fast enough to catch him from behind. Against Colgate, he broke seven tackles on the way to a touchdown run. He was so unstoppable against Holy Cross that afterward their shaken coach, Dr. Eddie Anderson, said: "Trying to stop Davis is like trying to stop a runaway express train."

His signature game probably came at the end of his sophomore season. In the Cotton Bowl Classic against Texas, Syracuse came into the game undefeated and had already been named consensus national champion. But they needed to beat Texas to convince the nation that they were truly the best team in America.

All his life, Davis purposely avoided talking about race—"I love Jackie Robinson, but I cannot be Jackie Robinson," he once said—but the treatment he received at the Cotton Bowl was particularly galling. His teammate John Brown said that he and Davis were refused service at the hotel and forced to sleep in a room behind the kitchen with two cots. Several Texas players screamed racial epithets at them. Brown admitted that it was too much for him to take; during the game he took a swing at a Texas player who had called him that name one time too many.

"I couldn't take it," he would say. "I wasn't as good at that as Ernie."*

---

* In the days after the game, Texas president Logan Wilson wrote a furious letter to the NCAA demanding that they investigate charges that the Texas players had engaged in "dirty play"—charges he called "irresponsible, false and slanderous." There had been no actual charges made by Syracuse; he was mostly referring to newspaper reports, particularly in the *New York Daily News*, where sports editor Gene Ward wrote, "Texas went out to win at all costs, and its efforts transcended the bounds of decency, camaraderie and sportsmanship."

And how did Ernie Davis fight back? The same way he always did: by being transcendently good. He had a pulled hamstring and an injured back, but he still caught an 87-yard touchdown pass in the first quarter, still the longest touchdown pass in Cotton Bowl history.

He then scored on a 1-yard touchdown run and caught the 2-point conversion. Later he intercepted a pass and caught another 2-point conversion. Syracuse won the game 23–14, and Davis was named the most valuable player. The awards banquet was a whites-only affair. They let David accept the award but did not let him stay for dinner.

By the time he was a senior, Davis was widely regarded as the best college football player in America. The question remained: Could an African American player win the nationwide Heisman Trophy vote?

Many sportswriters didn't think so. But Davis prevailed by 53 points, the closest Heisman vote up to that point. And here was what made Davis even happier: He won it over Ohio State fullback Bob Ferguson, who was also Black.

The times, Davis told a friend, really were changing.

ERNIE DAVIS'S PRO CAREER IS ONE OF THE SADDEST STORIES IN football history. The Washington Redskins had the first pick in the NFL Draft. Only the Washington Redskins, because of their racist owner, George Preston Marshall, had never had a Black player. "We'll start signing Negroes," Marshall bellowed, "when the Harlem Globetrotters start signing whites."

Ah, but as Davis said, the times *were* changing. There was intense pressure on Marshall—specifically from President Kennedy's White House—to sign Black players or face dire consequences, including losing the right to play at publicly funded DC Stadium. Marshall reluctantly sent to NFL commissioner Pete Rozelle a letter saying he would acquire two African American players for the 1962 season.

But Davis would not be one of them. Nobody knows why for sure, though the prevailing theory is that Marshall simply did not want his top draft pick and headline player to be Black. Instead, he traded the pick to Cleveland for the versatile Bobby Mitchell* and a draft pick.

In Cleveland, coach Paul Brown was beyond overjoyed. Because of Marshall's narrow-mindedness, he suddenly had what the press was universally calling "the most unstoppable backfield in the history of football" in Ernie Davis and Jim Brown.

Alas, Ernie Davis never played a down for the Browns. The summer before what was to be his rookie season, he was diagnosed with acute monocytic leukemia. He died less than a year later. More than 10,000 people attended his funeral in Elmira. He never won his No. 45 for the Cleveland Browns. The number was still retired in his honor.

---

* Mitchell became the first Black player in Washington and, after switching to receiver, became one of the game's most dynamic players. He said Marshall was openly racist—he once made Mitchell sing "Dixie" with the rest of the team. Mitchell is in the Pro Football Hall of Fame.

NO. 58:

APP STATE UPSETS MICHIGAN

"It was an ugly kick. It should have been blocked. But you know what?
I might have missed a pretty kick. I'd rather make an ugly one."

—APPALACHIAN STATE KICKER JULIAN RAUCH

———

SEPTEMBER 1, 2007

Every single day, Appalachian State football coach Jerry Moore had his team practice blocking kicks. It was an obsession for the guy. Appalachian State kicker Julian Rauch vividly remembers going out there every day to kick his field goals and feeling like he was just a prop.

"I really don't think Coach Moore cared if I ever got a field goal off," he says. "For him the field goal period was about his guys trying to block them. I think he figured, 'Hey, by default, somebody's gotta kick those.'"

Moore told them, every day, that field-goal-blocking practice would pay off.

———

THERE WAS NO BETTING LINE WHEN APPALACHIAN STATE WENT to play at Michigan. No number seemed big enough to the oddsmakers. Michigan was the No. 5 team in America and had real dreams of a national title. Appalachian State was terrific in their own little world of Division I-AA. But . . . come on. Michigan had enormous offensive lineman Jake Long, who would be the first pick in the following year's NFL Draft. Michigan had blazing receiver Mario Manningham—"Super Manningham," everyone called him. Michigan had running back Mike Hart, who had just finished fifth in the Heisman voting. Michigan had the most wins of any Division I team ever, and they had 109,218 rabid supporters in the crowd.

Appalachian State starting quarterback Armanti Edwards—a 5-foot-11, 170-pound sophomore—said the trip to Michigan was his first time on an airplane.

Michigan scored right away. The band played. The crowd cheered. This would be easy. Then Appalachian State had the gall to score, but fine, Michigan drove right back down the field to take the lead again. The band played. The crowd cheered. This would be easy.

But on the sideline, the Appalachian State offensive linemen seemed to know different.

"I remember them saying a lot of choice words," Rauch says. "They were like, 'We can dominate these guys!' They were saying, 'These guys don't have what it takes.' Their feeling was, yeah, we were smaller, but we were faster too. And we could compete. We weren't afraid."

The next twenty or so minutes were a blur. Michigan couldn't stop Appalachian State's five-receiver spread offense. Edwards threw his second touchdown pass. Then he threw his third. Then he ran one in for a touchdown. The score at halftime was 28–17.

Still, everybody figured they would fade, right? Michigan's superior size and strength would wear them down. The Wolverines did come back. In the fourth quarter, Mike Hart went on a winding, breathtaking 54-yard run and Michigan led by a point.

Then Edwards threw an interception with 4:31 left. The game seemed over. Relief washed over Michigan Stadium. This wasn't the wild party they had come for, but a win was a win was a win.

Only then, crazy stuff happened. Michigan's Jason Gingell went out with less than two minutes left to kick a field goal that would give the Wolverines just a little bit of breathing room. Except . . . well, what did Jerry Moore drill his team on again and again and again?

App State's Brian Quick, a freshman, broke through the line and blocked Gingell's kick.

Michigan's lead was still 1 point. The Mountaineers went on a wild 69-yard drive with no time-outs, and with thirty seconds left, Moore sent Rauch out to kick a 24-yard field goal. When Rauch went out there, he didn't feel nervous. That wasn't at all the feeling. Earlier in the game, his 46-yard field goal attempt had doinked off the upright and ever since then he'd been begging the fates for another chance.

"I'd say 85 percent of what I was feeling when I went out there was 'I want to redeem myself,'" he says. "Maybe 15 percent was 'Oh boy, here's a game winner.'"

When the ball was snapped, Michigan's Morgan Trent came racing around unblocked from Rauch's right. At the very last second, as he was kicking, he saw Trent flying in. His Appalachian State practice instincts kicked in and he stayed with his motion. But he did kick just a little bit high on the ball, causing it to come out at a lower trajectory than he wanted.

Oh no, he thought, and he listened for the thud that signified a block, a thud he'd heard again and again during Appalachian State practices.

There was no thud. The kick was good. Appalachian State led with twenty-six seconds left.

Michigan made one last dramatic drive. They moved the ball deep into Appalachian State territory, and with six seconds left, Gingell came out to kick the game-winning 37-yard field goal. And Rauch on the sideline had this feeling come over him.

We're going to block this kick, he thought.

And, like magic, Appalachian State's Corey Lynch raced in through the left side, blocked the kick, picked up the ball, and started running as 109,000 people watched in shocked silence. He desperately wanted to score the touchdown . . . but was chased down at the 7-yard line. No matter, the clock had run out and Appalachian State had won.

Back in Boone, North Carolina, students poured out into the street and police cars turned on their sirens. The celebration was wild. And the phone lines at the Appalachian State bookstore lit up with merch requests. This will probably not surprise you: Many of the calls, they noticed, were coming from Ohio.

NO. 57:

MIRACLE IN MISSISSIPPI

"I can't even explain it. I guess they
wanted it more than we did."

—MILLSAPS SAFETY RAY KLINE

—

OCTOBER 27, 2007

S ooner or later, you run out of laterals. That's football's law of gravity. If you could just lateral your way out of trouble, well, that's
what everybody would do, and it would be chaos. Every play would look
like the tiny plastic figures spinning and gyrating and trembling and
falling in an Electric Football game.[*]

But no. Sooner or later, you run out of laterals.

Except . . . when you don't.

Cut to Harper Davis Field in Jackson, Mississippi, four days before
Halloween. The Millsaps College Majors played the Trinity University
Tigers in front of 3,974 fans. Both teams were ranked in the Division
III Top 25. Millsaps led the game by 2 when they gave the ball back to
Trinity on the 39-yard line with two seconds left.

It was too far to try a Hail Mary, so they quickly fashioned a chaos
Electric Football game play. "We stood right over there and put in the

---

[*] Every football fan I know was, at least briefly, utterly mesmerized by the infinite
possibilities of Electric Football. Imagine creating your own tiny football universe,
designing your own plays, seeing these little plastic players come to life. It doesn't take
long after opening the box, however, to realize that it doesn't work that way, that the
players go in circles and fall down randomly, and that the action looks nothing at all like
football. My own moment of disillusionment came when someone explained to me that
when the game's motor broke—as it inevitably did within just a few minutes—you could
get the same effect by simply putting the field on top of a working washing machine. That
sort of pierced the magic of the thing.

play," Trinity's Riley Curry would say, pointing to a spot on the sideline. "It was basically, 'Just run.'"

The play went like this.

> Trinity quarterback Blake Barmore threw a short pass over the middle to Shawn Thompson, who cut hard to his right to avoid three tacklers.
>
> Lateral 1: As tacklers closed in on him, Thompson tossed the ball backward to Riley Curry, who ran as fast as he could to the right sideline. He was being chased by six Millsaps defenders. One got his hands on Curry.
>
> Lateral 2: Curry underhanded the ball backward to offensive lineman Josh Hooten, whose expression showed that he had never been so directly involved in the action.
>
> Lateral 3: Hooten instantly and blindly flipped the ball over his head. He did not seem to have any plan in mind, but the ball found its way to receiver Michael Tomlin, who had nowhere to run.
>
> Lateral 4: Tomlin, an instant before he was smashed to the ground, pitched the ball back to another lineman, Stephen Arnold. They were somewhere around midfield.
>
> Lateral 5: Arnold smoothly pitched the ball back to Shawn Thompson, who you might recall was the original receiver on the play.
>
> Lateral 6: Thompson ran left to draw the defense that way and then neatly pitched the ball to receiver Brandon Maddux, who was running to the right.
>
> Lateral 7: Maddux made it to the right sideline, where three Millsaps defenders waited impatiently for him. He stopped briefly, probably because he was exhausted, then flipped the ball backward ten yards to Curry.

Lateral 8: Curry had nowhere to go, he was surrounded, and finally it looked like this play had run out of steam. He voluntarily jumped out-of-bounds, but while in the air he double-clutched and tossed the ball back to Maddux. Curry stayed on the sidelines and joked with friends, "Can you believe this is still going on?"

Lateral 9: Maddux was still too tired to run, so instead he threw the ball across the field to Blake Barmore, the Trinity quarterback.

Lateral 10: Barmore had a bit of running room—nobody had expected he'd get the ball back—and he ran all the way to the Millsaps 34. As tacklers converged on him, he threw the ball backward to Thompson.

Lateral 11: Thompson threw the ball back to Curry, the second time they connected. Curry reversed field and ran directly into three Majors.

Lateral 12: Curry, without even looking, passed the ball to Tomlin, who ran hard to his right. Jonathan Wiener,[*] a sophomore English major who was calling the game, said: "He could go!"

Lateral 13: Tomlin went as far as he could, to the Millsaps 30, and then he flipped the ball back to that lineman Josh Hooten, who had no idea what to do with the ball the first time they tried this.

Lateral 14: This time Hooten calmly threw the ball over his head to Maddux and looked to block somebody.

---

[*] Wiener gained a bit of his own fame after this play, having stories written about him in numerous publications, including the *New York Times*. For professional reasons, he changed his named to Jonathan Bruce and, as of this writing, is an evening news anchor for the ABC affiliate in Houston.

Sort-of-lateral 15: Maddux, who was on his third carry of the play, was still winded from his cross-field run earlier. He flung the ball across the field. It bounced at the 42-yard line—so technically this was not a lateral but a fumble—and it skipped into the hands of Curry.

At this point, the Millsaps players were exhausted and frustrated and just ready for this game to end. One player crouched 20 yards behind the play. Another had his hands on his hips, and he just watched Curry run while giving off an "I didn't sign up for this" vibe.

And Curry found a gigantic hole. He later said that he felt like the whole world had opened up for him. He ran to the 30, the 20, the 10, the 5 . . . and the only Millsaps player with a chance to tackle him was junior Jacob Hanberry. But in the end all Hanberry could do was shove Curry to the ground as he crossed the goal line to score the winning touchdown.

This was one exhausting miracle.

"I kept wondering, 'When is this going to end? I'm actually really tired of running around,'" Curry would later say. "But whatever. It all worked out."

NO. 56:

THE FAKE SPIKE

"I give him credit for that, Bernie.
But I threw it. So, I take credit too."

—DAN MARINO

—

NOVEMBER 27, 1994

There has never been another quarterback quite like my hero Bernie Kosar. He was this gawky 6-foot-5 guy. He couldn't run at all,* he didn't have much of an arm, and he had ghastly form.

And yet, somehow, the guy was terrific. He led the University of Miami to a national championship. He brought life to his (and my) hometown Cleveland Browns, leading them to three AFC Championship Games. How did he do it? Well, for one thing, he was supernaturally accurate. One story that made the rounds was how at Buffalo quarterback Jim Kelly's charity party, he was coaxed at the last minute to participate in a contest to see which quarterback could throw a ball through a car tire from 20 yards away.

Kosar stepped up and threw the ball cleanly through without touching any part of the tire. The other quarterbacks there, including Kelly and probably the greatest thrower in NFL history, Dan Marino, tried to do the same but could not. Finally, one other quarterback managed to barely squeeze one through, bouncing it off the side, and Kosar was called back for a sudden-death throw-off.

He calmly stepped up to the line and threw the ball cleanly through again.

---

* When Kosar was quarterback at the University of Miami, Jenny Kellner of the *Miami News* wrote that he "scrambles with the grace and speed of a giraffe on Quaaludes."

So Bernie had that supernatural precision, but even more he just had a brilliant football mind. He was constantly outthinking defenses. Even after his arm and body gave out, that mind never stopped working. In 1994, he signed with the Miami Dolphins to be Marino's backup and he would constantly offer ideas. One of those ideas he simply called the "clock play."

It's unclear how many times the Dolphins practiced the clock play— it's not actually clear they ever did—but at the end of a Jets-Dolphins game in 1994, Bernie Kosar saw the possibilities of the moment. The Dolphins trailed 24–21. They got the ball at their own 16-yard line.

And then Dan Marino did Dan Marino things. When he was right, wow, nobody ever threw the ball like Marino did. The ball would just jump out of his hand like a bird on a mission. In 1984, Marino's first full season, he threw for 5,000 yards at a time when only a handful of quarterbacks had even thrown for 4,000.* The NFL record for touchdown passes was thirty-six; Marino threw forty-eight. He threw like that, more or less, for the next fifteen years.

Marino started the drive by rifling a pass to Irving Fryar, another to Mike Williams, another to Keith Jackson, two to Mark Ingram. This was Marino at his best, a conductor working the field—first the strings, then the brass, then the percussion—finding whoever was open.

The last pass to Ingram moved the ball to the Jets' 8-yard line. There were thirty-three seconds left. This was when Kosar told Marino through his helmet transmitter, "Clock play! It's time!"

Marino immediately saw it. He shouted out, "Clock! Clock! Clock!" while motioning that he intended to spike the ball. It's unclear how many of his teammates even knew what he was doing.

---

* Even more absurd, Marino's 5,084 yards passing that year was more than DOUBLE the Dolphins' record. Miami coach Don Shula was famously conservative on offense, but once he got Marino, he created the most prolific passing attack in football history. I suppose that's the definition of a good coach.

It's very clear how many of the Jets defenders knew what he was doing. None.

Marino stepped to the line, took the snap, and dropped two steps back. The Jets players assumed he would spike the ball, so they relaxed. Then, suddenly—and it was sudden; Marino had the quickest release in football—the ball was out and headed to Ingram in the end zone. Jets rookie cornerback Aaron Glenn was not entirely fooled—he ran with Ingram—but he had his back turned and the ball zipped behind him and into Ingram's waiting arms. And the Dolphins won.

The Jets went into free fall after the play. They lost all the rest of their games, after which they fired coach Pete Carroll. At first, he blamed the fake spike. But years later—after he established himself as a winner by winning a national title at USC and a Super Bowl with the Seahawks—he still could not let go of the play.

He did an interview with ESPN about it twenty-two years later. The headline was "We Weren't Fooled."

I imagine Bernie Kosar laughing pretty heartily at that one.

NO. 55:

THE STAND

Sportswriter Harold Ratliff: "Do you think you're a genius?"

Bear Bryant: "No, Harold, I'm no genius.
But I'm a damn good football coach."

—

JANUARY 1, 1979

You may have heard that wonderful quote "He can take his'n and beat your'n or he can take your'n and beat his'n." Well, that quote is about Paul "Bear" Bryant.

Well, wait, it's actually more complicated than that. The quote originally was about Missouri coach Don Faurot. After the 1949 Gator Bowl, which Missouri lost to undefeated Clemson by a point, Clemson coach Frank Howard said: "That Faurot, he's so good that he can take his'n and beat your'n or he can take your'n and beat his'n."*

A couple of years later, someone took Howard's words and applied them to Bear Bryant. That someone was Texas humorist Boyce House. In his version, he was getting his shoes shined in College Station, Texas, and he asked a kid, "What kind of coach you got here?"

And the kid supposedly said: "He can take his'n and beat your'n, or he can take your'n and beat his'n."

That coach in College Station was Bear Bryant.

There was no shoeshine kid. There's a long and not terribly proud history in sportswriting of attributing witty and already existing quotes to shoeshine kids, cabdrivers, and bartenders. Still, the quote stuck to

---

* Howard was well-known for his homespun wisdom, perhaps most famously when asked what he thought about starting a rowing team at Clemson. "I won't support any sport where you sit on your ass and go backward," he said.

Bear Bryant. Legendary Florida A&M coach Jake Gaither said it about him. Countless sportswriters used the quote to get at what made him so special.

Over thirty-eight years of coaching at four different schools, Bear's teams always won. His only losing record over all that time came in his first year at Texas A&M in 1954, the famous "Junction Boys" year.* Every other year, his teams won and won big. His Kentucky teams in the early 1950s won a Sugar Bowl and a Cotton Bowl. His 1956 Texas A&M team went undefeated. His Alabama teams won six national championships.

How did he do it?

"I wouldn't tell you if I knew," Bryant wrote in his autobiography. "This is my book you're buying, not my blood."

MAYBE A HINT ABOUT WHAT MADE BEAR BRYANT SUCH A DAMN good football coach can be found in what might have been the most dramatic coaching moment of his life. By 1979, Bear Bryant was more legend than man. There was a poster on walls across Alabama of Bryant walking on water.

His Alabama team was playing undefeated Penn State in the Sugar Bowl with the winner all but certain to be declared national champion. Midway through the fourth quarter, Alabama had the ball and was up a touchdown. That's when the Crimson Tide did something that Bear Bryant's teams rarely did: They got confused. Quarterback Jeff Rutledge, facing intense pressure, tried to pitch the ball back to running back Tony Nathan. The pitch was off target and Nathan wasn't ready

---

* That year, Bryant held a brutal ten-day training camp in the scorching heat of Junction, Texas, in order to find players tough enough to play for him. Most of the team quit during the camp. One of the Junction Boys, Gene Stallings, would later coach Alabama to a national title.

for it. The ball fell to the ground and was recovered by Penn State at the 19.

Soon enough, Penn State had it on the 6-yard line with three chances to score the game-tying touchdown.

On the first play, Penn State quarterback Chuck Fusina flipped a pass to Scott Fitzkee at the 1. Fitzkee seemed sure to score, but somehow Alabama defensive back Don McNeal knocked him sideways and out-of-bounds before he crossed the goal line.

"I wanna tell you something, folks," the marvelous broadcaster Keith Jackson* told the television audience. "That was one whale of a defensive play by Alabama's Don McNeal because Fitzkee has momentum and McNeal just won't let him in!"

Still, Penn State had the ball on the 1, with two more chances to score.

On third down, Penn State gave the ball to Matt Suhey, who attempted to leap over the pile for the score. But Alabama's David Hannah and Curtis McGriff broke through and hit Suhey on his way up. Then Rich Wingo met him at the top of the pile and prevented him from getting in.

And that made it fourth down, with less than a yard to go. This time Penn State gave the ball to Mike Guman, who also tried to leap over the pile. Alabama's Barry Krauss jumped with him, and the two crashed into each other in midair. The collision was so violent that it momentarily knocked Guman unconscious and momentarily left Krauss feeling paralyzed on his left side.

Guman did not get in.

When Krauss got back to the sideline, he saw that his helmet was cracked.

---

* I keep a list of my favorite Keith Jackson quotes. At the top is his line about former Florida quarterback Danny Wuerffel: "He is the kind of guy who would sneak into your house and steal your favorite hat." I don't know what it means even now, but I love it deeply.

"At that instant, that frozen moment, I was only doing the job that had been taught me through thousands of drills in hundreds of practices throughout my Alabama career," Krauss would write in his autobiography, *Ain't Nothin' but a Winner.*

Alabama won the game 14–7, and Bryant won his fifth national championship at Alabama. The next year, he would win his sixth.

"Bear didn't coach football," Bryant's former assistant coach Bum Phillips said. "He coached people."

NO. 54:
BEDNARIK HITS GIFFORD

"A man gets hit and gets hurt."
—CHUCK BEDNARIK

—

NOVEMBER 20, 1960

In 1905, Harvard president Charles Eliot* called for the abolishment of football at the school. This was a jolt. Harvard had been a pioneering football school. Even before the Civil War, before the rules of football were agreed upon, the freshman and sophomore classes at Harvard would play a super-violent football-like game on the first Monday of the school year. They called it "Bloody Monday."

Then, the whole idea of a game that could be called "Bloody Monday" was why Eliot objected to the game in the first place. He wrote that "if a college or university is primarily a place for training men for honorable, generous and efficient service to the community at large," there certainly could not be room for "a game played under the actual conditions of warfare and with the barbarous ethics of warfare."

Football was teetering at that moment. If Eliot had banned it, the game might have been finished in America. But there was one football fan who was not about to let that happen. And that one football fan happened to be Theodore Roosevelt, the president of the United States.

He called for exhaustive rule changes to make football safer without

---

* Eliot transformed Harvard into, perhaps, America's preeminent university, but he was no sports fan. He once talked about eliminating baseball at the school because he heard that a pitcher threw a fine curveball. "I understand the curveball is thrown with a deliberate attempt to deceive," he said. "Surely this is not an ability we would want to foster at Harvard."

making it—and I quote—"too ladylike." Roosevelt's reforms would eventually lead to the forming of the NCAA.

And football raged on.

You cannot separate football and violence. You can make the game progressively safer, but part of the appeal, undeniably, is the violence, the danger, the courage it takes to play. Football fans feel this deeply. The violence attracts and repels and is ever present. Every game, every single one, is stopped multiple times as trainers treat things like broken bones, sprained joints, torn muscles, concussions, and sometimes scarier injuries.

We know that this is when television goes to a commercial break.

In many ways, the Charles Eliot–Teddy Roosevelt argument goes on. You have those calling football barbaric and those who insist that football has gone soft. You have those fighting to make football safer or even to outlaw it. And you have those fighting to keep football from losing its fire and fury and, yes, menace.

Some break from the game over the violence.

At the same time, the game has never been more popular.

"Football is controlled violence," Johns Hopkins professor emeritus Michael Mandelbaum writes. "But it is violence, which people have loved to watch since the gladiatorial contests in ancient Rome."

THEY CALLED CHUCK BEDNARIK "CONCRETE CHARLIE" BECAUSE, well, no explanation necessary. Concrete Charlie was a waist gunner in the Army Air Forces during World War II. Once, while flying over Nazi Germany, his plane took too much enemy gunfire, and when the pilot tried to land the plane, it skidded off the runway. Bednarik jumped out the window.

Then, as John Schulian wrote in *Sports Illustrated*, he lit a cigarette, went to the briefing room, and drank his whiskey straight.

Even in a time of tough men playing football, he was the toughest.

He played sixty minutes, both sides of the ball. "I was not one of the 60-minute men. I was the *last* of the 60-minute men," he growled. He played through so many injuries, he could not even remember them all. He was once fined $500 for punching Chuck Noll in the face and would have gladly paid double to avoid the mandatory apology. He pinned Jim Taylor to the ground at the end of the 1960 NFL Championship Game so that the final seconds could run out. "You can get up now," he told Taylor once the final whistle blew. The NFL had to create a new rule to keep players from doing that.

His most famous moment, certainly, was the ferocious and jaw-dropping hit he put on Frank Gifford in that Eagles championship season of 1960. Even now, you see that hit on grainy black-and-white film and you will involuntarily shout out, "Ouch." Gifford had caught a pass over the middle and was briefly in open space. He broke to his right, where Concrete Charlie waited.

Bednarik slammed his shoulder into Gifford, lifted him off the ground, and then pile-drived him into the turf. The hit knocked Gifford out cold, though Gifford—a tough guy himself—insisted that it was the back of his head hitting the turf that actually caused the damage.

The difference seems immaterial.

Gifford lay motionless on the ground for a long while, and a very famous photograph of Bednarik celebrating over his body appeared in newspapers across the country. Many criticized Concrete Charlie for that, but he said he was not celebrating the hit itself but rather the fumble it caused. "I saw we had the ball," Bednarik said, "and I said 'Yipee, we got it!'"

Again, the difference seems immaterial.

Gifford's *Monday Night Football* announcing partner Howard Cosell loved promoting the myth that the hit knocked Gifford out of football. It did not. He did miss the rest of that season and all of 1961. But he returned in 1962 and played three more years. He always said the hit was clean. "If our roles had been reversed," he said, "I would have done the same thing to him."

Bednarik played until he was thirty-seven. He never lost that Concrete Charlie toughness. Once, long after he retired, someone asked him if he could have held up against the superior athletes in the modern NFL.

"I wasn't rude or anything," he said. "But inside, I was thinking: 'I'd like to punch this guy in the mouth.'"

NO. 53:

MAHOMES MAGIC

"That wasn't quite like it was drawn up."

—KANSAS CITY CHIEFS COACH ANDY REID

—

DECEMBER 11, 2022

Here's the question I undoubtedly will get asked most when this book comes out: "What were the hardest moments to leave out?" That was the question asked most after *Why We Love Baseball* came out. That was the question asked most after *The Baseball 100* came out too. It's a pretty good guess that lots of you will ask after this one too.

I'm going to give you the answer right now.

The hardest moments to leave out were the 1,943,477 Patrick Mahomes moments that didn't fit in this book.

There has never been a football player like Mahomes. We often get caught up in the Greatest of All Time arguments but maybe there's an even higher level than that. There are just a few athletes who are so thrilling, so wonderful, so darned fun to watch, that their greatness almost seems beside the point. Was Dominique Wilkins the greatest basketball player ever? Certainly not. But who would you rather watch play than the man everyone called the "Human Highlight Reel"? Was Bo Jackson the greatest baseball player ever? Not even close. But in his short baseball career, he gave us as many thrills as just about anyone who played ten or fifteen years longer.

Mahomes might yet stake his claim as the greatest ever. But we can say this already: When it comes to making magic, he's already in his own world.

Let me take five minutes to think of five amazing Mahomes plays. OK, got them.

1. There was the left-handed throw he made against the Broncos.

2. There was the spinny, twirly thing he did against Tampa Bay in 2022: He rolled to his right, got in trouble, and then did a spin not unlike what Wonder Woman did on the old TV show. Then he flung a 2-yard touchdown pass to Clyde Edwards-Helaire.

3. There was the crushing 26-yard run against the Eagles in Super Bowl LVII when he had a high-ankle sprain and could barely walk.

4. There was the fourth-and-9 rollout bomb he threw to Tyreek Hill against the Ravens.

5. There was the crazy 27-yard touchdown run he had against Tennessee in the playoffs when he broke three tackles and had CBS's Jim Nance gushing, "Out of this world!"

6. I know I said five, but I'm on a roll now and can't stop. There was the Mahomes bomb he threw to Tyreek Hill on third and 15 against the 49ers in Super Bowl LIV—this when the Chiefs trailed 20–10 in the fourth quarter.

7. There was the play against Indianapolis when he ran backward away from the rush, should have been sacked 15-plus yards, and instead ran around and then threw a strike to Byron Pringle for a 27-yard touchdown. "Only Mahomes," announcer Al Michaels said.

8. There was the sidearm touchdown pass to Jerick McKinnon against the Bears.

9. There have been a series of "jump throws," where Mahomes throws the ball while dangling in midair, the best probably being the long one he threw to Mecole Hardman Jr. against Tennessee.

10. Or, no, the short one he threw to Marquez Valdes-Scantling against Jacksonville.

11. Or, no, wait, the one he threw to Travis Kelce against Jacksonville.

We could keep on going. But I think you see the challenge of picking one.

In fact, since I first wrote that list, Patrick Mahomes led the Chiefs to another Super Bowl title—upsetting three teams along the way—and there were at least a dozen other highlight moments. The best probably came in Super Bowl LVIII against San Francisco when he led the Chiefs on a game-winning 75-yard drive in overtime, a drive that included two crucial runs and, finally, a 3-yard touchdown pass to Mecole Hardman. The man is simply magical.

In the end, I've settled on this one even though it was not "important" in the way some of these others are. This is just the one that best expresses the Patrick Mahomes experience. The Chiefs were playing the Broncos in Denver in 2022, they led 6–0, and on third and 2, Mahomes dropped back to throw. The Broncos pressured him. He rolled to his right and was simultaneously chased by linebacker Jacob Martin and cut off by defensive tackle D. J. Jones. He seemed in a perfectly constructed "no one can escape," James Bond trap. Only the snapping alligators were missing.

Only then, Mahomes—without even looking—flipped the ball over his head as if he were throwing litter out of a moving car.*

The ball landed in the hands of a streaking McKinnon, who caught it in perfect stride and ran untouched for a 50-yard touchdown.

I simply cannot describe how glorious it was. There were so many great reactions to it, but my favorite came from McKinnon himself:

"I saw him going," he said. "And I was like, 'He's either going to run it or it's going to be some crazy shit.'"

Then he smiled. "And . . . crazy shit it is," he said.

---

* Please, do not do this.

NO. 52:

THE TYLER ROSE

"I was all set to wrap him up when he ran right over me.
Nobody has ever done that to me before."

—ISIAH ROBERTSON

E arl Campbell wouldn't talk about the run. We were sitting in the lobby of the Radisson Hotel in Augusta, Georgia, back in 1993. Campbell was in town to speak about his panic disorder. I had only just started writing sports, and I was shaking with nerves.

Earl Campbell was a folk hero to me.

I was eleven years old when the Tyler Rose, as Earl was known, burst onto the NFL scene. That's the right age for folk heroes, that time when the sun is brighter than it will ever be, and the sky is bluer than it will ever be, and you still believe in magic.

We talked about many things. Campbell had this approachable personality; I was taken by his gentleness. We talked about the pain he felt when his father died (he was eleven). We talked about how his mother raised him and kept him from getting into trouble. We talked about his high school days in Tyler, Texas: Campbell wanted to be a linebacker like Dick Butkus, but his coach saw his running genius even before Earl did. We talked about his Heisman Trophy days at the University of Texas.

We talked about his glory days with the Houston Oilers. He joyfully recounted my second-favorite Earl Campbell run; that was the 81-yard run he had against Miami in a Monday night game in 1978. He took a pitch right, eluded one defender, then headed for the sideline. And he ran untouched the rest of the way. My favorite part of the run came at about the 35-yard line, when Dolphins linebacker Steve Towle closed in. At that moment, Campbell turned to look directly at Towle.

"What were you thinking at that moment?" I asked.

"I was thinking, 'You can't possibly think you're going to catch me,'" Earl said.

The interview was a dream. Then I asked him about the Isiah Robertson run, and for the first time he looked away from me, looked down at the ground. A decided chill had descended.

"I don't talk about that," he said.

It happened in just the fourth game of his NFL career. So much was expected of Campbell. He'd been the first pick in the draft. He'd been compared with all the greats, with Jim Brown, with O. J. Simpson, with Tony Dorsett. He was very good in his first three games, but he did not have that breakout moment.

And then he did. The Oilers had first and 10 at the Rams 22-yard line. Campbell took a pitch left, stepped over a blocker, and then headed directly for linebacker Isiah Robertson, one of the best and toughest linebackers in pro football. When Robertson had been at Southern University, people started called him the "Black Dick Butkus." That was how he introduced himself when he joined the Rams.* He'd been to the Pro Bowl each of the previous five seasons.

Earl Campbell didn't think about any of that as he ran.

All he thought, as he saw Robertson standing there, was: *You can't possibly think you're going to tackle me standing up straight like that.*

Campbell lowered his helmet into Robertson's chest and drove through him, sending him three yards backward. It was probably the most savage hit a running back has ever put on a defender. Campbell then cut back to the middle of the field, where strong safety Dave Elmendorf tried to grab him but ended up only tearing the jersey off him. Finally, three Rams players pulled him to the ground.

---

* Robertson took the comparison so seriously that he named his Great Dane "Butkus."

When I asked Earl why he wouldn't talk about it, he shook his head and said that he'd heard that Robertson had never really gotten over that run, that people were always bringing it up to him, and that it had broken him in some way. Earl hated that. That was not why he played football.

Years later, they met, and Campbell apologized for the run. Robertson shrugged. "It's just football," he said.

Campbell was as fierce a runner as anyone—his first three seasons in the NFL can match up with anybody's ever—but he wanted me to know that did not define him as a person. That run had caused someone pain. That was the very last thing that Earl Campbell ever wanted to do.

NO. 51:

"BE BOP BAMBOOZLED (IN 3D!)"

"This is the proudest moment of my life."

—BOB COSTAS

——

JANUARY 22, 1989

Now, as we reach halftime on our list, the question on your mind is obviously: *Was there really a Super Bowl halftime show that featured an Elvis impersonator who didn't sing or look like Elvis doing the world's largest card trick in 3D?*

Yes, Virginia, there was an Elvis Presto and "Be Bop Bamboozled (in 3D!)."

BEFORE WE GET THERE, HERE ARE TEN STEPS TO TODAY'S OVER- the-top Super Bowl halftime extravaganza:

Step 1: In 1922, Walter Lingo, owner and proprietor of the Oorang Dog Kennels in LaRue, Ohio, came up with a curious promotional idea. He went to America's preeminent athlete, fellow Ohioan Jim Thorpe, and convinced him to put together a football team of Native American players. They called the team the Oorang Indians and entered them in the NFL.

Lingo was not especially interested in football; the whole point was to promote his kennels. And as such, he created the first professional football halftime shows. He'd feature Native American dances, shooting exhibitions, and kicking exhibitions; most of all, the show would highlight his Airedale dogs in action. In my favorite version of the show, Airedale Red Cross dogs would deliver first aid to actors dressed up as World War I soldiers.

Step 2: A few years later, a brilliant promoter named Earnie Seiler—the newspapers called him the "Mad Genius"—helped create a college bowl game in Miami to draw in more tourists. The game was called the "Orange Bowl" and Seiler, in order to get attention, began building bigger and more elaborate (and longer) halftime shows. He would drench the entire stadium with orange-blossom perfume to set the scene, and then, well, there was the time he had Peter Pan fly, the time he released a world-record number of balloons, the time he released doves from a huge replica of Uncle Sam, and so on. Every year, it got bigger. The Orange Bowl halftime show presaged the Super Bowl halftime show.

Step 3: In 1970, the Super Bowl had its first halftime performer—Broadway star Carol Channing. This was after three Super Bowl halftime shows featuring college marching bands.

Step 4: In 1976, the halftime show was handed off to a wholesome youth group called Up with People. Their mission was to bring the world together through song and dance and they ended up doing four Super Bowls.*

Step 5: In 1991, New Kids on the Block performed in Tampa. This was in the New Kids' heyday, and it was the first time that the Super Bowl halftime show featured a current superstar act.

Step 6: Michael Jackson performed at halftime in 1993. That changed everything. Suddenly, the Super Bowl was one of the biggest gigs in music.

Step 7: In 2004, Janet Jackson made the biggest headlines imaginable after her breast was briefly exposed during a "wardrobe malfunction." The uproar was overwhelming. "It's hard to believe that there's a war and famine in the world, and yet people made such a big deal about a breast," she would say.

---

* When Up with People did their FOURTH Super Bowl halftime show in 1986, the *Pittsburgh Press* warned: "If the perpetual cheeriness of Up with People makes you nauseous plan to be absent for the group's 12-minute halftime show."

Step 8: In 2007, Prince rather surprisingly acceded to a pregame press conference and was asked, "How do you feel about being at the Super Bowl?" At which point he whipped his guitar around from his back and broke into a searing rendition of "Johnny B. Goode." During halftime of Super Bowl XLI, he sang "Purple Rain" while awash in purple rain, and that's probably the highest height the Super Bowl halftime show has ever reached.

Step 9: After Prince, everybody wanted to do the Super Bowl, so he was followed by Tom Petty, then Bruce Springsteen, then the Who and Madonna and Beyoncé and Shakira and Rihanna. . . . The only true worldwide sensation who has not done the Super Bowl seems to be Taylor Swift, who as of this writing is dating Kansas City's all-world tight end Travis Kelce and was attending NFL games every week, including the 2024 Super Bowl Kelce's Chiefs won.[*]

YOU WILL NOTICE I LISTED ONLY NINE STEPS.

Well, here's the tenth: Elvis Presto and "Be Bop Bamboozled (in 3D!)."

In 1986, after the fourth Up with People halftime show, NFL commissioner Pete Rozelle decided it was time to shake halftime up a bit. "There are three words I don't ever want to hear again when discussing the Super Bowl: Up. With. People," he told his staff. Rozelle was not a particularly adventurous soul, but he wanted something new, so he started taking proposals from production companies. He undoubtedly expected to hear from huge places like Disney and Paramount, and he did.

He also heard from a guy named Dan Witkowski.

He had never heard of Dan Witkowski. How would he have? Witkowski was a stage magician in Minnesota. But one thing Witkowski

---

[*] I went on this Taylor Swift interlude entirely for our younger daughter, Katie, who will not read this book but will definitely search to see if I mentioned Taylor Swift in it.

had was chutzpah, so he made his pitch for a gigantic halftime magic show. And Rozelle, well, he liked the guy. Twenty-five years earlier, Rozelle had taken a chance on an unknown filmmaker named Ed Sabol, and that led to NFL Films. Rozelle gave Witkowski the gig.

Witkowski's magic show needed a music theme, of course. He decided to build it around 1950s rock and roll. "The whole 1950s thing was pretty big at the time," he told the website Mental Floss. "Baby Boomers were trying to relive their youth, so we hooked on that."

Obviously, with the 1950s rock and roll theme, the show needed an Elvis impersonator. Witkowski personally came up with the name "Elvis Presto." They found someone named Jody LoMedico to do the singing; he was not an Elvis impersonator (and was kind of offended by the notion), but people thought he sounded a bit like Elvis. Unfortunately, LoMedico refused to actually be the guy in the stadium—he wasn't going to spend three weeks out of town for the $1,500 they offered—so they hired an actor who had played Elvis on Broadway.

Then that actor found a better opportunity in Japan, so he backed out.

That left a dancer named Alex Cole, who had done the choreography.

None of this was going all that well.

"The guy who did Elvis," LoMedico would say, "whoever you are, I wasn't a fan, man."

While all this was going on, Coca-Cola approached the NFL with their own idea: They wanted to do the halftime show in 3D. They had all these leftover 3D glasses from a failed attempt to do the television show *Moonlighting* in 3D, and so this seemed a great way to get rid of those and maybe garner some attention.

Now what you had was a beautiful, confused, jumbled mess—

Twelve hundred dancers, 102 Harley-Davidson motorcycles, multiple pink Cadillacs, a mishmash of 1950s-adjacent music,* weird magic

---

* Though the theme was the 1950s, most of the music WAS NOT actually from the 1950s. There was the Stray Cats' "Rock This Town" (1981); the Contours' "Do You Love Me"

tricks nobody understood or could follow, a backup Elvis impersonator who didn't look like Elvis, a voice track from someone who didn't want to sound like Elvis, backup singers called the Magic Wandas, and all of it in stunning 3D, meaning that it was "stunning" how much of it didn't work. It was awful. And glorious.

"Couldn't we just see a marching band?" media writer Lynn M. Jackson asked.

No. The days of the marching band were gone. The days of the half-time extravaganza were upon us. And I think the whole amazing thing was best summed up by Bob Costas, who had the honor of hosting "Be Bop Bamboozled (in 3D!)."

"Now, before we go any further," Costas said as he slipped on his 3D glasses at the start of the show, "I'd like to say publicly: This is the single proudest moment of my life."

When I approached Bob about that proclamation thirty-four years later, he did not hesitate.

"It remains so," Costas said.

(1962); "Greased Lightnin'" from *Grease* (1971); and Shorty Long's "Devil with the Blue Dress" (1964). There was only one Elvis song performed by Elvis Presto, "Burning Love," and Elvis didn't sing that until 1972. The only 1950s song performed was Little Richard's "Tutti Frutti."

NO. 50:

LAWRENCE TAYLOR

"When I make mistakes, good things come of it."

—LAWRENCE TAYLOR

———

NOVEMBER 13, 1983

Lawrence Taylor would be the first to tell you: He was not exactly a student of the game. So many of the other great defensive players would spend hours and hours in the video room breaking down offenses, studying schemes, learning everything they could. You take a guy like the great safety Ed Reed: He knew opposing offenses as well as their quarterbacks, sometimes even better.

LT? Nah.

"At times," Taylor wrote in *My Giant Life*, "I didn't even know what defense we were in or what the offense was doing. But I always told the coaches, 'When I make mistakes, good things come of it.'"

He was an athletic superhero. That's all. Running backs and tight ends were not nearly strong enough to block him. Offensive tackles and guards were not nearly fast enough to catch him. And nobody on the field was as mean. In time, teams would try to create all sorts of double-team, triple-team, and quadruple-team blocking concoctions to disrupt him. More often than not, it didn't even matter.

"I guess," LT says, "I was a freak."

THERE'S NO WAY TO RECOUNT ALL THE SUPERNATURAL THINGS Lawrence Taylor did on the field. He once ran down the breathtakingly fast Randall Cunningham from behind. There was the time against the Rams when he ran down wide receiver Henry Ellard from—no exaggeration—the other side of the field. On Thanksgiving Day in 1982 against the Lions, he blitzed, ran through guard Homer Elias, then grabbed quarterback Gary Danielson by the jersey with one hand and flung him to the ground. It was jaw-dropping.

And in that very same game—and it should be added for context that he missed the whole first half with an injured knee—the Lions were trying to score the go-ahead touchdown. Danielson dropped back and threw to the end zone. Taylor stepped in front of the receiver, grabbed the ball, and raced down the sideline 97 yards, looking for all the world like Earl Campbell or Bo Jackson.

"I thought you had a bad wheel," a teammate yelled at him after the game.

LT smiled. "The ball in my hand took care of the pain," he said.

There was the time he smashed through the hapless New York Jets line, sacked quarterback Ken O'Brien, and said, with something resembling sympathy in his voice, "Son, y'all gotta do better than this."

Week after week, he did stuff like that. He knocked offensive linemen back into their own quarterbacks. He ran through tight ends and blocked fullbacks with such ease, it didn't seem fair. He knocked the ball free time after time. He once played a game against the Saints in which his shoulder was so injured, he had to wear a harness. He had three sacks and two forced fumbles. No defensive player ever had a better sense for the big moment and how to make that moment his.

He altered games. And he also altered *the* game.

"He changed the way defense is played, the way pass rushing is played, the way linebackers play, and the way offenses block linebackers," coach and broadcaster John Madden said.

Yes, it was Lawrence Taylor who made the left tackle one of the most important (and highly paid) positions in football. It was Lawrence Taylor who convinced teams that if they wanted their offense to go, they needed to invest whatever was necessary to protect the quarterback's blind side. In fact, as Taylor told Michael Lewis for *The Blind Side*, the very term for the quarterback's back side was invented for him. "It was called the right side," Taylor said. "It *became* the blind side after I started knocking people's heads off."

"He arrived in the NFL," the legendary football writer Paul Zimmerman said, "like an emissary from another planet."

Zimmerman always said that Taylor made the greatest defensive play he ever saw and so that's the play we'll include here. It happened in November of 1983. The game didn't matter at all; the Giants came into the game with just two wins and no playoff hopes. Washington, meanwhile, was on its way to a second consecutive Super Bowl. Washington quickly took a 10–0 lead.

Then Washington quarterback Joe Theismann dropped back to throw. Taylor and Theismann would become forever linked for a play that happened almost exactly three years later when Taylor came crashing in from the blind side and gruesomely snapped Theismann's leg. This time, Taylor rushed and was cut off by Washington's 300-pound All-Pro left tackle, Joe Jacoby.

Taylor flung Jacoby to the ground.

As Theismann began to run from the pocket, Washington's right tackle, George Starke, slid over to stop Taylor from chasing after the quarterback.

"Taylor knocks him to the ground without breaking stride," Zimmerman wrote.

By now Theismann was gone, 10 yards downfield; he was a speedy quarterback. He'd finished second in the Heisman Trophy voting*

---

* In 1970, the hype to win the Heisman was so intense that Theismann actually changed the pronunciation of his last name. He and his family had always pronounced it "THEES-man," but together with the Notre Dame marketing crew, they changed it so that it rhymed with Heisman. Even after he lost the Heisman, he kept the new pronunciation. "My wife married me under that pronunciation," he said, "and I'm going to stick with it."

while at Notre Dame, mainly as a running quarterback. He could move. But Lawrence Taylor chased him down anyway and made the tackle.

"That's 560 pounds of linemen he's disposed of and a 4.6 quarterback he's run down," Zimmermann wrote. "And it's in a hopeless cause."

There were no hopeless causes for LT. "If I can play in a game," he said, "I can control it."

NO. 49:

THE HALLOWEEN RUN

"I don't think I got hit much harder in the game than I did by my teammates in the end zone. I was lucky to get out alive."

—BILLY CANNON

—

OCTOBER 31, 1959

Billy Cannon grew up in Baton Rouge, just a few miles away from the campus of Louisiana State University. But he didn't dream of playing for LSU. No, he dreamed of playing at Texas A&M for Bear Bryant. All the best wanted to play for Bear.

Billy Cannon wanted to be the best.

But Bear didn't call. Cannon was a high school sensation, recruited by everybody. He scored 39 touchdowns his senior year. He set the Louisiana state record in the 100-yard dash and the shot put. Everybody wanted him. But not Bear.

Cannon always figured that was because of the various legal troubles he had gotten into in high school. (Those legal troubles would follow Cannon all his life.) But as it turns out, that was probably not the reason. See, LSU's coach, Paul Dietzel, had spent two years as an assistant for Bryant at Kentucky. That meant he was directly aware of Bear's more, er, questionable recruiting tactics. After Louisiana native John David Crow left the state to play for Bear Bryant[*] —and it was said he drove out of Louisiana in a brand-new Oldsmobile—Dietzel called Bryant.

In his autobiography, *Call Me Coach*, he recalled saying, "Coach Bryant,

---

[*] John David Crow won the Heisman Trophy while playing for Bryant in 1957. Incredibly, he would be the only Bear Bryant player to win the Heisman.

I don't really care what you and your staff do in Texas, Arkansas, or wherever. But in Louisiana, there are some things you are doing that are not legal. I want you to know that in the future, if any of your coaches break the rules in Louisiana, I'm going to turn you in to the NCAA."

"And," Dietzel recalled a half century later, "we never lost another athlete to Texas A&M."

That's how Billy Cannon ended up at LSU.

He quickly became an LSU great. In his junior year, he led the conference in rushing and touchdowns, led the Tigers to an undefeated season and their first national championship, and finished third in the Heisman voting.

After the punt return, though, he was something bigger. LSU was undefeated and No. 1 that Halloween day. They were playing undefeated No. 2 Mississippi. Ole Miss led 3–0 with about ten minutes left in the game. The field was mud.

Ole Miss's Jake Gibbs boomed a long and high punt to the LSU 11.

Cannon was unsure how to handle it. Dietzel had a strict rule that his players should never field a punt inside the LSU 15-yard line. But then the ball bounced straight up to Cannon, like a puppy hopping into his arms, and he felt helpless against its wishes. He began running and Ole Miss's Larry Grantham—who would later be elected to the school's Hall of Fame—closed in. Cannon faked left, cut right, and slipped by him.

Cannon stumbled briefly and then drove his way through two tackles. Like that, he was in an open field. He had only one man to beat, the punter and quarterback, Jake Gibbs.* This is how Cannon remembered it for the book *Billy Cannon: A Long, Long Run*:

"Gibbs thought I was going to the wide side of the field, so I gave a

---

* Gibbs, being a punter, did not try to tackle anyone else. He would go on to a ten-year baseball career as a catcher for the New York Yankees.

little head fake. Now, I've got to give Jake great credit on this: That was the only tackle he missed in his entire career."

The rest is history. Cannon was moving so fast that in the film of the play—still shown every Halloween in Louisiana—the camera loses track of him at one point. But it picked up Cannon by the end zone, where his teammates swarmed him in triumph. That run, surely, won Billy Cannon the Heisman Trophy. It is the most singular play in the grand history of LSU football.

Cannon's life after the run took many turns. He played some pro football, became a dentist, and raised five children with his wife, Dot, whom he first started dating in high school. He also lost all his money by gambling and making bad investments, and he was sent to prison for his involvement in an elaborate counterfeiting scheme.

"Maybe," *Sports Illustrated* wrote, "that one run—without it, Cannon never would have won the Heisman—ultimately made him too big a hero, and coping with the adulation eventually became too much for him."

Cannon himself made no such excuses. His life was his life. After being released from one prison in Texarkana, he went to another, the Louisiana State Penitentiary in West Feliciana, this time to be the prison's dentist.

The inmates called him "Legend."

NO. 48:

THE BALLAD OF DUKE

"No All-American team is complete without
the name Duke Slater on it."

—KNUTE ROCKNE

NOVEMBER 28, 1929

There are people in sports history who make sense . . . and those
who do not. Duke Slater is one of those people who makes no
sense at all. Everything about him feels fictional.

Slater was an All-American football player at Iowa in the 1920s.

He was a star in the NFL, one of the great blocking linemen of the
early days of the NFL.

He became a municipal court judge in Chicago.

In 1951, he was elected to the College Football Hall of Fame's first
class.

All of these things are remarkable on their own.

What makes them beyond belief is simply this: Duke Slater was
Black.

LET'S GET OUR TIMELINE STRAIGHT FIRST. DUKE SLATER PLAYED
college football at Iowa a half century before John Mitchell became the
first Black player at Alabama. Duke Slater was a first-team All-Pro in
the NFL decades before Jackie Robinson broke the color barrier in
baseball. He was the only African American in that College Football
Hall of Fame first class—four years before Rosa Parks refused to go to
the back of the bus, a dozen years before Martin Luther King said, "I
have a dream."

How have there not been *multiple* movies made about Duke Slater's life?

HERE'S A MOVIE SCENE: WHEN DUKE WAS FOURTEEN YEARS OLD, his father, George Slater, forbade him from playing football. George was a strict Methodist minister and football repulsed him. Duke tried to argue but his father would not listen. Football was out.

Do you know what Duke Slater did?

He went on a hunger strike until his father gave in.

DUKE SLATER PLAYED FOOTBALL FOR MANY YEARS WITHOUT A helmet because, as the story goes, when he first began playing, shoes cost $6 and a helmet cost $4. He could afford one of them. He chose shoes.

EVERYBODY PLAYED BOTH OFFENSE AND DEFENSE IN DUKE SLA-ter's day. Few, though, could dominate on both sides like Slater could. He stood about 6-foot-1, 215 pounds, and was lightning quick. And so, on offense, he cleared pathways like no one else. And on defense he seemed to be everything, everywhere, all at once.

Back in Iowa, his Clinton High School team once played powerhouse West Aurora High School, a team that had not lost in three years. The people there that day said that Duke won the game single-handedly. After the game, according to Slater's teammate Burt Ingwersen, some angry West Aurora fans approached him and backed him up against a tree.

"They were going to be rough," Ingwersen told Slater biographer Neal Rozendaal. "I guess they weren't accustomed to seeing a great Negro athlete."

And you know what Duke did? He got down into his blocking stance and challenged any of them to charge at him. One by one they did, and he gently blocked them and tackled them, delighting them all.

"Duke," Ingwersen said, "sure could win friends."

IN 1921, SLATER WAS AT IOWA WHEN HIS HAWKEYES PLAYED Notre Dame—again, a team that had not lost in three years. Duke was ferocious. "Slater figured in play after play," the South Bend News-Times reported. Iowa won the game 10–7. On Iowa's game-winning touchdown run, Slater blocked no fewer than three Notre Dame defenders.

"That fellow Slater just about beat my team single-handed," Notre Dame's legendary coach Knute Rockne said.

IN 1922, THERE WERE NO RULES—SPOKEN OR UNSPOKEN— against African Americans playing professional football. It wasn't common, by any means. There were only three Black players in the league. But they were prominent players:

- Fritz Pollard both coached and guided Akron to an undefeated season in the league's inaugural season of 1920.

- Paul Robeson, who would become an international star as a singer and actor, was Pollard's teammate in Milwaukee.

- J. Mayo Williams—everybody called him "Inky"—later became one of the most successful record producers in music history.*

Duke Slater wasn't interested in playing professional football. He had been offered an assistant coaching job at Iowa, and that seemed a

---

* It was later said that his nickname "Inky" came from his rare ability to get African American musicians to sign with him. It isn't true: They called him Inky going all the way back to his days at Brown.

more stable life. Then Walt Flanigan, owner of the Rock Island Independents, offered Slater a position both as a player and offensive line coach. There was a little extra money attached and Duke became a professional football player.

In his third game, Rock Island beat Evansville 60–0—Jimmy Conzelman set an NFL record with 5 touchdowns—and Slater was so dominant (he even blocked a punt) that the next week reporters kept asking Rochester coach Doc Alexander how he planned to stop Duke.

"Who do you birds figure Slater is anyway?" Alexander grumped. "Do you people figure he's the first lineman that ever played football? Well, I'm here to tell you our regular man will play against him—and no one else will."

One sportswriter couldn't help but mock Alexander's boast: "A few minutes after Captain Alexander spoke, we heard other members of the squad talk about Slater and, judging from their line of chatter, the 'Duke' is going to find two or more to do business with next Sunday instead of one."

Rochester couldn't find enough people to block him. Rock Island won 26–0. There's no counting how many tackles Slater made in the game. You get the impression from the newspaper accounts that he made all of them.

BY 1927, SLATER WAS THE ONLY BLACK PLAYER IN THE NFL. DUKE was so good that the Chicago Cardinals wouldn't have thought of letting him go.

"Duke Slater's level of excellence single-handedly prevented a color ban from forming in the NFL," Rozendaal wrote.

That's not to say that Slater was immune to racism. Far from it. Every game, it seemed, some opponent took an extra hit or unleashed a racist slur. He rose above it. Leo Kriz, who had played with Slater at Iowa, remembered a teammate on the football New York Yankees taking cheap shots at Slater.

"Duke just looked up at the fellow and said in a quiet voice, 'Look, man, don't do that, because I don't want to hurt you,'" Kriz said. "The guy stopped the dirty play right there."

DUKE'S GREATEST GAME HAPPENED ON THANKSGIVING DAY 1929, Chicago Cardinals versus Chicago Bears. This was hyped up as a matchup of the two greatest backs of the age, the Bears' Red Grange and Slater's Cardinals teammate Ernie Nevers.

Slater prevented the matchup from taking flight. On defense, he and his Cardinals swarmed Grange and kept him from doing much of anything.[*] And on offense, Duke blocked so ferociously that Nevers had one of the greatest individual days in the history of professional football. Nevers scored 6 touchdowns.[†]

But it was hardly an individual performance. Bill Bidwill, whose father owned the Cardinals when he was young, would recall the story of Nevers simply pointing at spots in the Bears line and having Slater smash them open.

"Duke Slater, the veteran colored tackle, seemed the dominant figure in that forward wall which had the Bears front wobbly," the *Chicago Herald-Examiner* wrote. "It was Slater who opened the holes for Nevers when a touchdown was in the making."

SLATER BECAME A PRACTICING LAWYER EVEN WHILE PLAYING IN the NFL. After he retired, he became a judge. He opened the door for

---

[*] As it happened, it was Red's brother, Garland Grange, who scored the Bears' only touchdown of the day.
[†] Nevers also kicked four extra points, giving him 40 points, still the record for most points scored by one player.

African American players to sign at Iowa; one of them, Emlen Tunnell, would be the first Black player elected to the Pro Football Hall of Fame. Slater joined him there but, sadly, that didn't happen for more than a half century.

George Halas named Slater the "Rock of Gibraltar."

Red Grange called him the greatest lineman he ever faced.

The University of Iowa named the field at Kinnick Stadium for him.

Yes, a folk hero to the end.

Four years after Slater retired, the NFL officially and shamefully joined baseball as a fully segregated league.

NO. 47:

THE MIRACLE IN MOTOWN

"I throw it high."

—AARON RODGERS EXPLAINING THE SECRET

—

*DECEMBER 3, 2015, AND JANUARY 16, 2016,
AND JANUARY 8, 2017*

Nobody should be able to perfect the Hail Mary pass just like nobody should be able to win consistently at roulette or routinely pick Lotto numbers or always find a parking spot near the door of a movie theater. The pass is called a "Hail Mary" because it is a prayer, a last gasp, an act of desperation, and nobody should be able to perfect an act of desperation.

This is what makes Aaron Rodgers so absurdly confusing.

There have been, as of this moment I am writing these words, thirty-six successful Hail Mary passes over the past fifty years, depending on how literal you want to be about what makes a Hail Mary. Aaron Rodgers has thrown three of them.

As wild as that number is, it's the inevitability that really blows the mind. None of the three Hail Marys looked like desperation. They all looked pretty well planned out.

The first and probably best of the Rodgers Hail Marys happened in Detroit in 2015. It's called the Miracle in Motown. The Packers trailed 23–21 and had the ball on their own 39-yard line with time for one play. Rodgers dropped back, saw two Lions defenders burst through the line, ran backward to get away from them, stopped as they closed in, broke free, worked into the clear, and heaved the ball from the 36.

"Will it get there?" broadcaster Phil Simms asked, and it was the most logical question to ask because few mortals can throw the ball 70 yards in the air. None, perhaps, could throw it that far and that high in such a moment.

The Lions had five defenders in the area, which was good. None of them covered tight end Richard Rodgers, though, which was bad. Richard Rodgers leaped and made the touchdown catch. It didn't seem like luck at all.

Six weeks later, the Packers faced Arizona in a wild playoff game, and they trailed by a touchdown. This play was not as spectacular. The better one happened a few seconds earlier when, on fourth and 20, Rodgers dropped back into his own end zone, rolled left, and fired a 60-yard dream of a pass to receiver Jeff Janis.

But a Hail Mary is a Hail Mary so . . . the Packers had the ball at the Arizona 41 with five seconds left. Arizona had seen what happened in Detroit and decided they wouldn't give Rodgers the chance to do that again. Instead of dropping everyone back, they sent six rushers in a full-on blitz. Rookie linebacker Markus Golden broke through the line and had what looked like a clear shot on Rodgers. But Rodgers spun away. Golden stayed with him and closed in for the tackle when Rodgers, entirely off-balance, just threw the ball as high and far as he could.

Nobody can throw the ball 60 yards in the air from that position.

But we've already established this: There's nothing beyond Rodgers's arm. The ball flew to the end zone. Two Cardinals defenders—Rashad Johnson and Patrick Peterson (who will probably be in the Hall of Fame someday)—were the only ones there.

Then suddenly somebody named Jeff Janis—who had caught two passes for the Packers all season—ran between them, leaped, and pulled it in for a touchdown.

"That," announcer Cris Collinsworth said in the moment, "might be one of the great throws ever made."

Arizona fans will want it noted for the record that the Cardinals ended up winning that game in overtime. So noted. But that's two Hail Marys for Rodgers.

The third came almost exactly a year later, again in a playoff game. This was at the end of the first half instead of at the end of the game, with the Packers already leading. Still, Green Bay had the ball at the New York 42 with time for one play. The Giants did not pressure Rodgers—two of their pass rushers collided, knocking each other out of the play—so he was able to casually roll to his right and wait for his receivers to get downfield. Rodgers unloaded the pass from just beyond midfield. Again, it was more than 60 or so yards in the air and so impossibly high.

The ball flew to the back of the end zone, where Randall Cobb had slipped behind the defense. He pulled it in for the touchdown. Aaron Rodgers, man.

"Unbelievable!" Joe Buck yelled. But the crazy part was, it wasn't unbelievable at all.

NO. 46:
KENNY WASHINGTON SIGNS

"You folks haven't seen anything
until you see Kenny Washington
play football."

—SANTA CLARA ALL-AMERICAN JOHN SCHIECHL

———

MARCH 21, 1946

In the early 1930s, with the Depression raging, the National Football League wanted nothing more than to become like Major League Baseball. Who could blame them? Baseball was far and away the most dominant sport in the country. Baseball got the most coverage, had the most fans, drove the most conversations.

The NFL, meanwhile, was viewed as a rinky-dink operation filled with thugs and mercenaries.

With things around America looking utterly bleak, the NFL doubled down on its imitation of baseball. They split the league into two divisions, mirroring baseball's American and National Leagues. They set up a championship game that was meant to be a pro football World Series. They added four teams in baseball markets—Boston, Cincinnati, Pittsburgh, and Philadelphia—and named the first three after the local baseball teams.

And they fully stopped drafting or signing Black players for twelve years.

There were many great Black players ignored over those years, but the most prominent was certainly UCLA superstar Kenny Washington. In 1939, Washington led the nation in total offense, he was equally brilliant on defense, and he willed UCLA to an undefeated season. He even received notable Heisman Trophy support from West Coast writers. His UCLA teammate Jackie Robinson called him the greatest long passer in the history of football.*

Washington still went undrafted out of college. There were some media efforts to get a team to sign him, but no one did. Washington said Bears owner George Halas kept him around for a month after a college all-star game to figure out a way to sign him but was blocked by Washington's overtly racist owner, George Preston Marshall. We will never know how serious Halas was; the first great Black player in pro football, Fritz Pollard, insisted that Halas was as determined to ban Black players as Marshall.

Plus, in 1970, when Halas was asked why the league had been segregated, he rejected the question out of hand and insisted there was no ban. Halas said the reason there were no Black players in the NFL was "probably due to the fact there were no great Black players then."

THE STORY OF FOOTBALL'S REINTEGRATION REVOLVES AROUND the city of Cleveland. In early 1945, a Cleveland sports fan named Arthur McBride—who had become a millionaire mainly by organizing the newsboys who delivered the *Cleveland News*†—decided to bring to Cleveland a new football team to play in the new All-American Football Conference. He didn't want just any team either; he paid a record price for a guy by the name of Paul Brown; then he named the team after Brown.

The Browns, he insisted, would become the greatest football team in the world.

---

* In addition, Washington was an amazing baseball player: Longtime baseball coach Rod Dedeaux would always say that Washington was a better ballplayer than his teammate, a guy named Jackie Robinson.

† This could not be less relevant, but the news was absorbed by the rival *Cleveland Press*, a paper I delivered as a boy. This, alas, was after the days of us being organized, and the $5.35 I made per week had to suffice.

As you might imagine, none of this sat well with Dan Reeves, the owner of the NFL team in town, the Cleveland Rams. In truth, Reeves never liked Cleveland all that much anyway—he had bought them because "it was the only team available"—and he felt certain that he could make riches galore by moving to Los Angeles and playing in majestic 100,000-seat Memorial Coliseum. The Browns' arrival gave him the excuse he needed to make the move.

When NFL commissioner Elmer Layden seemed skeptical of the move, Reeves banded with some allies among the owners and got Layden fired. New commissioner Bert Bell was more accommodating. The Rams announced their move to Los Angeles in January of 1946. And within a few weeks, Reeves sent his general manager Chile Walsh to the Los Angeles Coliseum Commission meeting in what he assumed would be a simple rubber-stamp approval allowing his team to play in the Coliseum.

Then a man named Halley Harding rose to speak.

Harding had been a fantastic athlete—a football star in college, a professional basketball player, and a Negro Leagues shortstop for the Indianapolis ABCs. After retiring, he became the sports editor of the *Los Angeles Tribune*. Walsh did not know who he was when he first started speaking. He would not forget Harding.

Harding began by reminding everyone that the Coliseum was publicly owned, meaning it was paid for by his wife and African American taxpayers. He offered a brief history of the NFL's ban of Black players, singling out George Preston Marshall as the primary cause. He then spent a couple of moments retelling the story of Kenny Washington and called it singularly strange that he was ignored by the NFL despite his greatness. People in the room started to get riled up.

"Is it true," one of the commissioners, Roger W. Jessup, asked somewhat angrily, "that other players would refuse to play with or against our Kenny Washington?"

"I do not believe it is true, no," Harding said.

Another commissioner, Anson Ford, stood to applaud Harding's stand. And then the commission president, Leonard Roach, looked at an ashen Chile Walsh and asked: "Will you return to answer the question if the Rams will give Negro players an opportunity to play?"

"We will take any player of ability we can get," Walsh said quickly, and then directly to the point he added, "Kenny Washington is welcome to try out for our team anytime he likes."

The very next day, Walsh publicly invited Washington to try out.

Two months later, on March 21, the Rams signed Washington. Even then the NFL adamantly denied that there had ever been a ban, and *Los Angeles Times* writer Dick Hyland felt obligated to include this odd paragraph in his story:

"The National Football League has never had a rule against the use of Negro players and no precedent is being set by Washington's signing, despite the fact that no member of his race has played in the league since 1933."

Shortly afterward, the Rams signed Washington's friend Woody Strode* and the two men broke the NFL color barrier on September 29, 1946.

KENNY WASHINGTON WAS NOT THE FIRST BLACK PLAYER TO APpear in a pro football game in 1946, however. That happened back in Cleveland, when the Browns played their first game against the Miami Seahawks in front of more than sixty thousand curious fans.

For Browns coach Paul Brown, the only thing that mattered to him was excellence. When he looked at the All-American Football Conference constitution, he saw no rules against signing Black players. So he offered a tryout to his former tackle at Ohio State Big Bill Willis, who

---

* Strode would go on to a fine Hollywood acting career; he was nominated for a Golden Globe for his portrayal of the gladiator Draba in the 1960 film *Spartacus*.

stood 6-foot-2, 210 pounds, and was so fast that he ran sprints on the Ohio State track team.

"He was like a black panther when he was playing for me at Ohio," Brown said.

The next day, Brown offered a tryout to back Marion Motley, who had played for him in the Navy during World War II. Willis and Motley were both spectacular as the Browns destroyed the Seahawks 44–0. Both are in the Pro Football Hall of Fame. Football writer Paul Zimmerman would always insist that Motley was the greatest football player he ever saw.

AND WHAT OF KENNY WASHINGTON? ALAS, HE WAS SIGNED SIX years too late. Had he signed coming out of college in 1940, nobody doubted that he would have been an all-time great.

But by 1946, Washington was a shell of himself. He'd badly hurt his knee playing semiprofessional football. Dick Hyland, who had written admiringly about Washington as a college star, wrote a sad column with this conclusion: "I am most tempted to predict, flatly, that Kenny will not make the grade or class of ball played in the National Football League."

He wasn't entirely right: Washington did have a few bright moments in his NFL career, including a breathtaking 92-yard run against the Chicago Cardinals that hinted at what might have been. But he wasn't entirely wrong either. Kenny Washington was a part-time player for three years. He wasn't the same. After his NFL career, he tried to go back to baseball, but as one scout told the *Los Angeles Times*, "All those years of football took too much out of him."

Kenny Washington opened the door. But, alas, the door opened too late for him.

NO. 45:
"I CLOSED MY EYES"

"There was literally nothing that John Mackey couldn't do. If he had
taken off and started flying, all of us would have just nodded."

—TEAMMATE BILL CURRY

—

NOVEMBER 20, 1966

John Mackey was angry that day. His Colts, who still had dreams of
going to the first Super Bowl, had been lackluster during their
game against the lowly Lions. Quarterback John Unitas threw five interceptions before Colts coach Don Shula finally benched him. The
Colts defense missed tackle after tackle. Their kicker Lou Michaels
missed three field goals.

"We weren't ready to play. I can't explain it," Shula said afterward.

In the fourth quarter, Baltimore trailed 17–0. The backup quarterback, Gary Cuozzo, flipped a diagonal pass out to the Colts' tight end,
John Mackey, in the flat.

How do you sum up the sheer brilliance of John Mackey? You can
talk about how he is in the Hall of Fame, how he was the starting tight
end on the 50th Anniversary All-NFL team and so on, but even such
plaudits fall short. He was something new. As NFL Films' Steve Sabol
wrote, he took the tight end position from a "biplane to the space
shuttle."

Mackey stepped around the Lions' free safety, Wayne Rasmussen.
And with that, he was faced with the entire Detroit Lions defense—
Alex Karras and Mike Lucci and Roger Brown and Wayne Walker and
Bruce Maher and Bobby Thompson.

"When I saw all those defenders coming," Mackey said, "I made up
my mind that I was going to punish *somebody*. They had about seven or

eight guys there to make the tackle. I closed my eyes and said, 'I'm just going to ram into them.'"

That's precisely what he did. Mackey just blasted his way forward without concern for his own safety or the safety of the others.

"Mackey," says Ernie Accorsi, who was the Colts' public relations director in the 1960s, "was faster than anybody. And he was stronger than anybody. He could run around defensive backs, but that didn't interest him. I'd see him slow down so he could run over them."

Mackey closed his eyes and ran forward and smashed through the entire Lions team. And when he opened his eyes, he was free, all alone. He had come through the other side and all that was left was to sidestep Dick LeBeau and run the final 30 yards for one of the greatest individual-effort touchdowns ever. In all, ten different players had had a chance to tackle him.

The funny part is, only nine of those players were Lions. The tenth was his own teammate Lenny Moore, who was trying to block a defender. But when Mackey got rolling, he did not discriminate, and Mackey crashed through Moore too.

"Well, it didn't matter what team you were on," Mackey's teammate Bill Curry would say. "You didn't want to get in John's way."

NO. 44:

PLANO EAST VERSUS JOHN TYLER

"I done wet my britches."

—ANNOUNCER DENNY GARVER

—

NOVEMBER 26, 1994

There's a wonderful scene near the end of the movie *The Princess Bride* in which Westley is brought back from the dead—well, technically, from being *mostly* dead—and he has no idea what's going on. He asks a flurry of questions of the two men who revived him.

"Let me explain," Inigo Montoya says. "No, there is too much. Let me sum up."

That's all we can do with the messy, chaotic, rambling, labyrinthine, and bewildering high school football game between Plano East and John Tyler, one that led one of the announcers, Denny Garver, to shout out the lead-in quote: "I done wet my britches."

We cannot explain. We can only sum up.

This was a Texas Class 5A regional semifinal game between Plano East High School, just north of Dallas, and John Tyler High, about a hundred miles to the southeast. The game was played at Texas Stadium in Irving, where the Dallas Cowboys played. Both teams came into the game undefeated.

We probably don't need to talk about how big high school football is in Texas. We'll leave that to Plano East coach Scott Phillips: "It's bigger than life."

For the longest time, the game wasn't especially competitive. In a one-minute span in the fourth quarter, John Tyler's Marc Broyles returned a fumble 90 yards for a touchdown and Dave Warren returned a fumble 35 yards for another touchdown. That gave John Tyler a seemingly insurmountable 41–17 lead with three minutes left in the game.

"Seemingly insurmountable" is a sportswriting phrase that tells you something wild is coming.

In the announcing booth, you had Garver, a mailman by day, and you had longtime Texas broadcaster and actor Eddy Clinton. They were joined by Lake Highlands football coach Mike Zoffuto, who was there to scout the game; his team had already punched its ticket to the regional final.

With 2:36 left, Plano East quarterback Jeff Whitley connected with Terrance Green for a touchdown. That cut the deficit to eighteen.

"Dadgummit," a somewhat peppier Clinton said, "thataway to go, Jeff Whitley!"

Plano East's onside kick bounced off a John Tyler player and Plano East recovered. With 1:29 left, on fourth and goal, Whitley threw a 5-yard touchdown pass to Jonathan Braddick. After a successful two-point conversion, the deficit was ten.

Another onside kick. This time John Tyler's Roderick Dunn touched the ball and Plano East got it back again. They drove down the field in about thirty seconds, converting on a fourth and 10 on one play, and scored on another Whitley-to-Braddick pass.

"Yes, sir!" Garver shouted. "Good gosh almighty!"

Absurdly, even after failing on the two-point play, Plano East now trailed by only four.

Plano East lined up for another onside kick. "Can the improbable happen a third time?" Clinton wondered. Yes. Once again Dunn tried to recover the kick and saw it bounce off his hands. Plano East got the ball back.

"Break out the Oreos, baby!" Garver shouted.

This time it took Plano East only three plays to score the touchdown. It came on a 23-yard touchdown pass from Whitley to a wide-open Robert Woods running down the sideline.

"God Almighty they've done it, they've done it, they've done it!" Garver shouted, and then added, "Everybody on their cars on the radio back in Plano, y'all've done missed the greatest comeback of all time!"

There can be no argument. To come back from 24 points down in the final three minutes in a flurry that had to include three successful onside kicks and four touchdown passes? Unprecedented. Absolutely.

However, the game wasn't over yet. There were still twenty-four seconds left. And that guy Roderick Dunn, who had twice fumbled the onside kicks, stood back to return the kick with fury in his heart.

"I was thinking," Dunn would say, "if they kick it to me, I'm doing my best to make it to the end zone."

They kicked it to him. He got the ball at the 3-yard line.

"All right," Garver said, "just stick it to him."

Nobody could stick it to him. Dunn ran to his left and then, at about the 20-yard line, he made a hard cut to the middle between seven Plano East players. Not one of the seven touched him. Dunn broke into the clear and was surrounded by blockers. He ran all the way for the touchdown that won the game.

In the booth, Zoffuto, who had spent most of the game quietly being entertained by Clinton and Garver, seemed to grasp the gravity of the moment first. All this happened so long ago. Zoffuto died in 2012 after a battle with dementia. Garver died in 2017. Eddy Clinton is in his seventies and he still appears in commercials around Dallas. All the players in the game—Dunn and Whitley and Braddick and the rest—are all in their late forties, grown-ups with lives and memories of the greatest high school football game ever played.

Zoffuto's words echo still.

"Oh, gosh. I don't believe it," he said. "I'm sick. I want to throw up."

NO. 43:

BEAST QUAKE

"He just ran through the whole team."

—SEATTLE'S BRANDON STOKELY

—

JANUARY 8, 2011

I t was always startling when you stood next to Marshawn Lynch because, honestly, the guy just wasn't all that big. I mean, sure, 5-foot-
11, 215 or so pounds of pure muscle, isn't exactly small; he was no
Oompa-Loompa. But when you watched Marshawn Lynch run through
people, you would have sworn he was eight feet tall and had to weigh a
couple of tons.

That was just Beast Mode.

"Beast Mode," Lynch explained, easily jumping into the third person,
"is simply when Marshawn can't get tackled by one defender."

Time after time in his marvelous career, Lynch would go into Beast
Mode and defenders would scatter and fly like bowling pins. In the
middle of the 2010 season, the Buffalo Bills—who for some odd reason
believed that they had too many good running backs—traded Lynch
to Seattle. He struggled to make much of an impact on his new team at
first.

Then the Seahawks made the playoffs despite a 7-9 record; they remain the only team in NFL history to make the playoffs with a losing
record. Not only that, but because they won the staggeringly weak NFC
West Division, they got to play their first playoff game at home even
though New Orleans had a much better record.

The Seahawks were the rarest of things: a 10-point home underdog
in the playoffs.

Seattle fans will tell you they are the loudest fans in the NFL.* And
with the crowd at its most feverish, the Seattle offense played an
inspired game. Quarterback Matt Hasselbeck threw four touchdown
passes. The Seahawks led 34–30 with a little more than three minutes left.

Then Seattle called the running play "17 Power."

"I don't know if it was even in the game plan," Seattle tackle Sean
Locklear said after the game. "That's old-school power football."

"With Power," Lynch said, "we're running straight downhill. You
know we're coming. We know where you're going to be lined up at. Now
all you've got to do is stop it. I'm saying I'm better than you."

And . . . Power 17 totally did not work as drawn up. The Saints' defensive linemen stood up the blockers and allowed linebacker Scott
Shanle—who outweighed Marshawn Lynch by 30 pounds—to rush in.
Shanle had made this sort of tackle countless times in his career. He
had had ten tackles in the Super Bowl two years earlier. It should have
been a 1- or 2-yard run.

But Lynch smashed right through Shanle.

Defensive lineman Sedrick Ellis tried to get in the way but was
shrugged off. Will Smith grabbed at Lynch's feet, but he ran through
like he was dancing through tires in practice. Another lineman, Remi
Ayodele, grabbed at his leg; Lynch kept going. All-Pro safety Darren
Sharper got his arms around Lynch. But Marshawn blasted through
again.

Cornerback Jabari Greer came crashing in for the tackle.

He was barely a speed bump. Lynch hardly even slowed down.

And then, the coup de grâce that came at the expense of poor Tracy
Porter, who tried to pull Lynch down. Instead, Lynch gave him a stiff

---

* There has been a long rivalry between football fans in Seattle and Kansas City over
which group is most passionate. Kansas City has the record for pure decibel level at
142.2. But Seattle fans (well, more specifically, University of Washington fans) invented
the Wave.

arm that sent Porter flying about five yards. Nobody watches this play, nobody, without shouting out, "Ooooh!" when Lynch lays that stiff arm on Porter.

Defensive end Alex Brown tried to make a last-ditch dive at Lynch's left, but there was simply no stopping him, not with him in Beast Mode. At about the 3-yard line, Lynch turned and leaped backward into the end zone after a 67-yard touchdown run that still leaves the mind numb.

"It was all him," Locklear said.

And here might be the best part: The crowd got so loud during and just after that run that the Pacific Northwest Seismic Network station registered a small tremor.* That's how it became known as the Beast Quake.

---

* In an effort to get Taylor Swift into this book as often as possible, I must note that her concert in Seattle during the 2023 Eras Tour registered an even larger tremor.

NO. 42:

GALLOPING GALE
CARRYING THE MAIL

"My dad was there in the rain. He described every touchdown to
me when I was very small and continued to for the rest of his life.
He also memorized every line from the movie *Bullitt*."

—JEFF GARLIN

—

DECEMBER 12, 1965

What is it about those great athletes from the mid-1960s? They
have become something larger than legend. Think about it: Koufax. Mays. Chamberlain. Russell. Ali. Rudolph. Pelé. Palmer. Nicklaus. Butkus. Sayers. Each evokes memories that transcend games, that rise above statistics or accomplishments or awards.

"My dad was there in the rain," comedian Jeff Garlin says.

Yes, that was the point of those glorious athletes. They made you feel lucky to be there, to be alive in their time. The rest of us can only watch grainy film of Gale Sayers running. Even then, yes, you feel the electricity; you stare in wonder at the timeless moves; you gasp at the beauty. That's how magical Gale Sayers was. But as the great Frank Deford once wrote:

"Sometimes, no matter how detailed the historical account, no matter how many eyewitnesses, no matter how complete the statistics, no matter how vivid the film . . .

"Sometimes, I'm sorry, but . . .

"Sometimes, you just had to be there."

Oh, to have been there at Wrigley Field among the fedoras and flasks on that wet December day sixty years ago. Sayers scored 6 touchdowns against the 49ers. He might have scored 7 had it not been for a brief brush with imperfection.

The field was a swamp; it had rained all week in Chicago. Nobody could keep their footing—nobody, that is, but Sayers. In the first quarter, he took a screen pass and proceeded to make a series of gorgeous moves, one sending 49ers Pro Bowl linebacker Matt Hazeltine grasping at a ghost and falling into the mud. Sayers ran 80 yards for the score.

On the next touchdown he leaped over his own blocker, Jim Cadile, and outran two 49ers into the corner of the end zone. The third was easy. He merely paced himself and waited for tackle Bob Wetoska to knock cornerback Jimmy Johnson out of the way, then breezed in.

The fourth touchdown was 50 yards and required just one cut and a little Gale Sayers acceleration. The fifth touchdown was a 1-yard plunge face-first into the mud.

The sixth is the most famous, the 85-yard punt return. Sayers caught the punt and ran right. San Francisco's Ken Willard had a chance for the tackle and grabbed Sayers's leg, but Sayers shook him off. Then came the sublime moment: Sayers between three 49ers, one going for the shoulder, one rushing in from the left, one trying to pull him down from behind.

He made one move, one almost imperceptible move, and all three missed.

You can watch it a thousand times and never unlock its mysteries.

Sayers was so excited after scoring that he did something he never did. All his career, when Sayers scored, he would just flip the ball to the official. But this time, he threw the ball in the stands and did a little dance.

That was touchdown number 6.*

"That was the greatest exhibition I have seen by one man in one game," said the Bears' George Halas, who, by then, had seen it all.

Halas decided at this point to pull Sayers from the game even though

---

* In one of the great "wrong time" moments in NFL history, Green Bay's Paul Hornung scored 5 touchdowns on the very same day.

he was one touchdown shy of breaking the record set by Ernie Nevers against the Bears back in 1927.

"I would have loved to have left him in," Halas said. "But I never would have been able to forgive myself if he had gotten hurt."

Sayers did get a chance to score that seventh touchdown anyway. Late in the game, he went back in to return a punt and caught the ball at the 19. He started to run and then he saw an opening. Gale Sayers never needed much. "Give me 18 inches of daylight," he famously said. "That's all I need."

Sayers headed for the opening, and he just knew that he was going to score another touchdown. He just knew it. Only then, the most unlikely thing of all happened.

Gale Sayers slipped in the mud and got tackled.

"I think about it every so often," he told me many years later. "I think that's the only time I ever slipped on a football field."

NO. 41:

"I LOVE BRIAN PICCOLO"

"Some people are born unlucky.
Others just play behind Gale Sayers."

—BRIAN PICCOLO

—

MAY 26, 1970

The made-for-television movie *Brian's Song*, which has made more men cry than daughters' weddings, gets almost all of it right. But there's one part that the movie only hints at and doesn't fully capture.

Brian Piccolo utterly hated being the backup to Gale Sayers.

Nobody ever wanted to be a star professional football player more than Brian Piccolo. The game consumed him and obsessed him and tormented him. Piccolo hadn't been given the athletic gifts that he so craved. He was listed at 6 feet tall but probably wasn't. He couldn't keep on weight. He didn't have blazing speed. All he could do was outwork anybody and everybody, and that's what he did. He went to Wake Forest and led the nation in rushing and touchdowns. He even got a few Heisman votes.

Then he made it clear to anybody who would listen that he would do anything to play pro football. He would change positions. He would become a pass catcher. He would block his heart out. And . . . nobody wanted him. The NFL Draft was twenty rounds in those days; there were two hundred eighty players selected. Fifty of them were running backs. Brian Piccolo was not selected.*

---

* Gale Sayers was actually the third running back taken in the 1965 draft. The first was a player who got a brief mention in *Brian's Song*: Tucker Frederickson. In the movie, Piccolo talks about how he was one of the best high school running backs in the state, but the best back in the state, Tucker Frederickson, went to the same school. It wasn't technically

"It was the low point of my life, I guess," he would say.

Piccolo went looking for an NFL team. He was very strategic about it, looking to pick a team where he would have his best chance to start. Cleveland called, but the Browns already had Jim Brown and Leroy Kelly, so that was a nonstarter. He immediately wrote off other teams too.

Then there were the Bears. They had the worst rushing attack in the NFL in 1964. Their main running back, Jon Arnett, was turning thirty. Piccolo had found his team. He signed with Chicago days after getting married to Joy. Their honeymoon was kicked off at a Bears press conference.

"I'm going to do everything I can do to help the Bears win," he said.

Piccolo was aware, of course, that the Bears had drafted Gale Sayers out of the University of Kansas. Piccolo didn't know Sayers but believed, deeply, that he would win the job through sweat and heart. Then he tore his hamstring and spent the 1965 season on the taxi squad. He helplessly watched Sayers, perhaps the most spectacular rookie running back ever, score an NFL record 22 touchdowns* and dazzle everybody.

"I think he can play pro football," Bears tight end Mike Ditka said of Piccolo after the season. "But I'm not sure he can with us. He may have come to us at the wrong time."

Piccolo took it all hard. "I think what bothered me most is when I would meet some people and someone would say, 'He's with the Bears,' and no one else knew it," he said sadly. He didn't like Sayers either; he thought Sayers arrogant and aloof. The 1966 season was not much better than 1965. He got three carries all season.

---

true; Frederickson did not go to the Piccolo's high school. But he did play at a rival high school only fifteen minutes away in South Florida.

* Sayers's touchdown record lasted ten years until it was broken in 1975 by O. J. Simpson. The record for touchdowns in a season, as I write this, is 31, set by LaDainian Tomlinson in 2006.

In 1967, things changed a bit. Piccolo realized that Sayers was not arrogant but instead just extremely shy. Sayers began to better appreciate just how much Piccolo wanted to succeed. The two became friends. And then they became roommates, the first Black-white roommates in the history of the Chicago Bears.

Piccolo began to play more. But the main dynamic stayed the same: Sayers was the superstar and Piccolo played only when Gale needed a rest.* This bothered Piccolo intensely. He still hungered to play, to be a starter, to carry the ball, to score touchdowns. By now, yes, he loved and admired Sayers but he still resented that the entire offense was built around him. Piccolo thought that the Bears couldn't win with Sayers as a one-man show.

Then, in 1968, during a game between the Bears and 49ers, Sayers took a handoff and was quickly swarmed by three San Francisco players. One of them, Sayers's friend Kermit Alexander, dived at a blocker but ended up undercutting Sayers, wrecking his knee. Alexander was inconsolable. He was one of the players who helped carry Sayers off the field, and after the game he couldn't even speak through tears.

Piccolo was hurting for his friend. But . . .

"This is something I've dreamed of since I signed with the Bears," he told reporters after he gained 121 yards on eighteen carries and four catches. "I don't like the way I got it. But it's the opportunity I've been waiting for."

This moment is at the heart of *Brian's Song*. Because while Piccolo was happily embracing his first opportunity to be a featured back in the NFL—"I won't get you 60 yards on one play like Sayers, but I'll get you 6 yards ten plays in a row," he gleefully told reporters—he also relentlessly pushed Sayers in his effort to come back.

---

* In fact, it was Sayers who always determined when Piccolo would play. He would wave to the sideline to say he was coming out. Piccolo said he had the rare distinction of never being put in the game by a coach.

Gale Sayers did come back, and in 1969 he once again led the NFL in rushing. Piccolo once again was mostly consigned to his much-despised role of understudy, though he did find himself on the field more often as a lead blocker for Sayers. "I think I'm a pretty good blocker," he told a reporter. "Just say I'm contributing my share."

They had one grand game together that year. On November 16 they both started against Atlanta. Sayers wore his usual number, 40. Piccolo wore number 41. Sayers rushed for 96 yards and scored a touchdown. Piccolo carried the ball twelve times, caught two passes, and scored a touchdown himself.

Two days later, Brian Piccolo was at Chicago's Masonic Hospital with a monthlong cough that just wouldn't go way.

"Five years, I've been playing with the Bears, and none of those big guys ever put a scratch on me," he said. "Now I'm sitting in the hospital, feeling like a fool."

Soon after, he underwent surgery to remove a cancerous tumor from his chest. He was optimistic for a time after that, promising to gain back the 25 pounds of muscle he had lost and return to the team for the fall. But soon afterward, he had to check back into the hospital and undergo a second surgery and then a third.

"At one point football was the most important thing," he told a reporter. "But when you're lying on your back, and you wonder whether you're going to live or die, and you're thinking about your three little girls, you discover there are more important things than football. You look at the world a little differently."

IN LATE MAY 1970, GALE SAYERS WENT TO NEW YORK TO ACCEPT the George S. Halas Award as the most courageous player in the NFL. He spoke a bit about the determination it took to return to the NFL after his injury. He thanked various people, including "my teammate, roommate and friend, Brian Piccolo."

And then, with the six hundred people at the Pro Football Writers of America dinner utterly silent, he spoke words that still echo. Some of these words were used in the *Brian's Song* speech. Some were not. Sayers always wished that Billy Dee Williams, who played him in the movie, had not stuttered and stopped so many times during the speech because that was not how it had played out in real time.

"I gave a hell of a speech that night," he would say.

He ended it like so:

> *You flatter me by giving me this award, but I tell you here and now that I accept it for Brian Piccolo. Brian Piccolo is the man of courage who should receive the George S. Halas Award. It is mine tonight; it is Brian Piccolo's tomorrow. I love Brian Piccolo, and I'd like all of you to love him too.*
>
> *Tonight, when you hit your knees, please ask God to love him.*
> *Thank you.*

Brian Piccolo died three weeks later. He was twenty-six years old. No Chicago Bears player has worn number 41 since then.

NO. 40:

REGGIE WHITE

"Whoever said Reggie White has slowed down never had to block him."

—PATRIOTS LINEMAN MAX LANE

—

JANUARY 26, 1997

Here's a little story that starts with Reggie White sacking Cardinals quarterback Neil Lomax. It's unclear when exactly this happened. White sacked Lomax three times in a game in 1985, so it could have been then, but White also sacked Lomax ten other times in various games through the years.

Anyway, Reggie White sacked Neil Lomax. This was one of his 198 NFL sacks, second in league history to Bruce Smith. But he also had 23.5 sacks in the USFL and thirty-two sacks while in college at Tennessee.

All in all, nobody in the history of football has taken more quarterbacks to the ground.

"Neil," White said as he looked down on Lomax, "Jesus loves you."

"I know," Lomax said. "So, what's your problem with me?"

REGGIE WHITE ALWAYS KNEW WHAT HE WANTED: AS A CHILD, HE told his mother that he planned to be a football player and a Baptist minister. So, he became a football player and a Baptist minister. His two destinies of crushing quarterbacks and saving souls did not always seem harmonious—he was at the center of many jokes after he insisted that God had told him to sign with the Green Bay Packers and then admitted that he would have signed with the 49ers if they'd offered more money—but in every way, Reggie White was the truest of believers.

"I am on a mission from God," he used to say. "And football is my platform."

He was 6-foot-5, 291 pounds, strong enough to toss offensive linemen aside like they were throw pillows and fast enough to race around them before they got out of their stances. "He ran the 40-yard dash faster than I did," kick returner Vai Sikahema marveled.

There was no way to block him with one man. Often, two weren't enough.

"Once I watched Eagles game film with him in his home in the Philadelphia suburbs," Paul Zimmerman wrote. "And he pointed out the minefield he had to dance through on practically every play. It was like watching a matador trying to take on three or four bulls."

Reggie White was thirty-five years old and already a fully developed legend when he played in his first Super Bowl. There was some talk that he was diminished by then, and it was true that he was no longer the athletic marvel he had been. For only the second time in his career, he had not reached double digits in sacks.

But what made Reggie White the greatest defensive player in the history of professional football was that his greatness transcended sacks. John Madden believed he was even better against the run than he was against the pass. More than any of it, though, he had a unique ability to lift his teammates, helping them play the best football of their lives.

The 1996 Packers gave up the fewest points in the NFL. That was the first time a Green Bay team had done that in thirty years, going back to the days of Vince Lombardi. And nobody had any doubt who was at the heart of that defensive effort.

"Reggie White is probably the most unselfish team player I've ever been around," his Packers defensive coordinator Fritz Shurmur said.

"The guy is like God in pads," his teammate Don Beebe said, "yet you meet him and he's the most humble person you'd ever encounter. . . . I think what having a guy like that on the team does is, the athletes who are sitting on the fence, who could go either way, go on the side of good. Because Reggie's watching."

IN SUPER BOWL XXXI, REGGIE WHITE FELT UNCHARACTERISTI-cally weak. He waited for the rush, that sudden jump of adrenaline and power and, yes, divinity—White believed it was the hand of God—that always came when he needed it most. Only this time, in the biggest game, the energy burst would not come. He felt overheated and worn down, and he turned to the sideline and asked for someone to take his place for a bit.

"I can't tell you what was happening out there," he said. "I didn't feel too good."

Late in the third quarter, the surge finally arrived. His Packers led by 2 touchdowns after Desmond Howard's 99-yard kickoff return, but the Patriots offense had just driven for a touchdown and they seemed geared up, and New England quarterback Drew Bledsoe dropped back to throw.

White reached out his left hand and knocked Max Lane to ground. He then drove forward into Bledsoe and took him down. On the next play, he broke hard right, refused to let Lane knock him off course, and sacked Bledsoe again.

"After that," he said, "I knew we were going to win."

Later, he got his third sack, the Super Bowl record, and he felt exactly as he hoped to feel. He felt young. He felt strong. He felt so alive. "I know that strength could not come from within me," he said after the game. "It comes from somewhere else."

When the Packers won the game, he looked up to the heavens and said to Vince Lombardi, "Vince, we brought you back the trophy." He then ran around the field clinging to the Vince Lombardi Trophy. He didn't want to give it up.

NO. 39:

CHICAGO 73, WASHINGTON 0

"I would prefer doing football to anything else."

—GEORGE HALAS

—

DECEMBER 8, 1940

People rarely saw George Halas happy. Words like "joy" or "delight" or "contentment" were not in his playbook. There was no time for such foolishness. There was more football to do.

What did it mean to "do football"? Well, George Halas, in his long football life, did everything. He played. He coached. He raged. He negotiated. He owned. He was there from the beginning, going back to 1920, when the football team he organized for the Staley Manufacturing Company became a charter member of the American Pro Football Association. Halas was at the very first meeting. He had plenty to say.

By 1922, when the APFA became the National Football League, Halas had already moved his Decatur Staleys to Chicago and renamed them the Bears. And then the NFL followed his lead. Halas was not exactly an innovator; he just worked harder at winning than anybody else.

"No one who ever gave his best regretted it," he famously said, and he backed up those words with eighteen-hour days of obsessing over every imaginable detail and demanding that coaches and players match his work ethic. The Bears were the first NFL team to have grueling daily practices. They were the first NFL team to have intensive film-study sessions. They had to win every year and they did: In the NFL's first twenty-seven seasons, the Bears had only one losing record and won seven championships.

But happiness? No. Victories raced by Halas like a passing El train.

Losses stayed with him, none more than the loss in the 1937 NFL Championship Game to his most intense rival, George Preston Marshall, and his Washington Redskins. That loss haunted him.

Then, in 1940, he saw his chance to get back at Marshall. The difference in that 1937 game had been Washington's brilliant quarterback Sammy Baugh. Halas had to get himself a quarterback like that. Two years after the loss, Halas drafted a skilled passer out of Columbia named Sid Luckman. He also drafted a powerful center, Bulldog Turner, and a speedy halfback everybody called One Play McAfee because he was always just one play away from breaking away for a touchdown. All three are in the Pro Football Hall of Fame.

Halas felt certain he had his best Bears team. But when they played Baugh and Washington during the season, they lost. Halas and his players were sure that they had been cheated out of victory by the officials, and they said so. This led Marshall to call the Bears a bunch of crybabies.

Halas pounced on the quote. He clipped every newspaper article he could find that featured Marshall's insult and blew them up to five times their normal size. He then pinned them up all around the locker room.

During practices he would shout: "So, are the Chicago Bears just a bunch of crybabies?"

When Chicago and Washington met again three weeks later for the 1940 NFL Championship, the Bears could barely contain their fury. Then, before the game, Halas uncharacteristically offered up a riling speech. He usually just said something simple like "Go get 'em."

"Gentlemen," Luckman recalled him saying, "I know that you are the greatest football team in America. I want you today to prove to Mr. Marshall, the Redskins plus the nation that you are. They call us crybabies. Let's play the caliber of football to make them know what I know—that you are the greatest football team ever assembled in this country."

"We broke down the dressing room door getting to the field," Luckman said.

Luckman did not exaggerate by much. It's hard to imagine a team with more concentrated fury and furious concentration than those Bears. The 73–0 score is now famous. The Bears' Monsters of the Midway defense intercepted eight passes and held Washington to five yards rushing and was so ferocious that at some point Baugh was pulled from the game for his own safety. ("That was the most humiliating thing I've gone through in my life," he told reporters later of the game.)

The Bears' T-Formation offense—which was freshened up that week by a visit from one of the great innovators of the formation, Stanford's Clark Shaughnessy*—racked up 381 rushing yards. This was not (contrary to legend) the first time that the Bears used the T-Formation offense. But the Bears' offense was so unstoppable that this game more or less ended the single-wing offense. Within a year, pretty much every team was using it across America.

The Bears scored so many touchdowns that at one point referee Red Friesell asked Halas if he would mind going for two rather than kicking the extra point.

"Why?" Halas asked.

"We're running out of footballs," Friesell said.

At some point in the game, Luckman overhead Halas say, "I wonder what Mr. George Preston Marshall is doing at this stage." The joy in his voice was unmistakable. While there were some people on the Bears' sideline who wondered if maybe they should stop trying to score, Halas

---

* Shaughnessy had just led Stanford to an undefeated season by installing his T-Formation. "The Bears already used the T-Formation," Shaughnessy said. "But the Bears had no deception. No variations. I worked out an offense, using ruled graph paper. . . . We added the man in motion and the counter play. I didn't get much money, the Bears didn't have much money, but I was having fun."

certainly was not one of them. He did pull his starters, but, hey, if the others wanted to keep on scoring, who was he to stop them?

The part that really struck Luckman was the smile on Halas. He never before and never again saw his coach smile like that. "I found Halas almost delirious with joy," Luckman would say. It took 73–0 to make Papa Bear happy.

NO. 38:

PIONEER OF THE SACK

ESPN: "Is there anything you regret and wish you could do over?"

Deacon Jones: "Yes. I'd kill more quarterbacks."

———

SEPTEMBER 10, 1969

Before every college game at South Carolina State, David Jones led the team in a fiery and passionate prayer.

"What's Deacon praying about anyway?" one newcomer asked a teammate.

"That he won't kill anybody today," the teammate replied.

WHEN DEACON JONES WAS YOUNG, HE SAW JACKIE ROBINSON play in a spring training baseball game. Jones felt a fury he couldn't even explain. He grew up in a segregated Florida town called Eatonville, where he endured indignity after indignity. He recalled once being chased by a car full of white football players. They threw bottles at him, and one hit him in the head and briefly knocked him out. When he came to, he thought only of blood.

In the baseball game, as he often told the story, he saw an opponent purposely step on Robinson's hand. After the game, he and his friends found Robinson and talked to him.

"Your hand gonna be OK?" Jones asked.

"Yes," Robinson said.

"I guess you get used to it," Jones said.

"No, son," Robinson said as he looked Jones directly in the eye. "You don't ever get used to it."

"Then how do you deal with it?" Jones asked.

"We beat them on the field," Robinson said.

| | | | | |

THE DEACON WAS A MARVELOUS ATHLETE. EVEN AT 6-FOOT-5,
235 pounds, he ran a sub-ten-second 100-yard dash in college at South
Carolina State.* He also kicked a 48-yard field goal. Even so, it's not
entirely clear how the Los Angeles Rams found him. NFL teams didn't
spend much time or effort scouting Historically Black Colleges and
Universities.

But the Rams took him in the fourteenth round, and once he got to
camp, nobody could take their eyes off him. He was an offensive lineman at first, and right away, in his first game against the 49ers, he
blocked two Pro Bowlers—Charlie Krueger and Matt Hazeltine—on
the same play.

"The single play did not electrify anyone in the stands," Maxwell
Stiles wrote in the *Los Angeles Mirror*. "But it created quite a buzz among
the coaches."

Jones might have been an all-time-great offensive lineman, but his
heart wasn't in blocking. His heart was in hitting people. The rage he
grew up with, well, he needed to do something with that. He wanted to
hit people and hit them very hard.

"What do you do for a living?" Deacon Jones was often asked by
strangers.

"I kill quarterbacks," he would say.

He said that he chose to kill quarterbacks for a living because if he
had taken another path, he might have committed actual murder.

The Deacon made killing quarterbacks an art form. The first thing he

---

* Deacon Jones later got his scholarship at SC State revoked after he took part in a lunch
counter demonstration. He transferred to Mississippi Vocational College, which later
became Mississippi Valley State. This deserves mention because that means two of the
twenty or so greatest football players who ever lived—Deacon Jones and Jerry Rice—
played their college football at Mississippi Valley State. I don't think any other college can
match that.

would usually do was slap the side of the offensive lineman's helmet. The head slap was meant to disorient the blocker, though Deacon Jones was so big and so strong that sometimes it would knock them down. "It was like getting hit by a truck," Forrest Gregg said.*

Then, with the blocker momentarily dazed, he raced around and crushed quarterbacks. Nobody did it better. Football historians have studied the films and counted an incredible 128 Deacon Jones quarterback tackles behind the line from 1961 to 1968.

Thing is, nobody thought to count them back then. And the big reason why nobody thought to count them, probably, was that they lacked a name. "Quarterback tackles behind the line" is hardly exciting. And "quarterback kills"—even for a sport like football—seemed over the line.

So, in 1969, Deacon Jones unveiled a new name. He called it a "sack."

He had been calling his quarterback hits sacks privately for a while. Then the wonderful *Los Angeles Times* columnist Jim Murray imagined Deacon Jones as the "Right Honorable Secretary of Defense." And when asked how he and his Rams intended to prevent teams from throwing the ball, Secretary Jones said: "Our responsibility is to see to it that the enemy doesn't get it off the ground. . . . We call this 'Operation Sack.'"

A few days later, after the Rams beat the Packers, Jones told the press that his big regret was that he missed a chance in the first quarter to sack Bart Starr. When reporters asked how he came up with the sack name, Jones laughed.

"Sacking a quarterback," Jones said, "is just like you devastate a city or you cream a multitude of people. It's like you put all the offensive players in one bag, and I just take a baseball bat and beat on the bag."

It caught on with astonishing speed. Almost immediately, sportswriters everywhere used the term liberally; it was like everyone had

---

* The Deacon Jones head slap is totally illegal now. It's actually hard to believe it was ever legal.

just been waiting for the sack to get a name. Everybody starting counting sacks; players began using sack totals in salary negotiations; leading
sackers became stars. As Murray wrote, before the Deacon, "defensive
players were as anonymous as spies. They were the unknown soldiers
of football, known but to God—and the line coach."

With one turn of phrase, Jones opened up an entirely new world for
defenders.* The sack has created countless stars, from Reggie White to
Bruce Smith to Lawrence Taylor to Michael Strahan to Jared Allen to
the Sackman, Richard Dent, to the Jets' famed defensive line, "The
New York Sack Exchange." All of them owe a nod of gratitude to the man
who started it all.

"I came out of a hellhole," Deacon Jones said. "Thank God I had the
ability to play a violent game like football. It gave me an outlet for the
anger in my heart."

---

* It's actually quite remarkable how powerful the invention of a statistic can be. In
baseball, relief pitchers, like defensive linemen, were all but unknown and then
sportswriter Jerome Holtzman invented the save, and suddenly relief pitchers were
winning MVP Awards and Cy Young Awards and getting big contracts.

NO. 37:

MIRACLE AT MICHIGAN

"I don't care what they got. We're not losing this game."

—COLORADO COACH BILL McCARTNEY BEFORE THE FINAL PLAY

———

SEPTEMBER 24, 1994

No matter how many times you watch the 1994 Colorado-Michigan game, there will be at least one moment when you will think: *Wait, how did Colorado win this game again?*

Like, here's one: Colorado trailed 26–14 with about five minutes left. The Buffaloes finally got a drive going; quarterback Kordell Stewart drove the team all the way to the Michigan 4. With a score here, yes, you could see how the game was still in the balance.

Instead, Stewart fumbled the ball and Michigan recovered in the end zone for a touchback. The 106,427 fans unleashed the loudest roar imaginable, a roar that said: *Whew, that was close. But, finally, this game is over!*

Wait, how did Colorado win this game again?

Well, first they stuffed Michigan on three plays. Then Stewart and running back Rashaan Salaam—the Heisman Trophy winner that year—drove the Buffaloes back deep into Michigan territory. Salaam blasted it in to cut the deficit to five with 2:16 left. But they didn't have any time-outs left, so they were forced to try an onside kick.

And . . . the onside kick failed.

Wait, how did Colorado win this game again?

All Michigan needed was a first down to put the game away, and the Colorado defense helped out by jumping offside, giving the Wolverines third and 2 at the Colorado 37-yard line. Then four things happened in short order:

1. Michigan's offensive line jumped early.

2. The officials added five seconds to the clock for some unclear reason.

3. Michigan running back Tim Biakabutuka gained three yards to make it fourth down.

4. The Wolverines' ultraconservative coach Gary Moeller decided to punt from the Colorado 39 rather than try to put the game away.

Yeah, that's right: They punted from the 39-yard line. Colorado got the ball back at their own 15. There were fourteen seconds left.

Wait, how did Colorado win this game again?

THE PLAY ROCKET LEFT WAS DESIGNED BY A COACH NAMED EL-liot Uzelac. He had come up with it while working as a volunteer assistant coach for the Cleveland Browns. The idea was to hurl the pass *near* the end zone and then have one receiver tip the ball back into the end zone.

"We practiced it over and over," Colorado coach Bill McCartney would say. "But that was the only time we ever ran it."

Colorado could not run Rocket Left from their own 15. Even Kordell Stewart with his seemingly unlimited arm could not throw the ball near the end zone from way back there. But on first down, Stewart rifled a 21-yard pass to Michael Westbrook. He then rushed to the line and spiked the ball to stop the clock with six seconds left.

You will remember—especially if you are a Michigan fan—that the referee had put five seconds back on the clock after a penalty.

Now, from the 36, Stewart had a fighting chance to throw the ball far enough for Rocket Left. He dropped back 10 yards. Michigan rushed only three, so he had time to wait for everyone to get downfield.

Stewart then reared back and threw the ball from the 27—73 yards away from the end zone.

Even Bill McCartney, the ultimate believer, did not believe he could throw the ball that far. "I was hoping for a penalty," he would admit after the game.

But Stewart threw the ball 73 yards.

At the goal line, the ball first hit something and deflected up in the air. For years, it was reported that the ball hit the hands of Colorado receiver Blake Anderson. That's how Anderson remembered it, and to this day, people around Boulder call him the "Tipper." Years later, though, Michigan defensive back Chuck Winters said that, no, actually he thinks the ball deflected off his shoulder pad. Anderson shrugged. It all worked out.

Two players most clearly followed the ball after it was tipped.

One was Ty Law, Michigan's All-American cornerback who is now in the Pro Football Hall of Fame.

The other was Michael Westbrook, Colorado's All-American wide receiver.

Law, though, was out of position. The ball bounced almost directly over his head. He spun and tried to get to it, but Westbrook had the better angle. Westbrook came down with the ball and was able to fight off Law's efforts to wrestle it away.

"Touchdown!" ABC's Keith Jackson shouted, and, after letting the crowd tell the story, he went on, "There is no time remaining. . . . There are no flags on the field . . . only despair for the Maize and Blue, joy and exaltation for the Buffaloes of Colorado."

This is how it goes with football miracles. Despair and exaltation.

"It was lucky," McCartney would admit more than two decades later.

"That wasn't lucky," Westbrook insisted. "I don't believe in luck."

NO. 36:

HE'S ALL THE WAY HOME!

"Johnny the Jet Rodgers just tore 'em loose from their shoes."

—NEBRASKA ANNOUNCER LYELL BREMSER

—

NOVEMBER 25, 1971

This seems like a good time to let Dan Jenkins, the greatest college football writer of them all, have a word. And what better place for it than when talking about the sheer wonder of Johnny Rodgers.

"If the typesetters are not careful," Jenkins wrote in the pages of *Sports Illustrated*, "Nebraska's Johnny Rodgers may leap right out of this sentence, and then, like the hummingbird that he is, go flitting through ads, photographs, along the margins of the pages, in and out of stories and maybe right out the back cover if that is what it takes to beat somebody."

On November 25, 1971, Oklahoma and Nebraska—two football-mad schools and heated rivals—played a football game that people were calling the "Game of the Decade" . . . even though the decade had only just started. Nebraska was No. 1 in the country. Oklahoma was No. 2. They were both undefeated, naturally, but more than that, neither team had even been tested. Texas was supposed to give Oklahoma a fight and then lost by 3 touchdowns. Colorado was supposed to stay with Nebraska and instead lost 31–7.

Nebraska had the nation's top-ranked defense.

Oklahoma set an NCAA record that year by averaging 472 yards rushing per game.

The two most exciting players in college football were there—Johnny Rodgers for Nebraska, Greg Pruitt for Oklahoma.

College football tends to have several Games of the Decade every decade. "This Year's Game of the Decade," *Sports Illustrated* labeled Oklahoma-Nebraska before it was played. Two years earlier, Texas and Arkansas had played a Game of the Decade with President Richard Nixon in the audience.* A year before that, Purdue and Notre Dame had played a Game of the Decade; two years before that it had been Michigan State and Notre Dame; three years before that it had been Oklahoma and Texas.

Most of the time, such games do not live up to the hype.

This, though, was a spectacle, back and forth: Nebraska led early; Oklahoma took the lead; Nebraska took it back; Oklahoma took it back. It was wild and thrilling and epic. Oklahoma's offense tore through the previously impenetrable Cornhuskers' defense. Nebraska's Jeff Kinney scored 4 touchdowns, including the game winner. There was only one penalty the entire game.

But as more than fifty years have drifted by, one play remains.

That is Johnny Rodgers's "All the Way Home" return.

"Here's [Joe] Wylie's kick. It's high. It holds up there," Nebraska announcer Lyell Bremser said. "Rodgers takes the ball at the 30."

"The Sooner coverage was down fast," Jenkins wrote, "so fast that all of the 63,385 in Owen Stadium, not to mention the TV audience, must have felt Rodgers would have been much wiser to consider a fair catch."

Bremser: "He's hit but got away, back upfield at the 35."

Jenkins: "Heavens to Omaha if Rodgers didn't catch it with Greg Pruitt right on him. He took the blow, spun around on his own 30-yard line, and planted his left hand on Tartan turf to keep from falling."

Bremser: "He's to the 40. The 45. The 50. He's to the 45. . . ."

Jenkins: "He set sail to the right. But just as quickly he darted back

---

* Nixon infamously declared Texas the national champion after the game ended, ticking off Penn State, which was also undefeated at the time. "I'd like to know how the president could know so much about college football and so little about Watergate," Penn State coach Joe Paterno would say two years later.

to the left, through a whole cluster of wine-colored Sooner jerseys. There the minuet ended."

Bremser: "To the 40. To the 35. To the 20! To the 10 . . . He's all the way home!"

Jenkins: "It was one of those insanely thrilling things in which a single player, seized by the moment, twists, whirls, slips, holds his balance, and, sprinting, makes it all the way to the goal line."

Bremser: "Man, woman, and child, did that put them in the aisles! Johnny 'the Jet' Rodgers just tore 'em loose from their shoes!"

Now the 1971 Oklahoma-Nebraska game is not called the Game of the Decade.

It is called the Game of the Century.

And it's mostly because of that Johnny Rodgers punt return. That play still lives. A few years ago, I was at a Nebraska football game, and in the parking lot I saw kids who couldn't have been older than twelve—their *parents* were probably too young to vividly remember the game—playing football in the parking lot. One boy kicked the ball as high as he could, and another caught it out of the air.

"Man, woman, and child!" he shouted as he ran.

NO. 35:

THE DIESEL

"I want the ball."

—JOHN RIGGINS

———

JANUARY 30, 1983

John Riggins was so many things in his mercurial career. He was a small-town farm boy from Kansas. He was a Mohawk-wearing rebel. He was an underachiever and the hardest-working player on the field, overweight and the most fit player on the field, a salary holdout and a touchdown machine, a fashion icon and the hardest-nosed player you ever saw, a total goofball and a guy who read British poet Robert Service's "The Law of the Yukon" as part of his Pro Football Hall of Fame induction speech.

In other words, John Riggins was too many things to be just one thing. But just after New Year's Day 1983, with the playoffs about to begin, he stormed into the office of Washington offensive coordinator Joe Bugel and said, "I want the ball."

"Don't tell me," Bugel said, and he pointed toward the office of head coach Joe Gibbs. "Tell him."

Riggins then stormed into Gibbs's office.

"I want the ball," he told Gibbs.

"You got it," Gibbs said.

That's when John Riggins became the Diesel.

HERE IS THE LIST OF TWENTY-FIRST-CENTURY RUNNING BACKS who have carried the football thirty-five-plus times in three consecutive games:

Yeah, that's not a misprint. There should be nothing after that colon. It hasn't happened.

OK, right, but the game has changed, right? How about the 1990s? Here's that complete list:

Right. Still zero. The 1980s? Nope. The 1970s? Nope. How about the 1950s or 1960s? Certainly it happened back then, you know, with Jim Brown and Jim Taylor and John Henry Johnson and all those guys.

Nope. It's never happened. Heck, Jim Brown had only one game in his entire career where he carried the ball thirty-five times. Jim Taylor had none.

The week after John Riggins demanded the ball, Washington played Detroit in a wild card playoff game. Riggins got the ball twenty-five times and gained 119 yards as Washington rolled to an easy 31–7 victory.

"Is that enough for you?" Gibbs asked Riggins afterward.

"No," the Diesel said.

So, OK, fine, in the next week's playoff game against Minnesota, Washington gave Riggins the ball thirty-seven times. He gained 185 yards and scored a touchdown. "The man's a machine," his quarterback Joe Theismann said in wonder. "If there's not a hole there, he makes one."

These were not fancy runs. Most of the time, Washington called their most basic play, 50 Gut, which Washington center Russ Grimm described this way: "You give the ball to Riggins, he picks the hole, and you just let the big guy run."

The following week, Washington played Dallas in the NFC Championship Game. Second verse, same as the first. Washington called 50 Gut so many times that at some point Theismann didn't even need to say the words. Riggins carried the ball thirty-six times for 140 yards and 2 touchdowns. Washington was going back to the Super Bowl for the first time since being pounded into oblivion by the undefeated '72 Dolphins.

"How ya feeling?" Gibbs asked Riggins.

"I want the ball," the Diesel said.

| | | | | |

WHAT DO YOU DO WHEN THE MOMENT OF TRUTH COMES? THIS IS the question that every coach faces. The game is in the balance. The next play will decide things. Do you go for a surprise in the hopes of fooling the other team? Do you use your best player as a decoy and count on someone else?

In the fourth quarter of Super Bowl XVII, Miami led 17–13 and Washington faced a fourth and 1 from the Miami 43-yard line. The game had been two monster trucks crashing, two running teams trying to outwill each other. Washington decided to go for it. Here was the moment of truth. And Joe Gibbs did not hesitate.

He would give the ball to Riggins.

The play was not 50 Gut but instead 70-Chip, which sent him left.

The Dolphins defensive play was called Bullets and Spears.

"Trouble was," Leigh Montville would write in the *Boston Globe*, "there were not enough bullets and nowhere near enough spears."

The blocking was overpowering. The offensive linemen called themselves the Hogs,* and they took pride in giving Riggins openings, though, as Grimm said, "He doesn't really need them." This time, Riggins was past the first-down marker when he faced off against Miami's 5-foot-11, 190-pound Don McNeal.

You can guess how that went. McNeal hit Riggins high and got steamrolled. The Diesel was in the clear and he was moving so fast that safety Glenn Blackwood, one of the Dolphins' faster players, could do nothing

---

* The whole "Hogs" thing began when Bugel, in order to motivate his offensive linemen, started giving out a weekly "Porker Award" to the lineman who got down in the mud and played the hardest. "I've hung up a picture of the ugliest razorback hog you ever saw with his snout in a feed bucket," Bugel said. "The lineman who plays best will have his name placed by that hog's picture." The linemen quickly took pride in the award and started calling themselves the Hogs. And fans started wearing pig snouts to games.

but watch him pull away. The touchdown broke the Dolphins and Washington won its first Super Bowl.

In all, Riggins carried the ball thirty-six times for a Super Bowl record 166 yards. That was three straight games with thirty-five carries. "That's on the verge of too many carries," he said afterward, but nobody thought he meant it. He was saying it only because there wasn't another game to play.

Afterward, President Ronald Reagan called to offer congratulations.

"Last week," Reagan told Gibbs, "I was going to ask Riggins to change the spelling of his name. Now I was wondering if he would mind if I changed the spelling of my name. Put a couple more g's in it."

When Riggins heard this, he smiled.

"Ron's the president," he said. "But I'm the king."

NO. 34:

BEEBE AND LETT

"I know I could have just stopped. But I just couldn't."

—DON BEEBE

—

JANUARY 31, 1993

There are two questions that linger from Don Beebe's quixotic and inspiring chase of Leon Lett in Super Bowl XXVII.

First and most obvious: What drove Beebe to such extremes?

Second and less obvious: What the heck was Jimmie Jones doing?

We'll take them in order. There were about five minutes left in the game, and the Cowboys were up 52–17. The game had been close for a while; Beebe dropped a touchdown pass that would have tied up the game 14–14 with four minutes left in the first half.

Then things went very bad very quickly for Buffalo. Troy Aikman fired a touchdown pass to Michael Irvin. Buffalo's Thurman Thomas promptly fumbled, setting up Aikman to throw another touchdown pass to Irvin. It was 28–10 at halftime, and other than Beebe's 40-yard touchdown reception in the third quarter, things kept getting worse and worse.

Buffalo was looking for a pride score. Frank Reich dropped back and didn't sense Dallas's Jim Jeffcoat coming on the rush. Jeffcoat hit him and the ball bounced free. Cowboys' defensive lineman Leon Lett scooped it up and ran free, surrounded by blockers. Lett was preposterously fast for a 6-foot-6, 290-pound behemoth and he was so sure that he would score the touchdown, he already had a touchdown dance in mind.

"Michael Jackson had just done the halftime," he would tell NFL Films. "So, I was going to do the 'Billie Jean' dance."

Then came Don Beebe. He had run a deep pass pattern and was 20 or 25 yards away when the ball popped free. But he refused to give up on the play. On the television screen, he did not even appear on the screen until Lett had reached the 25-yard line. At the 20, Beebe was still 5 yards behind Lett. But he kept coming.

"I wasn't gonna quit," Beebe would say. "That's what I was thinking all the way."

Beebe didn't have a fully formed plan for how to bring down Lett. "I was going to jump on his back," Beebe said, a ploy that probably wouldn't have worked. But at the 10-yard line, Lett held his arms out in celebration. That put the ball directly in Beebe's sights.

At the 1, Beebe reached for that ball and knocked it out of Lett's hand. The ball harmlessly rolled out-of-bounds, making it a fumble and touchback, giving the ball back to the Bills.

What kept Don Beebe going? The game was over. The play seemed hopeless.

"That's the way I was coached," he would say. And maybe, in the end, we can understand that. Wouldn't we all like to be Don Beebe, fighting to the end even when the game is lost?

Jimmie Jones, on the other hand, that's harder to understand.

Jones was a rotation defensive lineman for two Super Bowl champion Cowboys teams. He himself had a great day in that Super Bowl, recovering two fumbles and even scoring his own touchdown.

On the return, Jones escorted Lett to the end zone. He had, as they say, one job: to make sure that nobody chased Lett down from behind. Unfortunately, and for reasons that are not entirely clear, he kept looking to the *left* of Lett, undoubtedly assuming that any threat would have to come from that side of the field.

Then Beebe ran by him on the *right* side. Beebe couldn't have been more than two feet away from Jones when he raced by. ("He could have swatted me like a fly," Beebe would say.) But Jones was so focused on his left that he never saw Beebe, not even after Beebe had knocked the ball free.

Leon Lett took a lot of grief for his hot-dog maneuvers at the goal line,* and he took those with grace and humor. "Who chases down a guy down 30 points like that?" he would say. "I mean, you honor that guy."

Right. But Jimmie Jones should have made the block.

---

* Though not from Beebe himself. "A lot of people in Buffalo have said to me, 'I'm glad you knocked the ball out of the guy's hand. He was showboating,'" Beebe told *Sports Illustrated*. "I say, 'Wait a second here. The guy's a defensive lineman, he's probably never scored, and here he is about to score a touchdown in his first Super Bowl!'"

NO. 33:
THE GUARANTEE

"The Jets will win Sunday. I guarantee it."

—JOE NAMATH

—

JANUARY 12, 1969

By now everybody knows about Joe Namath's guarantee before Super Bowl III. What few know is, that wasn't even close to his most controversial quote of the week.

Let's go over the basics: Namath's Jets were massive underdogs against the Baltimore Colts going into the Super Bowl in Miami. The Colts had won fifteen of their sixteen games, including a 34–0 destruction of Cleveland in the NFL Championship Game.*

To many, the Colts being favored by 19.5 points felt conservative.

There's a very famous photograph of Joe Namath lying back in a lounge chair at a hotel pool surrounded by notepad-carrying reporters. The presumption by many is that he boldly predicted the Jets would win right then and there. He did not. Namath made the guarantee at the Miami Touchdown Club Awards Dinner on the Thursday night before the game.

And he made it impulsively.

Namath was giving his rambling speech, playing his role as Broadway Joe, the larger-than-life bachelor who threw touchdown passes all day and partied all night. He was, in the words of biographer Mark Kriegel, high on scotch, but he was also high on simply being Joe Namath, and he riffed on some of his favorite topics—the togetherness

---

* This was back when the NFL and AFL were still separate leagues. In 1970, the leagues would merge.

of the Jets, the stodginess of the NFL, the pleasures of being single in New York.

Then somebody in the crowd yelled that the Colts would shut him up on Sunday.

"The Jets will win Sunday," Namath shouted back at the heckler. "I guarantee it."

Was it a big deal? Well, not at first. The *Miami Herald* was the only one with the story on Friday morning: "'I Guarantee We'll Win'—Namath" was the headline. But honestly, Namath had been saying stuff like that all week. He bashed Colts quarterback Earl Morrall, offering a long list of quarterbacks who were better passers. He nearly got into a fight with the Colts' Lou Michaels. "He pointed to me and said, 'We're going to kick the hell out of you and I'm gonna do it,'" Michaels told Kriegel. He called Johnny Unitas over-the-hill. He said that the Jets faced had tougher competition in the AFL than the Colts. And lots of other stuff like that.

Namath blurting out the guarantee at a heckler hardly seemed like anything.

But . . . there was something so direct about the way he did it. *"The Jets will win Sunday. I guarantee it."* The story began to pick up steam by Saturday. Jets coach Weeb Ewbank was asked to respond.

"He guaranteed it, huh?" Ewbank said. "Well, I'm with him. Joe's an honest boy, and if he says that, he must mean it. I don't think he's whistling 'Dixie.'"*

Then the Colts were asked to respond.

"We can read," Colts coach Don Shula said.

"There's nothing I like to hit more than quarterbacks," Colts defensive lineman Billy Ray Smith said. "And when you get a mouthy one, it makes it that much better."

---

* Jets running back Emerson Boozer would later tell me that after the Jets watched the Colts on film, they ALL knew they were going to win. "We were just better than them," Boozer said. "We all knew it. We just didn't go around talking about it like Joe."

"He's never faced anybody like he's going to have to face in our defense," Unitas said.

"He's done his talking," Baltimore's Bubba Smith said. "On Sunday, we'll do our talking."

"I think we'll beat the Jets 50–0," one unnamed player told Baltimore columnist Bill Tanton.

The Colts, as everybody knows, did not win the game 50–0 . . . or win it at all. The Jets won a mostly dreary affair 16–7. Baltimore had so many chances but failed to score four times inside the Jets' 25-yard line and missed a field goal, and Morrall failed to see a wide-open Jimmy Orr on a flea-flicker play near the end of the first half. Meanwhile, Namath just calmly moved the team down the field with clever play calling and accurate passes.

"We made fewer mistakes," the Jets running back Emerson Boozer told me. Most of the time that, and not guarantees, is what wins football games.

NO. 32:

"HOW IN THE WORLD?"

"I think my career is more than just one catch."

—ODELL BECKHAM JR.

—

NOVEMBER 23, 2014

Here's the problem with doing something impossible: People will want you to do it again. Harry Houdini couldn't escape from the Chinese Water Torture Chamber once and move on with his life. No, he had to escape night after night in town after town. When Joey Chestnut consumed a world record sixty-eight hot dogs in ten minutes at the Nathan's Hot Dog Eating Contest in 2009, there was immediate pressure on him to eat more the next time and the next and the next.*

In the moments after New York Giants rookie receiver Odell Beckham Jr. made *that* catch—and how else can you describe it except as "*that* catch"?—he had no idea that it would stand forever, both in history and in his own life. It was all just instinct, you know? The Giants were playing the Cowboys on the Sunday night before Thanksgiving. First play of the second quarter. Giants had the ball on the Dallas 43.

Quarterback Eli Manning dropped back, glanced left, and then threw deep to his right. OBJ was sprinting down the sideline and was covered tightly by the Cowboys' Brandon Carr—a bit too tightly, in fact, as he tangled up a bit with Beckham and the referee threw the flag for pass interference.

---

* Which he did do. Multiple times. In 2013, Chestnut ate sixty-nine hot dogs. In 2016, he ate seventy-four hot dogs, then seventy-five the next year. In 2021, he raised the record to seventy-six.

When the flag came out, the natural instinct was to look away from the ball.

The ball did not seem catchable anyway.

Only then, Beckham sprang off his left leg, and while falling backward—looking a bit like a high jumper after clearing the bar—he reached over his head with his right hand and snagged the ball out of the air, not unlike the way a subway passenger grabs for a pole when the train suddenly jolts. Beckham then held on to the ball with three fingers and pulled it in to his chest while falling into the end zone.

"There's a flag," announcer Al Michaels said, and then: "Wait. He caught that? How in the world?"

How in the world? No matter how many times you watch that catch, those same words will come to mind: *How in the world?*

"That may be the greatest catch I've ever seen in my life," Cris Collinsworth said.

"Man, I just witnessed the greatest catch ever possibly," LeBron James tweeted.

"INCREDIBLE!!!" Hall of Fame receiver Michael Irvin tweeted, complete with three exclamation points.

Before that catch, Beckham was a supremely talented young receiver with a bright future. After that catch, though, he was something else: He was in the gallery of the gods with the greatest NFL receivers who ever lived. In the next day's *New York Daily News*, the paper ran a gallery of the greatest catches in the history of New York, all sports, and it placed Beckham's catch—which had happened only a few hours earlier—with Willie Mays's catch in the 1954 World Series and Derek Jeter's catch when he went flying headfirst into the stands and David Tyree's Helmet Catch in the Super Bowl.*

---

* I believe they missed one: Don Larsen catching his catcher Yogi Berra after Larsen threw the perfect game in the 1956 World Series.

"It was a moment that obviously changed my life for better or for worse, whatever you want to call it," Beckham would say.

Better *or* worse? How could that astonishing catch have made his life worse?

Well, the better part was easy to see. The catch made him famous. Soon he was doing a Buick commercial (a bridesmaid catches the bouquet OBJ style) and a Head & Shoulders commercial (numerous people do their own versions of that catch) and a Nike snow day commercial (he catches small barbells over his head). Beckham went to the Pro Bowl his first three years in the league. Every sports fan in America seemed to be talking about him.

The worse? Well . . .

"His world is based on hype and that one catch," Pro Bowl defensive back Stephon Gilmore once said of him.

The quote was meant to be a dig . . . and there was a hard edge to it. Beckham has been a good receiver since those first years. As I write these words, he has made almost six hundred catches, many of them jaw-dropping. That's one heck of an NFL career, in the top 5 percent probably of all-time receivers.

But in the afterglow of *that* catch, being a "good receiver" feels like something of a letdown. It isn't fair. But this is what comes with making the greatest catch in NFL history when you have just turned twenty-two years old and are full of potential.

"Whom the gods wish to destroy," the English critic Cyril Connolly wrote, "they first call promising."

A few years ago, Beckham said that he didn't mind the catch following him everywhere because "it gives me motivation to do something crazier." He probably won't, though. That's the trouble with doing something impossible. You have to be OK with just doing it once.

NO. 31:

"FOOTBALL CHOSE ME"

"Now I want to introduce you to the third-best
running back that ever lived."

—WILLIAM SANDERS INTRODUCING HIS SON
AT THE HALL OF FAME CEREMONY

——

JANUARY 5, 1992

No one—and I do mean no one—will ever again be introduced into the Pro Football Hall of Fame by their father as the *third-best running back that ever lived*. But Barry Sanders didn't mind. It sort of tickled him. People could never ever fully grasp how little he cared about fame, how little he cared about records, how little he cared about immortality or history.

Barry Sanders ran merely to make the next guy miss.

He knew all his life that he would never make it into his father's top two.

BARRY SANDERS WAS NOT A RUNNING BACK THE WAY OTHER greats were running backs. No, he was a dancer and a hypnotist and an illusionist and a ghost. He disappeared and reappeared, split in two and rejoined, stopped instantly like the Road Runner at the edge of a cliff and then took off so fast that his cleats would smoke.

"He made defenders look like fools," said Gale Sayers, perhaps the only one who could truly understand what it must have felt like to run like Barry Sanders.

But even Sayers admitted that he did not understand Barry. Perhaps no one did. Sayers loved to run. And Barry? Well, he did not use the word "love" often when talking about football.

"I started playing football at the age of nine," he said, "and it was something I felt like I had to do. It was once said that man can do what he wants, but he cannot will what he wills. In a lot of ways, I think football chose me.

"I had to play. It wasn't that I wanted to play. I *had* to play."

This was so hard—impossible, even—for people to comprehend. How could someone run like Barry Sanders, the most joyful back the game has ever known, and by all indications not *feel* that joy himself, that thrill, that wonder? Even his famously modest touchdown anti-celebrations—when he crossed the goal line, he would flip the ball to the official and display no sign of triumph—left some people baffled.

"How do you juke people, spin, make adults fall down, get into the end zone," former basketball star Jalen Rose asks in the documentary *Bye Bye Barry*, "and just give the ball to the ref? That's a decompression that 99.9 percent of us just don't have."

The explanation was always the same: "That's just Barry." This was a guy who in high school pulled himself out of a blowout game rather than carry the ball a couple more times to clinch the Wichita high school rushing title. This was a guy who—after rushing for an astonishing 2,628 yards in his junior year at Oklahoma State, a record that might never be broken—wanted someone else to win the Heisman Trophy. This was a guy who in his rookie NFL season with the Lions pulled himself out of a game when he was 10 yards shy of leading the NFL in rushing.

And this was a guy who, in the end, walked away from football at age thirty-one when he was still healthy and unstoppable and maybe just one season away from passing Walter Payton at the top of the all-time rushing list.

That's just Barry.

To pick a single Barry Sanders run to represent all that he was is like picking a single quote to explain Shakespeare or a single note to explain Aretha Franklin. And yet there is a play that does stand out, not only for its brilliance but because of what it represented. Barry Sanders spent his career as a one-man show. The Lions over his ten-year career fluctuated between pretty good and pretty bad. He played in six playoff games, and his team lost five of them. He took the brunt of those losses because opponents focused all their attention on him, and as great as he was, even Barry could not beat eleven defenders by himself.

Except once. In 1992, the Lions played the Cowboys in a division playoff game. The Cowboys were a team on the rise—they would win three of the next four Super Bowls—and they never made any secret of their play: Stop Barry Sanders.

For a long time, they did. It just so happened that on this day, Sanders's teammates picked up the slack. Quarterback Erik Kramer threw three touchdown passes, much to the shock of the Cowboys defenders.

"I didn't think Kramer had it him," Cowboys linebacker Jack Del Rio admitted.

In the fourth quarter—with the Lions already up 31–6—Kramer handed it off to Sanders. He had just 22 yards, and now his only job was to stay in bounds and keep the clock running. But Sanders could never be dull. He ran right and eluded the grasp of Dallas's Tony Tolbert.

Then he ran into defensive back Robert Williams and bounced backward like a tennis ball hitting a wall. He stood there for an instant. While he stood there, a bunch of Cowboys moved in front of him, five in all.

And all five went crashing to the ground.

How? You don't explain such things. You just enjoy them. It was like Sanders had stopped time.

With the pathway clear, he took off running. And—this was the best part—one Cowboys defender, Tony Casillas, was still on his feet. But he, quite understandably, thought the play was over. So Sanders simply ran behind him, and Casillas turned his head and watched him go. If Casillas had been a comic strip character, the thought bubble over his head would have said: *What the @#$*?*

Then, to crown the run, Sanders made one more move that utterly paralyzed the last Cowboys defender, Ken Norton Jr. While Norton fell to the ground, Sanders scampered the rest of the way for a 47-yard touchdown run.

And then, like always, he flipped the ball to the official like he'd done nothing at all.

That was the only playoff touchdown Barry Sanders scored in his career.

In 1997, Barry Sanders ran for 2,053 yards, the fourth-highest total in NFL history. Some of his teammates said that getting to 2,000 yards was meaningful to Sanders. Barry himself never showed that. It did mean a lot to his father, William, who was in the stands when he did it, and he said, "It's an indescribable feeling for me and for myself."

Someone then asked him if Barry was now the greatest running back ever.

"No," he said. "I still think Jim Brown's the greatest running back I've ever seen."

A year later, Sanders retired.

"My desire to exit the game is greater than my desire to remain in it," he said.

People have wanted a deeper explanation ever since. But even after all the Sanders books and documentaries that have come out, the reason hasn't changed. The thing that compelled him to play football was gone. And without it, Barry Sanders was not going to play football.

He asked his father to present him into the Hall of Fame; throughout Barry's life William Sanders had been as talkative as Barry was silent, as boastful as Barry was humble, as eager to chase the spotlight as Barry was to avoid it. He relished the moment.

"First," he said, "I want to say hello to the greatest running back that ever lived, the number one running back that ever lived. He's not with us today. I think he's with his family in Los Angeles: Mr. Jim Brown. So, I want to say hello to him."

Yes, he began his speech meant to celebrate Barry Sanders by saying hello to Jim Brown, who wasn't even there. Barry couldn't help but smile. Finally, he introduced Barry as the third-best running back of them.

But wait. You ask: If Jim Brown was first and Barry was third, who was second?

"Well," William Sanders explained, "that would be me."

William Sanders was a roofer. He had never even played college football.

"Your grandfather," Barry would tell his sons as he laughed, "was something else."

NO. 30:

JIM BROWN

Question: "What's it like trying to tackle Jim Brown?"

Sam Huff: "I don't know. I woke up on the training table."

———

SEPTEMBER 22, 1963

Nobody towered over the game the way Jim Brown did.

They called him Superman. They called him indestructible. They called him a god. They were calling him the greatest player who ever lived by the end of his second pro season. He was a 6-foot-2, 230-pound rocket ship in an era when pretty much everyone else was a Volkswagen Beetle.

"He's like tackling a locomotive," the Rams' Glenn Holtzman said, pulling the most vivid image he could summon in the 1950s.

There are plenty of jaw-dropping Jim Brown numbers we could use to numerically display his dominance . . . but Jim Brown loathed statistics. "Every time I break another record," he said unhappily, "I become more of a statistic and less of a person."

So, instead, we talk about Jim Brown the titanic force. He is widely regarded, still, as the greatest lacrosse player ever. As a high school senior, he averaged 38 points per game in basketball. (Perhaps he will forgive this brief mention of a number.) He was offered a baseball contract by the legendary manager Casey Stengel himself. At Syracuse, he was nationally ranked in the decathlon. There was nothing athletically beyond his reach.

Football spoke to him most vividly because football, more than any other sport, allowed him to match his heart against those of others. And he never doubted that he had the biggest heart. He never doubted that the bigger the moment, the larger he would become.

"I am a god," he used to say to teammates. "I can't be hurt." He didn't mean that literally, of course; it isn't that Jim Brown thought his body was somehow invulnerable to injury. He meant it mentally. He meant it emotionally. He wouldn't let anyone hurt him. He wouldn't accept the pain that anyone was trying to inflict on him. He never missed a game. He would stay on the ground for a few seconds after each run, leaving the unenlightened to wonder if he could go on.

"Hey, you gonna get up?" a cheeky linebacker supposedly said to him once.

Brown looked and said quietly but with menace: "Yes, I'm going to get up. But next play, you won't." And as the legend goes, on the next play, the linebacker felt all of Jim Brown's wrath and needed to be helped to the sideline.

"You gang-tackled him, gave him extracurriculars," Chuck Bednarik, one of the game's all-time tough guys, said. "We would kick him. We would bite him. We would yell everything and anything we could think of when he was down. . . . He'd get up slow, look at you, and walk back to the huddle. He wouldn't say a word. And he'd just come at you again."

No, Jim Brown was never, ever going to stay down.

"When it was time to play," he said, "I was there."

He ran with the fury with which he lived. Brown had the speed to run away from defenders. Sometimes he did that. More often, he preferred to smash into them, make them feel his will, make them understand what it took to tackle Jim Brown.

"He told me, 'Make sure when anyone tackles you, he remembers how much it hurts,'" Hall of Fame tight end John Mackey said. "He lived by that."

Jim Brown always ran angry. But every now and again, someone would challenge him or disrespect him, and then he took his fury even higher. Once at Syracuse, the Cornell coach made some sort of comment about how his star player, George Pfann Jr.,* would show Jim Brown a thing or two on the lacrosse field.

"I circled the quote, taped it on his locker, and watched to see his expression," Brown's lacrosse coach Roy Simmons told the *New York Times*. "He read it, crumpled it up, and scored seven goals. I had to take him out, it was such a runaway."

Well, in 1962, the Cleveland Browns were blown out by Tom Landry's upstart Dallas Cowboys 45–21. The Cowboys held Brown to just 29 yards rushing and forced him to fumble. Not to get into numbers, but even that low total was misleading; the Cowboys held him to –1 yard until the final eight minutes, when they rested many of their starters.

It might have been the worst game that Jim Brown ever played as a professional. All of 1962 was a grind for Brown: He played with a sprained wrist; he clashed with legendary coach Paul Brown (who would be fired at the end of the year). It was the only season of his career that he did not lead the league in rushing. The Cowboys game was a low point.

In the second week of the 1963 season, the Browns faced Landry's Cowboys again.

And Brown was even more unstoppable than normal. In the first quarter, he ran off right tackle and at one point was in the middle of four Cowboys defenders and two of his own blockers. Brown had so many remarkable talents but perhaps the greatest of them all was his balance. You simply couldn't knock him off his feet. He just kept on going until everybody around him fell to the ground and he ran 71 yards in all, the second-longest touchdown run of his career. A little later, he ran for a 61-yard touchdown. In all he had 232 yards, five shy

---

* George Pfann, Cornell's lacrosse star, was the son of George Pfann, who was a Cornell football star in the 1920s and is in the National Football Foundation Hall of Fame. "My dad didn't want me to play football," George Jr. said. "He didn't want me to get hurt."

of his NFL record at the time, and when the game ended, an angry Tom Landry wanted to talk about how Brown wasn't much of a blocker.

This seemed a bit like saying that Aretha Franklin wasn't much on the violin.

"What about as a runner?" Landry was asked.

"I have no doubt," Landry admitted, "but that Brown is football's finest runner of all time."

NO. 29:

THE STATUE OF LIBERTY

"May the football star and the cheerleader live happily ever after."
—*GOOD MORNING AMERICA*'S CHARLES GIBSON

—

JANUARY 1, 2007

The Statue of Liberty is the oldest trick play in football. How old is it? Well, nobody can say for sure. But consider this: By the early 1910s, sportswriters were already referring to the play as the "old Statue of Liberty play" or the "time-worn Statue of Liberty play" or even the "time-honored Statue of Liberty." One newspaper story in 1916 said the play was famed "nearly a quarter century ago," which would have placed its origin within just a few years of Lady Liberty's dedication in 1886.[*]

The play is simple enough. In its most basic form, a player (usually the quarterback now, though it used to be anybody) drops back and gets into a throwing motion—looking a bit like the Statue of Liberty. The quarterback, in one motion, pretends to throw in one direction while surreptitiously handing the ball off to a player running in the other direction.

Amos Alonzo Stagg, who basically invented everything in football[†] around the turn of the century, might have invented the Statue of Liberty in 1896. Then Vanderbilt coach Dan McGugin claimed one of his players invented it around 1905. Then Fielding Yost, the great

---

[*] The Statue of Liberty was dedicated on October 28, 1886. Two days later, in front of seventy-five loyal fans, Harvard beat Dartmouth 70–0 during a heavy rainstorm in Cambridge.

[†] Stagg also played in the very first public basketball game; he was working at the Springfield, Massachusetts, YMCA when James Naismith invented the game there.

Michigan coach, is credited for inventing it or perfecting it or something. The point is, everybody used it back in those early days of college football.

Nobody saw it coming in 2007.

ON NEW YEAR'S DAY, BOISE STATE AND OKLAHOMA PLAYED A game for all time. The game was a festival of colors and sparks and magic tricks. Most of the magic tricks were performed by Boise State, a school playing in its first ever major bowl game. The Sooners—named after those nineteenth-century settlers who tried to stake claim to Oklahoma land sooner than they were allowed to—were playing in their twenty-eighth.

The Broncos were not about to let that—or the fact that the oddsmakers made them touchdown underdogs—upset them. The Broncos took a 2-touchdown lead before Oklahoma's players even knew the game had begun. The Sooners then steadied themselves and imposed their will and took the lead back. There didn't seem anything left for Boise State to do.

Ah, but Boise State had come into this game with a huge bag full of gadgets and contraptions and thingamajigs and Rube Goldberg machines to unleash on unsuspecting Oklahoma when the moment called for them. On fourth down and forever, when the game seemed lost, they ran a play called "Circus," which was a hook-and-ladder play; it scored a touchdown. Later they ran a play in which their quarterback went in motion and a receiver took the snap instead and he threw a touchdown pass to somebody else. It was all wild.

And then it was overtime in this fun house of a game. Oklahoma led by 1, and Boise State decided to go for the 2-point conversion.

"Statue left," quarterback Jared Zabransky announced in the huddle.

They really called it. It was the old Statue of Liberty play. Zabransky dropped back, looked to his right, and faked a pass in that direction.

But while he was doing that, he put the ball behind his back and handed it off to a sophomore running back named Ian Johnson, who ran to his left.

Nobody was even close as Johnson ran into the end zone for the conversion that won the game.

At this point, Ian Johnson knew just what he was going to do. The moment would never be more perfect. He threw the ball into the stands, did a quick interview with ESPN, then got on one knee in front of Boise State cheerleader Chrissy Popadics.

"Will you marry me?" Ian Johnson asked.

"Yes!" Chrissy Popadics yelled out.

That's how good a play the old Statue of Liberty is. Even after a hundred years, it still offers some delightful surprises.*

---

* Ian and Chrissy are still married and living in Boise. They have a daughter named Johannah. I went to see them a few years after the proposal, when Ian was trying to make it as a professional football player, and they seemed as happy and in love as the day Ian scored the touchdown.

NO. 28:

PAUL BROWN GETS REVENGE

"All the Browns can do is pass the ball."

—EAGLES COACH GREASY NEALE

SEPTEMBER 16, 1950

Innovations just poured out of Paul Brown. Every other day, it seemed, he was inventing something or other. The face mask? Yeah, he invented that. Coaches calling plays instead of quarterbacks? He was the first. Intelligence tests for scouting players? Paul Brown. Taxi squads of players to call up in case of emergencies?* Paul Brown. Full-time assistant coaches? Paul Brown.

He came up with innovations without even trying. His Browns were playing a game in the late 1940s, and quarterback Otto Graham dropped back to throw. He was almost immediately swarmed by the pass rush.

Running back Marion Motley, seeing his quarterback in trouble, raced over, grabbed the ball away, and took off running. To everybody's surprise, there was all sorts of open space; all the defenders had gone after Graham.

On the sideline, Paul Brown nodded and made a mental note.

Voilà. They had just invented the draw play.

"Whether they know it or not," NFL commissioner Pete Rozelle said, "nearly everyone in the game of football has been affected by Paul Brown."

---

* The first pro football taxi squads were *actual* taxi squads. Cleveland Browns owner Arthur McBride owned a taxi company. Paul Brown convinced him to hire good players he had cut to drive taxis so that when the team needed them, he could quickly bring them in.

But in 1950, when the Browns entered the NFL after winning four consecutive All-American Football Conference championships, there were doubters. It was one thing to beat up on the Chicago Hornets or the Buffalo Bisons or the Los Angeles Dons or the sad sack Baltimore Colts.* But this was the National Football League with the Chicago Bears and the New York Giants and the Philadelphia Eagles. This was real football.

Everybody was ready to see if the Cleveland Browns could hold their own.

And everybody would find out right away because Commissioner Bert Bell shrewdly arranged for the opening game of the season to match up the Browns with the two-time defending NFL champion Philadelphia Eagles. Those Eagles had the league's best offense and the league's best defense. They had won their two championships by shutouts.

Both teams stayed respectful in the week leading up to the game, but Philadelphia Eagles coach Greasy Neale was confident. He knew that his team was the best in the world.

Then, before the game, the Eagles' star running back Steve Van Buren got hurt. Neale didn't think it would make a difference. And he was right. Sure, the offense might have missed Van Buren, but it was the Eagles' defense that was overwhelmed. They simply had no idea what to do against the Browns' sophisticated passing game. Quarterback Otto Graham threw three touchdown passes and Cleveland won 35–10 in front of the largest crowd to ever watch an NFL game to that point, more than eighty-five thousand.[†]

----

* This was a different Baltimore Colts from the Johnny Unitas team that would later dominate the NFL. This Colts team folded in 1951 after only one year in the NFL. An entirely new Baltimore Colts team was founded two years later.

† The record for largest crowd to ever watch a regular season NFL game was set in Dallas in 2009 when 105,121—including more than thirty thousand standing-room-only fans—watched the New York Giants beat the Cowboys. But if you include preseason

"What coverage are they in?" Paul Brown asked his assistant coach Blanton Collier at some point during the game.

"Truthfully," Collier said, "I don't know. I don't think they know."

"That," a flabbergasted Bert Bell said after the game, "is the best pro football team I have ever seen."

That's the game that has gone down in history. But, in many ways, the cooler Browns-Eagles game came later in the season. It was in December, after a record snowstorm had hit Cleveland.

This time, Eagles coach Greasy Neale was not nearly as outwardly respectful as he had been before the first game. He told reporters that he loathed the Browns and that he wanted *any other team* to win the title except Cleveland.* He griped that the only reason the Browns had won that first game was because the Eagles had not had a chance to scout them and prepare for their passing game. The Giants had just shut out the Browns 6–0 and he felt sure the Eagles would do the same.

"All the Browns can do is pass the ball," Neale reportedly said.

Well, the Browns beat the Eagles again, this time by a much closer 13–7 score. They went on to win the championship, much to Neale's chagrin. But there's something else about that game, something so incredible that speaks to the competitive fury of Paul Brown.

Cleveland did not throw a single pass the whole game.

Not one. It is the only time since World War II that a team won a game without even one pass. When asked about that afterward, Paul Brown said, no, he hadn't done that on purpose. But you know he did. And he added:

"It was nice to repay Mr. Neale for shooting off his bazooka."

---

games, the attendance record was set in Mexico City when 112,376 watched Dallas play the Houston Oilers.

* "I've got no love for Ohio," Neale said. When reminded that as a Major League Baseball player he had spent eight years playing outfield for the Cincinnati Reds—including on the 1919 Reds that beat the infamous Black Sox in the World Series—he corrected himself. "I have no love for Northern Ohio," he said.

NO. 27:

MIRACLE AT THE MEADOWLANDS

NFL Films: "Can you walk us through that play?"

Larry Csonka: "No. I have no interest in
walking you through that play."

—

NOVEMBER 19, 1978

With 1:23 left in a bland late-autumn Giants-Eagles game, Philadelphia quarterback Ron Jaworski threw an interception that ended the Eagles' hopes. The Giants led the game 17–12 and the Eagles had only one time-out remaining. This would be a tough loss for an up-and-coming Eagles team and especially for their forty-two-year-old obsessive coach, Dick Vermeil.*

All the Giants had to do was fall on the ball three times to win the game. In those days, though, falling down on the ball was very much against the whole zeitgeist of the manly NFL. Coaches, players, and fans all thought kneeling was cowardly. Chiefs founder Lamar Hunt lobbied the league to institute a rule that if a team was stopped for a loss in the final two minutes, the clock would stop. None of the owners liked the rule suggestion, but they did share Hunt's disapproval of the kneel down.

The Giants' Joe Pisarcik did kneel on the first play. Well, it was more like he rolled over awkwardly. While he did that, Philadelphia

---

* Here is how obsessive Vermeil was: On July 4, 1976—the day of the American bicentennial celebration—he was studying film when he heard a band playing and fireworks. He furiously called his assistant Carl Peterson to ask what the hell was going on. "It's July Fourth," Peterson said. "It's our nation's birthday." To which Vermeil responded: "I don't care whose birthday it is. Tell that band to stop playing that damn music."

linebacker Frank LeMaster angrily smashed into running back Willie Spencer and knocked him backward. He was trying to create havoc, cause a fumble, start a fight, induce a penalty, anything to stave off the inevitable defeat.

"You know," fellow linebacker Bill Bergey told Philadelphia columnist Frank Dolson, "with the old team—I'm talking about the old Eagles, when Dick Vermeil wasn't here—it would have been, 'Let 'em fall down on the ball.' . . . Now Frank was trying to make something happen."

LeMaster's maneuvers had the desired effect. The Giants were outraged, words were exchanged, a near fight broke out, and all of this freaked out the Giants' much-maligned offensive coordinator, Bob Gibson. He was a fifty-one-year-old longtime assistant getting his first chance to be an NFL coordinator . . . and he needed a win. Many of his players were in open revolt against him. Reporters questioned his competence. Now he worried that falling down on the ball would lead to complications, so he changed strategy.

On second down, Gibson had Joe Pisarcik hand off the ball to future Hall of Fame running back Larry Csonka. He didn't want the ball. This was a man who had spent his career playing for the ultracompetent Don Shula, who always seemed to take the safest option. The reluctant Csonka bulled ahead for 11 yards, leaving third down and 2 and the clock rapidly winding down to zero.

Then the next play was sent in. It was another Csonka running play called "Pro-up 65."

The players in the Giants' huddle were dumbstruck.

"Don't give me the ball," Csonka pleaded.

"Let's just fall on it," center Jim Clack shouted.

Pisarcik didn't know what to do. It was only his second year in the NFL, and already he'd been excoriated by Gibson for changing plays in the huddle. His instincts told him to fall on the ball but what if that went wrong? It might mean the end of his NFL career. He was an undrafted quarterback out of New Mexico State. He had spent his first years playing for Calgary in the Canadian Football League. He needed this gig.

He called Gibson's play. It was a timing play: Pisarcik had to take the ball, reverse-pivot 180 degrees, and stuff the ball in the gut of a charging Csonka. Pisarcik broke the huddle and walked to the line apprehensively.

Anyway, that's how Eagles cornerback Herm Edwards saw it.

"There was just something strange going on," Edwards told me many years later. "It was an instinct. Maybe it was the way Pisarcik looked at Csonka. I don't know. I just thought, 'Uh-oh, these guys are not on the same page.' And I thought, 'Watch the ball.'"

The Eagles had an all-out blitz called, so Edwards was close to the line. He said the rest played out in slow motion for him. The snap between Clack and Pisarcik was not clean—the ball was snapped so hard that Pisarcik later found blood under his fingernails—so he did not have a handle on the ball as he turned to make the handoff. Instead of jamming the ball into Csonka's gut as he was supposed to do, the ball hit Csonka's hip and bounced free.

Then came the most unappreciated part of the Miracle at the Meadowlands.

Pisarcik had a chance to recover the fumble. The ball bounced up to him. But he was so off-balance after his collision with Csonka that he fell and couldn't get his hands on it. The ball bounced off his chest and took one little hop into the hands of Edwards, who scooped it up in stride as if that had been the design of the play all along.

"It's like the ball came to me," Edwards would say.

He ran the 26 yards all by himself. Only one Giant, tight end Gary Shirk, was even on the television screen when Edwards scored.

Even though it didn't mean a whole lot—the Giants weren't going to the playoffs anyway—it has to rank as one of the toughest losses in NFL history.

"We could write a book on losing," the Giants' Jim Clack said.

The next day, the Giants fired Bob Gibson. "It wasn't Bob's fault we fumbled," Giants director of personnel Andy Robustelli said. "But, uh, that wasn't the right call."*

---

* A week later, the Eagles beat the Cardinals and the game ended with quarterback Ron Jaworski falling on the ball four straight times. Each time, he found himself surrounded by three specially placed teammates whose sole job was to be back there in case of a fumble. It was the first use of the victory formation, which has been used in the NFL ever since.

NO. 26:

BRETT FAVRE PLAYS
FOR HIS DAD

"That's what I could do best—make a throw
from an awkward situation."

—BRETT FAVRE

—

DECEMBER 22, 2003

As he grew older, Brett Favre became something of a cliché. This seems to be the evolution of many of our greatest athletes. They begin as something entirely fresh and new, and as time passes, they become familiar and then they are imitated and then they are caricatured and then they become clichés.

When Brett Favre entered the NFL, he created a whole genre. He was the toughest player, the fiercest competitor, the boldest gambler, the most indestructible superhero, with the heart of a lion, the guts of a burglar, and an arm like a cannon, but more than that, as every commentator and analyst and fan seemed to say, he was "like a kid out there." He played with this effervescent joy and delight.

The biggest broadcaster in football, John Madden, spoke of him as if he were a god; it got to the point where the comedian Frank Caliendo made a name for himself simply impersonating Madden talking about Favre:

"Brett Favre is the greatest player in the world. If you pulled his legs off and poked out his eyeballs, he'd still be the best torso in football. That's how good Brett Favre is. I mean, Brett Favre can throw a football 200 yards underwater!"

Yes, perhaps it grew tiresome by the end.

But there was a reason Madden gushed like that. Brett Favre rocked the NFL. Every pass was a cliff-hanger, every game a light show. He threw into double coverage, triple coverage, quadruple coverage. He didn't care. He'd throw from any angle. The guy would be chased by rolling boulders, thrown off bridges handcuffed, hunted by Empire stormtroopers, and he'd always come out on the other side.

The young Favre . . . his uniform should have been a leather jacket.

Over his twenty-year career, he had countless moments: the across-his-body heave to Sterling Sharpe, the walk-off bomb to Greg Jennings in Denver, the "He did what?" pass to Antonio Freeman, the headfirst dive in Milwaukee, the run of joy after his Super Bowl pass to Andre Rison, on and on and on and on.

But the game he played for his father was something different.

I MET IRVIN FAVRE IN THE STRANGEST WAY. FAVRE'S FIRST SUPER Bowl in 1997 was in New Orleans, about an hour away from Kiln, where Favre grew up. Southern Mississippi, Favre's college, chartered a bus to take reporters on what I can only describe as the Brett Favre Tour Bus Adventure (with lunch included!). We went to Hattiesburg to see Southern Mississippi.* There we met an old college teammate of Favre's named Greg Reed.

"I remember the first pass," he told us. "It was cold, and I ran about 12 yards, and he threw it. And I turned around and the ball was coming at me, and I could hear it."

What did it sound like? we hungrily asked.

---

* The bus was filled with many reporters and television and radio people. These included Chris Russo, the famous talk show personality "Mad Dog," and I will never forget that about a half hour into our journey, he piped up and said, "Wait a minute. I don't want to go to Hattiesburg! Let me out." So they let him out in the middle of nowhere. I don't know how he got back, but last I checked, he was still rolling along on talk radio.

"A whistle, maybe? No, that's not it. I can't really describe it. I never heard anything like it. It just sort of whined, you know?"

Then we went to Kiln and saw Brett's childhood home; we visited the library; we went to a restaurant called the Rooster. There we met Brett's mom, Bonita, who told us a story about the time that the family's Saint Bernard was munched by an alligator.

Finally, we met Irvin. He was a nice man. He was a football coach himself and decided to make all three of his boys (Scott, Jeff, and Brett) into quarterbacks. Here's the kind of guy Irvin was: When he coached Brett at Hancock North Central High School, the team was loaded with talented running backs. So Irvin installed a wishbone offense, rarely letting Brett throw.

"If I had wanted to showcase my son, I could have let him throw," he said. "But I did what I thought was best for the team. That's what I wanted to get across to Brett. Always do what's best for the team."

Four days before Christmas in 2003, Irvin Favre had a heart attack while driving near his home. He was fifty-eight years old.

As it turned out, Brett was not scheduled to play that day; the Packers were playing Oakland on a Monday. He met with the team—he would call that the most emotional meeting he'd ever been involved in—and came out deciding to play against the Raiders. "I know that my dad would have wanted me to play," he said.

Favre was having a good but trying season. He would lead the league in touchdown passes and finish third in interceptions; two of those interceptions were pick-sixes.* He talked often about how nothing seemed to be coming easy.

That night, though, while playing for his father, Brett Favre was better than he had ever been or would ever be again. In the first half, he threw for 311 yards and 4 touchdowns. He fired the ball downfield

---

* As of this writing, Favre has thrown more pick-sixes—thirty-two—than any quarterback in NFL history. But the Rams' Matthew Stafford is only two behind.

repeatedly, with his usual daring, challenging the Raiders' secondary again and again. He completed three 40-yard passes. He hit on six third and long plays. It was so awesome and heart-wrenching that Raiders fans, not exactly known for their hospitality, stood and applauded and some even cried a little. Didn't we all?

"I've got two heroes," Favre's teammate Mike Wahle said after the game. "My dad and Brett Favre."

NO. 25:

THE HOLY ROLLER

"There's nothing real in the world anymore!"

—RAIDERS ANNOUNCER BILL KING

—

SEPTEMBER 10, 1978

For a while in the 1960s and '70s, there were so many supernatural Raiders plays that people said owner Al Davis must have sold his soul. The plays all seemed to have names too: There was the "Heidi Game" and "Sea of Hands" and "Ghost to the Post" and "Old Man Willie" and "Monday Night Mayhem" . . .

NFL Films' Steve Sabol was so moved by the Raiders' magic that he wrote a poem in their honor called "The Autumn Wind":*

The Autumn Wind is a Raider

Pillaging just for fun

He'll knock you 'round and upside down

And laugh when he's conquered and won.

The Holy Roller, I think, tops them all. It wasn't the most important Raiders play: Old Man Willie happened in a Super Bowl and others happened in the playoffs. The Holy Roller happened in an early regular-season game. But the Holy Roller best captures the brashness, the audacity, the rudeness, and the sheer gall of those Raiders.

---

* "The Autumn Wind" is an "adaptation" of Mary Jane Carr's 1941 poem "Pirate Wind." I put "adaptation" in quotes because in many places the poems are identical, though I greatly prefer Steve's final two lines to Carr's, which were: "He'll snatch your hat as quick as that / And laugh to see you run!"

That gall reflected Al Davis, whose rise to football mythology defies explanation. Davis didn't play football, not even in high school. He bullied, conned, and charmed his way into the sport. Out of college, he tried for a coaching job at Adelphi University on Long Island and the head coach told him no, they weren't hiring, but they would keep him in mind if something opened up. He figured out a way to get a meeting with the school president, and a few minutes later the head coach got a call from the president saying: "You've got yourself a new assistant coach."

He kept hustling his way up. In the Army, he convinced General Stanley Scott of Fort Belvoir to let him coach the football team. He found an assistant coaching job at the Citadel, then one at USC, then one for Sid Gillman and the Los Angeles Chargers of the American Football League.

"Al had that knack of telling people what they wanted to hear," Gillman would tell Davis's biographer Ira Miller.

Then Wayne Valley, owner of the Oakland Raiders, hired Davis to be head coach. He did so for the most Al Davis reason imaginable: "I hired Al Davis because everybody hated his guts," Valley said.

Davis loved that scouting report.

"I don't want to be the most respected man in football," he would say many times through the years. "I want to be the most feared."

Oh, people feared him. For one thing, he was brilliant. His ability to scout players was uncanny. But more than that, they feared him because Davis would go to any length—*any length*—to win. Al Davis was the sort of man who would show up at celebrity golf tournaments to find out if any of the football players were unhappy with their teams.

This was a man whose entire persona was wrapped up in his motto: "Just win, baby."

All of that brashness is in the Holy Roller. It was the second game of the 1978 season. The Raiders—who had been in the AFC Championship Game for five straight seasons—had lost their season opener to the Broncos in a flurry of dropped passes and dumb penalties, and Davis was outraged. The next game against San Diego was worse: Linebacker Phil Villapiano said that most of the team had gone to a karaoke bar the night before and overdone it.

"We stunk," he said.

Raiders quarterback Ken Stabler threw three interceptions. Oakland fumbled the ball three times. A mediocre Chargers team lead by 6 with 1:07 left, and Oakland had the ball way back at its own 19.

Then Stabler got hot—as he so often seemed to do in such moments— and hit on five passes to move the ball to the San Diego 14 with ten seconds left.

Then came the play. Stabler dropped back and could not find an open receiver, and San Diego's Woodrow Lowe broke through the line and grabbed Stabler from behind.

Stabler, who was out of ideas, desperately shoveled the ball forward. Oakland's Pete Banaszak tried to pick the ball up at the 14 and perhaps run with it. But San Diego's Fred Dean dived at the ball too, and it squirted forward all the way to the San Diego 5. There it popped up into the hands of Oakland's Dave Casper. But he couldn't hold on to it, so he just sort of knocked the ball forward the remaining yards and then fell on it in the end zone.

The referee Jerry Markbreit signaled a touchdown.

Everything was chaos. Both coaches ran on the field. Nobody seemed sure what had happened. Replays would show that Stabler had purposely chucked the ball forward, meaning it should have been ruled an incomplete pass (and intentional grounding). Replays would show that Banaszak actually had not tried to recover the ball but instead batted it forward. That too was against the rules. Casper's recovery too could have been viewed as illegally fumbling the ball forward. There were several other potential violations on the play, so many that Chargers fans created a T-shirt calling the play "The Immaculate Deception."

All of this made Al Davis's heart sing.

And now we leave you with Oakland announcer Bill King's glorious call:

The ball, flipped forward,
is loose,
a wild scramble,
two seconds on the clock,
Casper grabbing the ball,
it is ruled a fumble,
Casper has recovered in the end zone, the Oakland Raiders have scored on
the most zany, unbelievable,
absolutely impossible
dream of a play!
Madden is on the field,
he wants to know if it's real,
they said 'yes,
get your big butt out of here,'
he does.
There is nothing real in the world anymore . . .

NO. 24:

WIN ONE FOR THE GIPPER

"You've all heard of George Gipp, I presume."

—KNUTE ROCKNE TO HIS TEAM BEFORE THE ARMY GAME

—

NOVEMBER 10, 1928

Maybe this is just me, but I always thought that George Gipp, star of the famous "Win one for the Gipper" story—the guy played by future president Ronald Reagan in the movies—was a wholesome lad who gave everything he had in every game he played until he was struck down in the prime of his life. I thought that was the whole point of the story.

Uh, no. That was most certainly not George Gipp.

As Willy Wonka said: "Strike that. Reverse it."

"What about you, Gipp?" Notre Dame coach Knute Rockne raged at his lethargic star when the team trailed Army 17–14 in 1920. "I don't suppose you have any interest in this game?"

"Look, Rock," Gipp was said to have responded while he puffed on a cigarette in a corner of the locker room. "I got $400 bet on this game, and I'm not about to blow it."

That story from Jim Lefebvre's Rockne biography, *Coach for a Nation*, gets you a bit closer to the real-life George Gipp, one of the more volatile athletes in college football history. He didn't even like football much; baseball was his racket.

But Gipp was an astonishing football talent. He could do everything, absolutely everything: He could run, he could throw, he could kick, he could tackle, he could block, and he could cover. He was, in fact, such a brilliant pass defender that Rockne insisted "not a single forward pass was ever completed in territory defended by George Gipp."

None of it seemed to matter much to Gipp. He would show up for practice or not show up for practice; it made no difference to him. He once showed up so late that Rockne yelled, "Gipp, just go on home."

"Fine, Rock," he replied. "But I ain't going home. There's a poker game I interrupted to get here."

There was always a poker game or a billiards hustle or a gambling opportunity for George Gipp. He needed the action. He constantly bet on his own games, sometimes offering wild odds just to get people interested. Before an Indiana game, he was so desperate to get money down that he offered a bet that he personally would outscore the entire Hoosiers team.*

In 1920, he was named the Notre Dame captain despite his ever-fluid feelings about the game. Then he was kicked out of school, probably for being caught in a bar, this in the time of Prohibition. Then he was reinstated because of pressure in the community.

Rockne tolerated all of it. He more than tolerated it. Norm Barry, a Gipp teammate, recalled to *Sports Illustrated* how Rockne would shout at Gipp for missing practices or showing up late for practices or any number of other indiscretions, but shouting was as far as he would go. "On Saturday," Barry said, "Gipp would be in the game."

Like much else about George Gipp, there are conflicting stories about how he caught pneumonia. What we do know is that coming into the Northwestern game, he was feeling sick, and Rockne didn't want him to play. But Gipp begged to get in—that Northwestern game had been declared "George Gipp Day"—and Rockne relented. The game was played in frigid conditions on a nearly frozen field and Gipp threw two touchdown passes. On the train back from Chicago, according to Jack Cavanaugh's *The Gipper*, he told his teammate Hunk Anderson, "I really don't feel good at all."

He died less than a month later.

_____

* Gipp did not outscore Indiana in that game, but apparently nobody had been willing to take him up on the bet.

∣ ∣ ∣ ∣ ∣ ∣

IN 1928, ROCKNE COACHED WHAT WOULD TURN OUT TO BE HIS
worst Notre Dame team. Rockne's record as coach at Notre Dame is
truly extraordinary. Not counting 1928, his teams went 100-8-5 and
had five undefeated seasons. Rockne's motivational talents surely have
never been matched. His quotes, even ninety-plus years after his death
in a plane crash, are still very much a part of the football coach's lexicon:

> *"Show me a gracious loser, and I'll show you a failure."*
> *"As a coach, I play not my eleven best, but my best eleven."*
> *"Build up your weaknesses until they become your strong points."*
> *"It's not the will to win that matters. It's the will to prepare to win."*
> *"Football is played with arms and legs and shoulders but mainly
> from the neck up."*

That year, 1928, Notre Dame came into its game against undefeated
Army as a massive underdog. As if this wasn't bad enough—Rockne
hated losing to Army under any circumstances—the game was to be
played at Yankee Stadium in front of seventy-eight thousand–plus
people. All the New York sportswriters would be there.

Rockne needed his best-ever motivational speech.

And you betcha, he came up with it:

> *"Now I'm going to tell you something I've kept to myself for years.
> None of you ever knew George Gipp. He was long before your time.
> But you all know what a tradition he is at Notre Dame. And the last
> thing he said to me, 'Rock,' he said, 'sometime when the team is up
> against it and the breaks are beating the boys, tell 'em to go out there
> with all they got and win just one for the Gipper. I don't know where
> I'll be then, Rock,' he said, 'but I'll know about it and I'll be happy.'"*

Well, anyway, that was how actor Pat O'Brien did it in the movie
Knute Rockne All American.

Is that how Rockne actually said it? Probably not, no. For one thing, he was not sitting in a wheelchair like in the movie. For another, the movie has him giving the speech at halftime; the best evidence suggests he gave it before the game. Beyond that, even Rockne wouldn't have been quite that maudlin. Contemporary accounts have him beginning with the line "You've all heard of George Gipp, I presume," and then he proceeded to, for the first time, reveal Gipp's dying wish.

Two days after the game, Frank Wallace—a former Notre Dame student and passionate Notre Dame fan and Rockne acolyte—wrote it this way for the *New York Daily News*:

> *Football people knew that Rockne would fire the boys up in his speech before the game. This is what he told them—"On his deathbed, George Gipp told me that someday when the time came, he wanted me to ask a Notre Dame team to beat Army for him."*
>
> *It was not a trick. George Gipp asked for it. When Notre Dame's football need was greatest, it called on its beloved "Gipper" again.*

Many people, through the years, have questioned Wallace's contention that "it was not a trick." Any number of those who knew George Gipp felt quite certain that he never would have made such a request, certainly not with his dying breath, and that he would have been much more likely to ask Rockne to place a bet for him. And it seems odd that Rockne would have waited *eight years* to reveal the wish and not, say, in 1922 when Notre Dame and Army were locked in a 0–0 draw or in 1925 when Army smashed Notre Dame 27–0.

Trick or no, Notre Dame did upset Army that day.

NO. 23:
THE PHILLY SPECIAL

"My career flashed before my eyes."

—EAGLES COACH DOUG PEDERSON

—

FEBRUARY 4, 2018

How many hours have football coaches spent designing trick plays? Countless, right? They have sketched out plays on napkins and graph paper, on scraps of paper and notebooks they keep by their beds at night. They have designed flea-flickers and Statues of Liberty, double passes and double reverses, fake field goals, fake punts, fake reverses, the entire gamut of laterals, all the rooskies,* and so on.

Trick plays are just so much fun. Like the "Annexation of Puerto Rico." That play was run (and named) in the kids' football movie *Little Giants*, but it has since become an NFL play, most joyfully run by the Carolina Panthers. The ball was snapped to quarterback Cam Newton; he slipped the ball between the legs of running back Richie Brockel. Newton spun around and ran to his right. Brockel, who had the ball, ran to his left untouched for a touchdown.

So much fun. How about Kansas's camouflage play in 2016? The Jayhawks were wearing their blue jerseys, and on a kickoff, they had returner LaQuvionte Gonzalez lie down in the end zone, which was painted the same blue as their jerseys. He blended into the scenery,

---

* The "rooskie" plays—which include the fumblerooskie, the puntrooskie, and the bouncerooskie, among others—usually involve surreptitiously leaving the ball on the ground for a teammate to pick up, though they can take on other forms. The idea is to run one way and hope the defense follows while a teammate runs the other way. In many ways, these plays date all the way back to the Hein Special, the first trick play, which happened in 1933. (See No. 93.)

chameleon-style, and then after the kick he popped up and took a lateral pass from the return man. That play didn't really work all that well, but it was still a blast.

In 1966, Colorado State was playing its undefeated rival, Wyoming. Quarterback Bob Wolfe threw the ball to Larry "Lemon Juice" Jackson,* an elusive 165-pound wingback. The pass bounced and Jackson stopped and hung his head at the incompletion. It was brilliant acting. All the Wyoming players stopped too, thinking the play was over.

But it was actually a backward pass, so the play was still live. Lemon Juice Jackson tossed a perfect pass to tight end Tom Pack, who ran alone the rest of the 33 yards for a touchdown.

The prettiest trick play of them all, I think, happened in Super Bowl LII, defending Super Bowl champion Patriots versus the Eagles. Philadelphia, somewhat surprisingly, led 15–12 and faced a fourth and goal from just outside the Patriots' 1. There were thirty-eight seconds left in the first half, and the conservative play would have been for the Eagles to kick a field goal and be satisfied with a 6-point lead going into halftime.

But that was not how the Eagles played. Coach Doug Pederson told his coaches, "We're going for it," and he sent his offense back on the field with a play.

Trouble was, he didn't like the play he'd called. He raced down the sideline to call time-out. Some of the Patriots thought he had changed his mind and would now kick the field goal. That was the furthest thing from Pederson's mind.

"Hey," quarterback Nick Foles said when he walked to the sideline. "You want Philly Philly?"

The look on Pederson's face when Foles said that was utterly glorious.

---

* People didn't actually start calling Jackson "Lemon Juice" until 1968. By then, the biggest thing going in college football was O. J. Simpson, with people calling him "Orange Juice" or, more simply, "Juice." With Larry Jackson's initials being "L.J.," the "Lemon Juice" nickname just fit.

777777777777

It was a look of panic and mischief and excitement and more panic. "My career," he would say, "flashed before my eyes."

Then Pederson said: "Yeah, let's do it. Let's do it."

Philly Philly. Its official name was "Philly Special," which is just what Foles said when he got to the huddle. Nobody said anything. When you run a trick play, you don't want to let on that anything suspicious is about to happen.

Foles stood in the shotgun and lifted his leg as if to call for the snap. Then he seemed perturbed by something. He walked over to his right tackle Lane Johnson, patted him on the backside, and seemed to be changing the pass-blocking scheme.

At that precise instant, the ball was snapped back to Eagles running back Corey Clement, who raced to his left as if he planned to run left. But then he flipped the ball up in the air, and it was caught by tight end Trey Burton,* who was running right.

Then, on the run, Burton lofted a pass to . . . a wide-open Nick Foles in the end zone.

It was utterly beautiful, more a dance number than a football play, which is exactly how it was drawn up. "That play was choreographed like few things you've ever seen," Eagles offensive coordinator Frank Reich said. "I felt like it was more like a production in a theater than something on a football field."

There have been more critical trick plays, more elaborate trick plays, and perhaps even more spectacular trick plays. But for pure beauty? The best.

"I still get nervous watching it," Pederson says.

---

* Trey Burton was an All-State quarterback in high school, and he started his college career at Florida as a quarterback. Of course, nobody on the Patriots was thinking about that in the moment.

NO. 22:

NEBRASKA GOES FOR TWO

"Football is a game. And you play games to win."

—TOM OSBORNE

—

JANUARY 2, 1984

When Tom Osborne went for two on that January day in Miami, I was about to turn seventeen years old, and I thought it was the most courageous call I'd ever seen a coach make on a football field.

As the years have gone by, well, I think it's more complicated than that.

Let's set the scene. It was 1984, and in those days, there was no "real" college football national champion. There was no playoff system or sports-wide structure to determine one. What they would do instead was play out the season and play out the bowl games, and then a bunch of sportswriters and a bunch of coaches (and various others as well) would pick the team that they thought the best. That team (or teams if the sportswriters and coaches didn't agree) was declared the *mythical* national champion. They actually used that word, "mythical." It was a different time.

The puzzle seemed fairly simple in 1984. Nebraska went into their Orange Bowl game undefeated. That team was absurdly good; they won games by comical-looking scores like 84–13 and 72–29 and 67–13. They averaged more than 50 points per game. Many were calling them the greatest college football team ever.

And their opponent, Miami, was . . . well, few put much thought into their place in the college football universe because few thought that Miami could beat Nebraska. The Cornhuskers were 11-point favorites. Then the Hurricanes, behind the brilliant passing of Bernie

Kosar, took a 17–0 lead. And suddenly the world of college football looked upside down.

But Nebraska came back, sparked by offensive lineman Dean Steinkuhler scoring on a fumblerooskie.* Nebraska scored 2 touchdowns in the fourth quarter, the second with forty-eight seconds left in the game, to pull within one.

And Osborne was faced with one of the biggest decisions in college football history.

Go for two and try to win the game?

Or kick the extra point and go for the tie?

Osborne did not hesitate. He would later say it wasn't even that hard a decision for him. He went for two. Former All-Pro quarterback John Brodie was in the booth for NBC that night and so he was able to offer the first opinion. "He's going for the win," Brodie said, "and I commend him for it."

That was certainly how I felt too. You can't settle for the tie there! Gill's 2-point conversion pass—the play was called "Triple Right 51 I-Back Flat"—was tipped by a Miami defender, and it banged off the shoulder pad of running back Jeff Smith and fell incomplete. The chance was lost. The game was lost. The mythical national championship also was lost; Miami was selected as champion by both the sportswriters and the coaches.

But Tom Osborne's hard decision was applauded across America.

"Fans Approve Attempt for Two Points" was the headline in the *Omaha World-Herald* in a story highlighted by a quote from Don Weaver of Beatrice, Nebraska: "He wouldn't settle for a tie because he's a winner."

---

* Here's the most famous fumblerooskie of them all: On this play, quarterback Turner Gill seemed to take the snap and run right. But what actually happened was that he let the ball fall to the ground, and while ran right, Steinkuhler scooped up the ball and ran left. The NBC cameras were completely fooled. A couple of the Hurricanes did figure out the play, but they couldn't tackle Steinkuhler until he got into the end zone.

"Osborne did the right thing," Mike Lupica wrote in the *New York Daily News*. "Remember Osborne, because on this night filled with heroes, he was one too. He went for it."

"He could have kicked the point and backed in as national champ," Tom McEwen wrote in the *Tampa Tribune*. "But the bold, proud Nebraska went for two points, the win and clear ownership of a national championship."

"Dr. Tom Osborne brought more honor upon himself with a decision that failed," Larry Felser wrote in the *Buffalo News*, "than he ever did in any game he ever won."

"No one can question the courage of Tom Osborne," Mark Janssen wrote in the *Manhattan (KS) Mercury*.

So, there is no argument, right?

Only, well, actually there was. . . .

"Those who worship at the shrine of macho would have us believe that Osborne has become some sort of an American folk hero," Joe McGuff wrote in the *Kansas City Star*. "The only problem is that all of this talk about guts is nonsense. . . . What Osborne did not do was make a gutty decision. The gutty decision would have been to kick the extra point and finish the season with the best record in major college football. . . . Going for two was the easy way out."

I remember first reading this, years after the play, and it kind of blew my mind. Others, like Pittsburgh's Bob Smizik, made similar points.

So, did Tom Osborne actually take the *easy* way out by going for two? Well, look at how he was celebrated even when the play failed.

And what would have happened if he had taken the tie? He would have been condemned and skewered by sportswriters and fans from sea to shining sea. We know this without the slightest doubt because in 1966 Notre Dame's Ara Parseghian settled for a tie against No. 2 Michigan State, and he never heard the end of it. Ever. But Notre Dame won the mythical national championship. After a while, few even remember the details. Pennants, as they say, fly forever.

This was the choice Tom Osborne faced. Sure, his players wanted him to go; the fans wanted him to go; the media wanted him to go; everybody wanted him to go. But if he had kicked the extra point and tied the game, the 1983 Nebraska Cornhuskers would be listed as the national champions. His players would forever be able to say they were on a national championship team.

And Osborne would have gotten hammered by everybody for years and years to come.

I still believe that Osborne made the right choice. I do. I think going for two is what you do when you're playing for history, as Nebraska was doing that day. But I no longer believe it was the courageous choice. No, it would have taken some serious guts to kick the extra point there.

NO. 21:
THE LOMBARDI SWEEP

"A seal here and a seal here . . ."

—VINCE LOMBARDI

—

JANUARY 2, 1966

Vince Lombardi understood that his all-consuming pursuit of perfection was ultimately doomed. He understood that perfection was unattainable. He knew the Saint Augustine quote: "This is the very perfection of a man, to find out his own imperfections."

But perfectionists don't get to choose their lot in life. Vince's father, Harry, was a perfectionist. His mother, Matty, was a perfectionist. At school, as David Maraniss wrote in the classic *When Pride Still Mattered*, "The Jesuits had taught him that human perfection was unattainable, but that all human beings should still work toward it."

"The satisfactions are few, I guess, for perfectionists," Lombardi wrote. "But I have never known a good coach who wasn't one."

Vince Lombardi, in so many ways, dedicated a lifetime to perfecting one play.

"My number one play," he said, "is the power sweep."

The Power Sweep—often now called the Packers Sweep or more specifically the Lombardi Sweep—was the engine that powered the Green Bay Packers and obsessed Lombardi. It was the play, he often said, that expressed who he was as a coach and who the Packers were as a team.

Lombardi put together the Packers Sweep over a lifetime. He picked up countless scraps and hints along the way. He first came across it as a player at Fordham* when he watched the University of Pittsburgh

---

* Lombardi was not a great player, but he was the right guard of a famous Fordham offensive line that was nicknamed "Seven Blocks of Granite."

run their own sweep out of the single-wing offense. Later, as a Giants assistant, he admired the Los Angeles Rams' version of the sweep.

Lombardi then tore the play down to its most basic elements, then tore it down again and then tore it down again. "Since his days at West Point," Maraniss wrote, "he had based his coaching philosophy on [Army coach] Red Blaik's belief that perfection came with simplicity."

Every single day, the Packers would practice one play simply numbered as 49 (that was the sweep right; it was 28 if the sweep was to go left). For the play to be perfect, every single player on the offense had to be perfect.

The center had to decide if he had time to cut off the lineman to his right; if so, he did that, but if not, he passed off the assignment to the right tackle and instead went after the middle linebacker.

The tight end had to be sure that under no circumstances would the linebacker on his side get inside penetration.

The fullback had to be sure to get out fast and run right at the defensive end and seal him off.

The right guard had to get all the way to the outside to make sure that he blocked anyone standing out there, whether it was a safety or a cornerback.

And so on. The left side of the line had their responsibilities, the receivers had their responsibilities, the quarterback's steps had to be precise, the running back had to follow the guard, and timing and precision were everything. This is, obviously, true for every play designed by every coach, but Lombardi took it to an obsessive extreme never quite seen before.

"If you look at this play," he said as he drew the Packer Sweep on a chalkboard, "what we're trying to get is a seal *here* and a seal *here* and try to run this *play in the alley.*"

"He'd never stop," said Bill Curry, who was the Packers' center in the mid-1960s. "He'd say 'Run it again,' then scream how we had to be the worst team he'd ever coached. Then he'd scream 'Run it again,' and tell

us how worthless we were. Then he'd scream 'Run it again.' I can remember whole practices where that was the only play we'd run."

This leads to the NFL Championship Game of 1965, Green Bay Packers versus the Cleveland Browns in the snow and sleet and fog of Lambeau Field. This was the Packers' third championship game in five
years. The Browns were defending NFL champs.

Cleveland led 13–12 at halftime. In the third quarter, the Packers
drove the ball into Browns territory.

Then the Packers called 49, Packers Sweep Right, and quarterback
Bart Starr handed off the ball to Paul Hornung. And it was like Lombardi's chalkboard had come to life. Ken Bowman sealed off defensive
tackle Jim Kanicki. Forrest Gregg turned his lineman inside. Fuzzy
Thurston pulled at precisely the right angle ("You've got to pull *flat* so
you don't interfere with the quarterback," Lombardi implored) and led
the play. Fullback Jim Taylor ran directly at left linebacker Jim Houston and knocked him out of the play.

Hornung powered forward for 20 yards.

Perfect. Well, was it perfect? Could it be perfect? *Run it again!* The
next play was 28, Packers Sweep Left, meaning that this time guard
Jerry Kramer pulled ahead of Hornung and he blocked two Browns.

Again, everybody did their jobs. But it was the sheer determination
of Gregg that Lombardi would remember. Gregg, as his job required,
looked for a linebacker to block. When he couldn't find one, he raced all
the way across the field and knocked a Browns defender backward.
Hornung was in the clear and in the end zone, a 13-yard touchdown
run that gave the Packers a lead they would never yield.

"Did you keep it pretty basic today, Vince, because of the weather?" a
reporter asked him afterward.

"Yes, we did," Lombardi said with a gleam in his eye. "But we're a
pretty basic football team."

At ten thirty a.m. the next morning, Lombardi was in his office
studying films in preparation for the 1966 season.

NO. 20:

TOM BRADY

"Tom has got a real good personality for a quarterback."

—PATRIOTS COACH BILL BELICHICK BEFORE BRADY'S FIRST START

—

JANUARY 19, 2002

Let's try, if we can, to go back in time to a moment before Tom Brady was Tom Brady, before he set every single passing record,[*] before he guided teams to ten Super Bowls, before he willed the Patriots back from that 28–3 deficit against the Falcons, before he led the league in passing and touchdowns at age forty-four, before people just called him GOAT as if "Greatest of All Time" wasn't his status but his actual name.

Let's try to go back to a moment when it was unclear if Brady was even a viable NFL quarterback.

During a driving snowstorm in New England, the Patriots played the Oakland Raiders in an AFC Divisional playoff game. It was a complete mess. There were eleven punts in the first half. The Raiders led 13–3 in the fourth quarter, and at that exact moment, there was no reason at all to believe that Tom Brady had the stuff to bring New England back.

Brady's story has been told and retold a million times. He platooned for a time with the more celebrated Drew Henson at Michigan. He was a sixth-round draft pick and was utterly devastated and infuriated by

---

[*] Every single record? Well, Tom Brady has the record for—deep breath—most passes attempted, most passes completed, most passing yards, most passing touchdowns, most playoff passes attempted, most playoff completions, most playoff passing yards, most playoff passing touchdowns, most game-winning drives, and longest touchdown pass. He does not have the record for most interceptions—that one belongs to Brett Favre—so I suppose there is a little bit of hyperbole in saying he set every single passing record.

the NFL's lack of belief. He spent most of his rookie year on the practice squad.* Going into his second year, the Patriots signed veteran quarterback Damon Huard, seemingly because they did not even trust Brady to be the backup to starter Drew Bledsoe.

Then a series of things happened. Brady surprised pretty much everybody by beating out Huard for the backup job. "Tom has a lot of natural leadership," Patriots coach Bill Belichick said to the media. "It was easy to see it was a natural thing for him, and he was very comfortable doing it."

Next, the Patriots lost their first two games . . . and in the second loss, Drew Bledsoe got hit hard by the Jets' Mo Lewis and had to be carried off the field. He had suffered a concussion. The next week, Tom Brady was the starting quarterback, at least for the few weeks that Bledsoe would need to recover.

He didn't immediately blow anybody away, to say the least. Brady didn't throw a touchdown pass in either of his first two games. In the second of those games, against Miami, he got sacked four times and fumbled a snap that led to a Dolphins touchdown. After that game, *Boston Globe* columnist Ron Borges, speaking for the consensus, wrote: "He did as good as he could against the Dolphins. What he did not do—and won't do anytime soon—is replace Drew Bledsoe."

Then things started to click a bit for Brady. He played fantastically the next two weeks, capped off by a brilliant audible call against Indianapolis that led to a 91-yard touchdown pass to Dave Patten, the longest in team history. "That's not coaching," Belichick gushed. "That's the quarterback."

In the following week, legendary coach Bill Parcells offered a rather remarkable bit of foreshadowing during his radio show. A caller talked about how good Brady looked, and Parcells scoffed. "Give me a break,"

---

* Patriots fans were much more enamored with another young quarterback, Michael Bishop, who had finished second in the Heisman Trophy voting while at Kansas State.

he said. "You won't know about him until he throws four interceptions, gets smacked in the face, and they break his nose. They lose the game, and everyone blames him, players, callers, and the coaches look at him funny. And by Wednesday's practice, he has to get the team ready for the next game.

"*That*," Parcells concluded, "is when you'll find out if you have a quarterback."

Sure enough that Sunday, Brady threw four interceptions as the Patriots lost to the Broncos. That made the Patriots 3-4 on the season.

And that is precisely when the Patriots found out that, yes, they had a quarterback. For the rest of the season, Brady's numbers were nothing special, but his presence certainly was. All anybody could talk about was how comfortable he seemed, how much in control he was, how much more together the whole team seemed with him at quarterback. The Patriots won eight of their next nine games and won the division.

And that led to the fourth quarter in the snow against the Raiders. He led the Patriots on an extraordinary 67-yard drive in which he completed nine passes in a row and then ran for the touchdown from 6 yards out.

But the Raiders still led 13–10 with less than two minutes left when Brady dropped back to throw from the Oakland 42-yard line. He couldn't find any open receivers. He raised his arm and started to throw but thought better of doing so, and as he tried to hold on to the ball, his old college teammate Charles Woodson came charging in from his right and he saw nothing but glory.

"As I was coming in," Woodson would tell NFL Films, "I thought, 'Right here, the game is over. He ain't gonna outrun me. He ain't gonna spin me. We're already playing Pittsburgh in the AFC Championship Game.'"

Sure enough, Woodson knocked the ball free. The officials ruled it a fumble. The Raiders recovered.

Then it went to replay review.

"Obviously, I'm thinking we lost the game," Brady said. "I didn't know the Tuck Rule."

Ah, there we go: the Tuck Rule. We probably don't want to go into all the vagaries of the rule, but two years earlier, the NFL had put in a rule that stated that any forward motion with the arm—even if the motion was done only with the intention of tucking the ball back toward the body—would be considered a forward pass. The rule would be abolished a few years later.

The officials ruled that Brady was trying to tuck the ball in and ruled the play an incomplete pass and the Patriots kept the ball. Then Adam Vinatieri kicked one of the most clutch field goals in NFL history, a 45-yarder through the snow and wind, to tie the game and send it into overtime. He then kicked a 23-yard field goal in overtime to send the Patriots to the AFC Championship Game.

There, Brady was knocked out of the game with an injured ankle and Drew Bledsoe led the team back against Pittsburgh into the Super Bowl. Belichick went back to Brady for the Super Bowl, and as he expected, Brady played smart and sensible football. Belichick designed a defense that transfixed and overwhelmed the high-flying St. Louis Rams, and the Patriots won.

"If you don't know by now," the Boston Globe's Bob Ryan wrote after the Tuck Rule game, "Tom Brady is not a gunslinger. He is not Sonny Jurgensen or Dan Marino or Kurt Warner. . . . He is one part pigskin surgeon, one part pigskin shop foreman, and one part pigskin efficiency expert. He is a game manager who simply has the knack for making a little go a long way in a football game."

Of course, Tom Brady turned into so much more than that. He turned into everything: the biggest winner, the fiercest competitor, the greatest leader, the most prolific passer, the smartest player on the field, and, yes, even a gunslinger who left Marino and the rest in the dust. But that unique thing he already had in the Tuck Rule game—the knack for making a little go a long way—well, he had that too for the rest of his career.

People have often said winning that game was luck. Then I think again of that line Martin Scorsese says at the beginning of *The Color of Money*: "For some players, luck itself is an art."

NO. 19:
RUNNING AT WARP SPEED

"I've already gotten a call from Moscow. They think Marcus Allen is a
new secret weapon, and they insist we dismantle it."

—PRESIDENT RONALD REAGAN

—

JANUARY 22, 1984

The play was called many different things in the next day's papers.
Most writers referred to it as "17 Bob Trail," which sounds like an
address for an all-night emergency veterinary hospital in the suburbs.

Some called it "17 Bob Tray" and some called it "17 Bob Trey." One
writer called it "17 Bob Trey Oh," sounding like one of the players realizing for the first time that the quarterback had called "17 Bob Trey"
and responded "17 Bob Trey! Oh!" One writer called it "17 Bob Train."

Here's the thing. The play itself—actually called 17 Bob Trey O*—
didn't matter.

Marcus Allen ran it totally wrong.

This was Super Bowl XVIII, Los Angeles Raiders versus Washington,
and the Raiders already led by 19 and seemed to have the game well in
hand. The call was for Marcus Allen to go left and follow his right
guard, Mickey Marvin, into the hole.

Marvin did his job and pulled into the hole. But Allen sensed a problem. Marcus Allen was a beautiful runner, and he was an instinctive
runner. At USC, he became the first college running back to ever rush
for 2,000 yards in a season. And he did it not with blazing speed or

---

* This has to be the most famous running play in Raiders history and maybe NFL history.
Not only was 17 Bob Trey O the Marcus Allen Super Bowl run; it was also the play call for
the Bo Jackson 91-yard Superman run from the Tecmo Bo chapter.

bulldozing power; he lacked both of those things. Instead, he gained those yards using a supernatural sense of everything around him. He just knew where trouble waited.

And in that moment, something told him to stop following Mickey Marvin.

We should not let Allen's lack of speed pass without comment. It was the criticism that followed him for his entire NFL career—a Hall of Fame career, it should be noted, in which he won a regular-season MVP and a Super Bowl MVP and rushed for 123 touchdowns, which was the NFL record when he retired.

Still, he never stopped hearing about his slowness. He'd run a dull 40-yard dash at the NFL Combine, and scouts gasped, and teams selected two running backs ahead of him in the NFL Draft. During that Super Bowl season, Allen's longest run was 19 yards, and it was said that Raiders owner Al Davis, who had built his entire football philosophy around speed, was losing enthusiasm for Allen.*

So, when Allen stopped following Marvin and did a 180-degree turn and started running the other way, it seemed like a doomed maneuver. Surely, he wasn't fast enough to pull something like this off.

But Allen never worried about his track speed.

"I'm as fast as I need to be," Allen told me.

He ran away from Washington's Ken Coffey, who tried to knock the ball free from behind. He saw an opening and blazed through it. Two Washington players—linebacker Neal Olkewicz and defensive back Anthony Washington—seemed to have good angles to get him. But

---

* The relationship between Davis and Allen would grow much worse. In 1986, Davis became enthralled with the ultra-speedy Bo Jackson and lost interest in Marcus Allen. "He's trying to stop me from going to the Hall of Fame," Allen said in a nationally televised interview. Allen sued for his right to leave the team. He then joined the Kansas City Chiefs, and he led the NFL in touchdowns and was named Comeback Player of the Year.

Allen ran away from them both. Nobody was going to catch him on this run.

"It's like everything was in slow motion," he said. "And I was running at warp speed."

In all, he ran 74 yards. It was, at the time, the longest run in Super Bowl history. And it would always be the longest run of Marcus Allen's career.

"You're not supposed to be this fast," Raiders running back coach Greg Pruitt said to Allen after the play. "What are you doing in the end zone?"

NO. 18:

THE TACKLE

"I knew two things. I knew the only way he was going to score was if I missed the tackle. And I knew I wasn't missing that tackle."

—MIKE JONES

—

JANUARY 30, 2000

On the day before Christmas 1998, the newspaper in Belleville, Illinois, ran a telephone poll with one question: "Should the St. Louis Rams fire their head coach, Dick Vermeil?"

The Rams were about to finish a dismal 4-12 season. This was one year after they had gone 5-11. The offense was terrible, yes, but the defense was, well, also terrible. Before taking the Rams job, Vermeil had been out of the coaching racket for fifteen years after burning out in Philadelphia, and he seemed out of answers. He had a career losing record as a coach. He was sixty-two years old.

Of the 111 people who called in, ninety-one said yes, absolutely, the Rams should fire him. The poll was most politely summed up by this comment: "He's a real nice guy. But the game has passed him by."

THE 1999 ST. LOUIS RAMS ARE INEXPLICABLE. NOTHING ABOUT them makes any sense at all. NFL teams will spend countless hours developing a plan, creating a mindset, building a team block by block. The Rams on the other hand just kind of threw a bunch of things at the wall and, Jackson Pollock–style, they came out art.

The Rams hired a first-time offensive coordinator named Mike Martz, who had a million ideas. They happened to be paying close attention when the Indianapolis Colts inexplicably grew tired of their all-time-great running back Marshall Faulk, so they traded for him. In the weeks leading up to the draft, they told everybody that they absolutely *had* to fix the defense, but then with their top pick, they drafted wide receiver Torry Holt.

And then the quarterback they had spent big money acquiring in the offseason—St. Louis native Trent Green—was badly hurt during the preseason and the Rams found themselves with no choice but to give the job to an unknown quarterback only three years removed from his job as stocker at a Hy-Vee supermarket in Iowa.

That quarterback was named Kurt Warner.

And suddenly—emphasis on that word "suddenly"—the St. Louis Rams had the best offense not only in the NFL but quite possibly in the *history* of the NFL. Faulk set an NFL record with 2,429 yards from scrimmage. Warner threw forty-one touchdown passes; only Dan Marino had ever thrown more. They put up 38 points against the Bengals, 42 against San Francisco, 41 against Atlanta, 43 against the Saints, etc. They scored fast and they scored from anywhere at any time and it was beyond thrilling.

The Rams went from being as blah as any team in the NFL to the "Greatest Show on Turf." And Dick Vermeil was on his way to the Pro Football Hall of Fame.

THAT RAMS OFFENSE WAS THE STORY ALL SEASON LONG. THE Rams' defense? Nobody really noticed them. They just quietly went about their business—no one more so than their hardworking linebacker with the plainest name imaginable, Mike Jones.

Jones went undrafted coming out of the University of Missouri. He was given a chance with the Oakland Raiders because their defensive coordinator, Gunther Cunningham, believed in his character. "He gives you everything he's got," Cunningham said. "And he's there every day."

Jones became a starter with the Raiders and then signed with the Rams. He did not have great speed; he did not pile up a whole lot of tackles; he never made a Pro Bowl. But his teammates loved him. More than that, they admired him. Nobody played harder. Nobody cared more.

"Mike was always first at work," Holt said. "Sometimes he'd be in a suit; he'd have a briefcase. He was about his business."

"If we need a play," his teammate London Fletcher said, "we know Mike will make it."

At the end of Super Bowl XXXIV in Atlanta, the Rams needed a play. They led Tennessee 23–16 with five seconds left. The Titans had the ball on the 10-yard line. Tennessee quarterback Steve McNair threw a quick slant pass to their best receiver, Kevin Dyson. He caught the ball at the 4-yard line and seemed certain to score.

"As soon as I caught it," he said, "I was thinking pay dirt."

Only then Jones wrapped his right arm around Dyson's waist and used his left arm to grab Dyson's left knee to make sure he didn't go anywhere. And Dyson was tackled just short of the goal line as the clock expired. And the Rams won the Super Bowl.

"Mike held on to him with everything he had," the Rams' Isaac Bruce said.

"That right there was the greatest tackle in Super Bowl history," Keith Lyle said.

"One tackle," D'Marco Farr shouted, "and we're on top of the world."

There was something beautiful about that impossible Rams season ending like that, not with fireworks and flashes and glitter. No, it ended when their humble and quiet blue-collar linebacker did his job and made the tackle.

After the game, I asked Jones how he felt.

"Tired," he said.

NO. 17:

THE MUSIC CITY MIRACLE

"The NFL is not made up of Hall of Famers, although we would
all like to be. I'm just happy to be remembered."

—KEVIN DYSON

—

JANUARY 8, 2000

Dr. Kevin Dyson started in just fifty-eight games in his injury-shortened NFL career before going on to a life in high school education. No, it was not exactly the career he wanted after being the first wide receiver selected in the 1998 draft, but Dyson is philosophical about that. Hey, not everybody can be Randy Moss.

Still, for twenty-two days in January of 2000, Kevin Dyson was the center of the football universe. He was a key figure in two of the twenty or so greatest plays ever.

In Super Bowl XXXIV, yes, he was stopped 1 yard short of the end zone.

But three weeks earlier, he had stood on the sideline brooding about his Tennessee Titans' heartbreaking loss.

"Dyson, you're in," he heard Tennessee Titans special teams coach Alan Lowry shout. He felt sure he'd heard wrong. There were sixteen seconds left in the wild card game, and the Bills were about to kick off after taking a 16–15 lead. Dyson was not part of the kickoff return team. Sometimes they would use him if they expected the opponent to try an onside kick. But that obviously wasn't happening here.

"Dyson," Lowry said again, "you're in."

He looked around. The game had taken a huge toll on the team. Derrick Mason, their normal kick return man, was out with a concussion. His backup, Anthony Dorsett, was cramping up and could barely stand, much less walk. Dyson had been cramping too but now he was healthy enough . . . and, anyway, there was nobody else.

"We're running Home Run Throwback," head coach Jeff Fisher told him. "You know how to run that, right?"

Then, according to legend, Dyson shrugged and said: "Um, I wasn't really paying attention during those practices."*

Dyson had a basic idea about the play. It was Tennessee's last-gasp kickoff trick play. Lowry had been thinking about Home Run Throwback for almost twenty years, going back to 1982, when he was coaching for the Dallas Cowboys. This happened during the players' strike; he was at home watching undefeated Southern Methodist play Texas Tech. With seventeen seconds left in the game, Texas Tech kicked a game-tying field goal that seemed certain to wreck SMU's chances for a national championship.

SMU's Blaine Smith was back to receive the kickoff. The ball came to him, and he fumbled around with it until the Texas Tech coverage was on him. At that instant he picked the ball up and fired it across the field to Bobby Leach, who raced down the sidelines untouched for 91 yards and the game-winning touchdown.

The play blew Lowry's mind. He called his friend Tony Marciano, who was on the SMU staff, and said: "What the heck is that play? You gotta show me that play."

Eighteen years later, Lowry was finally ready to call it.

The Bills kicked the ball up in the air and fullback Lorenzo Neal backed up to catch it. He was not supposed to be the one catching the ball—Neal was not exactly known for his sure hands—but he was a respected leader, and he wanted the ball. He caught it at the 25.

He then ran to his right and handed the ball off to Frank Wycheck

---

* When asked about this story on a YouTube show called "National Vintage League," Dyson said that the story has been exaggerated, but he admitted that his response to the coach was "probably wasn't reassuring." He used to watch the play and think, *We're never going to run this.*

the way you might give someone car keys when you want them to drive. Wycheck took a few steps to his right. As the play was drawn up, he was supposed to throw it across the field to Isaac Byrd, who had some kick-returning experience. Maybe.

"I think," Wycheck would say. "I'm not really sure."

Nobody was sure. Byrd thought his job was to go block somebody, so that was what he did. Wycheck had to throw the ball to somebody, though, so he turned and fired it across the field to Dyson, who had drifted down the field. Dyson raced back to catch the ball.

"That looked like a forward pass!" announcer Mike Patrick shouted, and unquestionably it *did* look like a forward pass because of the way Dyson had caught the ball. Dyson began running. He had not returned a kick in his NFL career. And he never would again.

Right away, up in the Tennessee radio booth, color commentator Pat Ryan saw the open field. "He's got something!" Ryan shouted.

His partner, Mike Keith, was not so sure. Keith, like Mike Patrick, had thought Wycheck's pass was probably a forward lateral. But he didn't see any flags on the field, so he called it as straight as he could.

"Fifty! Forty!" Keith said.

"He's got it!" Ryan shouted. "He's got it!"

"Thirty! Twenty!" Keith said.

"He's got it!" Ryan shouted.

Dyson knew that his job was to run as far as he could and then step out-of-bounds so that their thirty-seven-year-old kicker, Al Del Greco, could try for the game-winning field goal. But there was nobody in front of him. There was nobody around him. He saw the end zone.

When he got to the 10-yard line, Keith made the call that still rings in Nashville.

"Ten! Five! End zone! Touchdown Titans! There are ... no ... flags ... on the field! It's a miracle! Tennessee has pulled a miracle! A miracle for the Titans!"

A miracle for the Titans. Well, it was sort of a delayed miracle because the replay officials studied the video like it was the Zapruder film. You could understand: This was a nearly perfectly constructed optical illusion. Because of the way Dyson had to go back for the ball and the way he caught the ball, it definitely looked like a forward pass. There are people, particularly people in Buffalo, who will forever insist that it was forward.

But if you follow just the ball, you see it almost perfectly paralleled the 25-yard line, making it a legal lateral.

The Music City Miracle sent the Titans on a spectacular ride. They beat Peyton Manning's Colts. They crushed the Jaguars in the AFC Championship Game. Then Kevin Dyson fell 1 yard short in the Super Bowl. Two legendary plays in one month.

After he retired, Dyson went back to school and got two master's degrees and a doctorate in education, leadership, and professional practice. He became a high school principal. And when you ask him how he feels about his place in football history, he just smiles and says: "It's nice to be remembered. How many players are remembered?"*

---

* Kevin Dyson actually had one more really cool moment. In a game on September 22, 2002, against Cleveland, Kevin scored on a 7-yard touchdown pass from quarterback Steve McNair. In that same game, Kevin's brother Andre, a defensive back for the Titans, scored on a 16-yard interception return. It was the first time brothers had scored touchdowns in the same game.

NO. 16:

THE GAME NO ONE LOST

"I feel like I've been to the mountaintop.
But, gracious, I'm not sure I looked over it."

—KELLEN WINSLOW

—

JANUARY 2, 1982

Late in the fourth quarter, or maybe it was in overtime, San Diego Chargers tight end Kellen Winslow caught another pass and couldn't get up. This had happened a few times, actually. Winslow caught thirteen passes on that muggy day in Miami, and each one seemed like it would be his last. He was hurting everywhere. It didn't seem like his body could take any more.

"Closest thing to dying I know," Winslow said after the game, quoting Muhammad Ali after his Thrilla in Manila fight against Joe Frazier.

He made this catch and stayed on the ground.

Then Miami rookie cornerback Fulton Walker went over, lifted him, and held him upright for a moment, as if they were slow dancing.

"Stop helping that man up!" enraged Miami coach Don Shula screamed from the sideline, but his Dolphins did not listen.

Some things matter more than winning, no matter what Lombardi might have said.

THEY WERE VERY DIFFERENT TEAMS. THE DOLPHINS WERE OLD-school. They pounded you with their Killer B defense, the nickname building on the fact that several of their best defenders—Betters, Baumhower, Brudzinski, and the Blackwood brothers—had names that started with B.

The Chargers were futuristic. They threw the ball all over the field like no team ever had. People called them "Air Coryell" after their pass-happy coach, Don Coryell.

The game looked like a blowout at first. The Chargers took a 24–0 lead before the first quarter even ended. Shula, realizing that you can't pound your way back from a 24-point deficit, inserted his passing quarterback, Don Strock, and Strock threw on almost every down. They pulled within 2 touchdowns. Then, with thirty seconds left in the half, San Diego kicker Rolf Benirschke just missed a 55-yard field goal.

Strock took the field once more and moved the team to the San Diego 40 with six seconds left. Shula considered a long field goal try but then thought of something else.

"Hook and Ladder?" Shula asked Strock. The quarterback shrugged. Shula loved the Hook and Ladder play—had loved it since his playing days—even though the thing never worked, not even in practice. But, you know, what the heck?

Strock threw a 15-yard pass to Duriel Harris, who was surrounded by four Chargers defenders. That was the hook.

In one motion, Harris caught the ball and flipped it to a streaking Tony Nathan, who caught the ball and raced down the sideline. That was the ladder.

"What a play!" NBC announcer Don Criqui screamed even before Nathan had crossed the goal line. "What a play! Hall of Fame! Hall of Fame football play! That goes to Canton!"

What a play. The sound of the crowd after the play was enormous. And it wouldn't die down. The Orange Bowl was so filled with cheering during halftime that the Dolphins players in the locker room couldn't even hear Shula giving second-half instructions.

"I've never heard anything like it," Strock told *Sports Illustrated*'s Rick Reilly. "It was like we were still on the field. We were in the locker room, what, ten, fifteen minutes? And it never stopped."

Madness followed. The Dolphins tied. The Chargers took the lead on a 25-yard pass from quarterback Dan Fouts to Winslow. Winslow's mouth was bleeding from a hit. He'd broken two sets of shoulder pads.

His left shoulder was bruised, and he could barely move his right shoulder, and he couldn't turn his neck. He was cramping from the heat. But he wouldn't come out.

Strock struck back, connecting on a 50-yard touchdown pass to tie the game again.

Fouts threw an interception. Tony Nathan scored to give Miami their first lead.

And the Chargers were reeling. They punted, Miami moved into field goal range, and it looked like the game was decided.

"We thought they were dead," Miami's Joe Rose said. "It was like, 'C'mon, throw in the towel. It's hot, we're tired, let us win the game.'"

But this game had a different destiny. San Diego's Louie Kelcher forced a fumble. Fouts drove the Chargers down the field again, hitting Winslow on the big third-down play that led to his slow dance with Fulton Walker. Two plays after that, Fouts tried to throw to Winslow again, but he threw it too high. That's when James Brooks—all of 5-foot-9, 175 pounds—sneaked behind Winslow and caught the ball in the back of the end zone.

And the game was tied with fifty-eight seconds left.

The rest of the game was . . . I guess the only thing you can compare it with is the end of a dance marathon that simply will not end, even as the dancers pray that it will.

The Dolphins could have ended it when kicker Uwe von Schamann lined up for a 43-yard field goal.* Kellen Winslow ran into the game. He was not normally on the kick-block team—he had never blocked a kick in his life—but he had to try. He was battered, bruised, cramping, and exhausted.

And that son of a gun blocked the kick.

Then he was carried off the field for the fourth time in the game.

---

* Von Schamann was a beaut. When he was at Oklahoma, he was sent out to try a 41-yard field goal to beat Ohio State. The Buckeyes crowd shouted, "Block that kick! Block that kick!" and you know what von Schamann did? He waved his arms to lead the crowd, like he was a conductor leading the cheer. Then he nailed the 41-yarder to win the game.

The Chargers had the next chance to win it, thanks to a brilliant third-down catch from . . . well, whom do you think?

"Superman," Don Shula said when asked what he thought of Winslow's performance.

Benirschke promptly missed the 27-yard field goal.

Back to Miami. Back to Uwe von Schamann. This time he had a 34-yarder to win it, and he was thinking about only one thing: kicking it high enough so that it cleared Kellen Winslow. Unfortunately, while trying to kick the ball high, he actually kicked the ground first and San Diego's Leroy Jones blocked the ball.

Exhaustion and humidity soaked the air. Strock and Fouts each had passed for 400 yards. They combined for seven touchdown passes. Five different players had 100 yards in receiving. For the last time, Fouts drove the team down the field. He hit Charlie Joiner on a long pass that took the ball to the Miami 10. Joiner couldn't get up after the play.

Benirschke came out to kick the 29-yard field goal.

And this time, the kick was true.

"We're so glad to get out alive," Coryell would say.

"This one will hurt for a long time," Shula would say.

Sports Illustrated called it "the game no one should have lost." And I think they almost got there. Yes, in the moment, the Chargers won, and the Dolphins lost.

But as time has gone by, something funny has happened. Most people have forgotten who won and who lost. What difference does it make? The Dolphins' Hook and Ladder is legend. Kellen Winslow couldn't even keep up with all the people who watched that game and then named their kids after him. When Miami Dolphins fans were asked years later to vote for the most memorable game in franchise history, this was the game they selected. When Dan Fouts is asked about never playing in a Super Bowl, he says that he played in something bigger.

He's right. He played in the game no one lost.

NO. 15:

HAIL FLUTIE

"One thing I vividly remember thinking as I was watching the players celebrate after the play—with me being fourteen and going through puberty and knowing what football means—I remember thinking: 'Oh my gosh, I wish I was one of these guys this weekend. They're going to have sex.'"

—COMEDIAN GARY GULMAN

—

NOVEMBER 23, 1984

We're going to let Gary Gulman, the brilliant comedian who is also the most Boston guy I know, take us through the Doug Flutie Hail Mary because he was fourteen years old when it happened, a delightful age for one of college football's most delightful plays.

Gary was not a huge college football fan because, realistically, there was not much high-end college football in New England. There weren't any traditional college football powers up there, not unless you wanted to go back to the ancient days of Harvard before World War I, when Percy Wendell was team captain and Percy Haughton was the head coach. Lots of Percys back then.

No, Boston was a pro sports town, its psyche mostly built around the perpetual anguish of the Red Sox. There was no room for much else, certainly not anything involving colleges.

Only then, Doug Flutie came along.

"No, we didn't think much about college football," Gary says. "Then all of a sudden you got this little guy from Natick running around and throwing these long passes, and they're beating Penn State and Alabama and Clemson, and it's like: 'Hey, what is this?'"

It's hard to explain what a lightning bolt Doug Flutie was in New

England. Boston had its basketball heroes in Bill Russell and Larry Bird and its hockey hero in Bobby Orr and plenty of baseball heroes like Ted Williams, but none of them were *from* Boston. None of them talked like your neighbor in Nahant or Needham or Newton or Norfolk or Norwell or Natick.

"You have to understand, it was like, 'We know this guy,'" Gary says. "It wasn't that way with the other big Boston stars. We didn't *know* Larry Bird. But Flutie, he was one of us. We knew people in Natick. We knew all about it."

Yes, four of the 26.2 miles of the Boston Marathon are run through Natick. Now here was this guy, the ultimate Natick hero: three-sport star, straight-A student, favorite of every coach and teacher. And he was small too, a perfect New England underdog. Heck, Boston College was the only school to even offer him a scholarship. Boston College was nowheresville then. They went winless in 1978. They hadn't been to a bowl game since World War II.

But then Flutie came to Newton and right away he was a revelation. As a freshman, he got into a glorious passing duel with Pitt All-American Dan Marino. As a junior, he finished third in the Heisman Trophy voting.

By the autumn of his senior year, he had all of New England dreaming with him.

Game after game, he performed miracles, large and small. Boston College beat Alabama and made it all the way to No. 4 in America before losing heartbreakers to West Virginia and Penn State and tumbling a few spots in the polls.

Then the game happened, Boston College versus University of Miami. It was a made-for-television extravaganza; the producers at CBS wanted a nationally televised matchup between Flutie and Miami's star quarterback, Bernie Kosar. The network paid Rutgers $80,000 to drop their game with Miami and set the Boston College–Miami game for the day after Thanksgiving.

| | | | | |

GARY GULMAN WAS AT HIS AUNTIE JUDY SIEGEL'S HOUSE THAT day. Judy was not his aunt. She was his mother's best friend. But family is what you make of it, and so he was there with a whole mess of people who were "family," including his uncle Bob (not his uncle) and their son, Richard, and a family called the Greenes. Gary particularly loved Richard. He was a huge sports fan who once, as a teenager, got an old-man mask, wore it to a Red Sox game, and carried a sign that read, "Last Red Sox 20 game winner."

They were all locked into the game, even the non–sports fans. The quarterback matchup was just so captivating. You had Miami's 6-foot-5 Bernie Kosar, an awkward and precise passer from Cleveland. You had Flutie, 5-foot-10 at most, flitting about and zinging passes through double coverage. The numbers boggle the mind. Flutie threw for 472 yards and 3 touchdowns that day. Kosar threw for 447 yards and 2 touchdowns. Two different receivers had 200-yard games. There were six lead changes in the final twenty-one minutes.

"It was so exciting, but it was almost too much," Gulman says. "It was like that Miami–San Diego game, if you remember that, except I didn't care who won that game. I just enjoyed it as a fan. This one was a bundle of emotions, one touchdown after another, one great pass after another, up and down."

Boston College led 41–38 with less than four minutes left when Miami faced a third and 21 from their own 10-yard line. Kosar dropped back and was almost sacked in the end zone for a safety. Instead, he escaped and hit a 20-yard pass. Later, the Hurricanes converted on fourth down, Kosar hit four more passes, Melvin Bratton scored the touchdown with twenty-eight seconds left, and the game sure seemed over then.

"At that moment," Boston College coach Jack Bicknell said, "I had no hope. . . . I had this game in my pocket as a loss."

"You know what I thought?" Gulman asks. "I thought, 'Sure, they're going to lose. It's OK.' By that point, I'd already been Red Sox–ed and Patriots-ed enough to know that in New England sports, things don't usually pan out. I thought, 'It's OK. They'll still play in a bowl game.' By fourteen, I was already expecting the worst."

But you know which Boston guy still did believe?

Right: Doug Flutie.

"I've been thinking since I was ten years old that I was charmed," Flutie said, and that was exactly the way he carried himself, as if something good was always about to happen. Boston College moved the ball to midfield with six seconds left.

The play call was 55 Flood Tip.

Flutie dropped back 10 yards, and then Miami's Jerome Brown closed in on him. Flutie raced to his right to get away, set himself at the 37-yard line, and unleashed the longest and highest throw he could summon against a 30 mph South Florida wind.

The clock went to zero with the ball in the air.

The play was called Flood Tip because the Eagles were supposed to *flood* the zone with three receivers and then *tip* the ball in the air to give a teammate a shot at making the play. But Flutie's throw traveled so far and so fast that two of the three receivers couldn't catch up to it.

One receiver—Gerard Phelan—did catch up to it. He had somehow slipped behind Miami defensive backs Darrell Fullington and Reggie Sutton. And he watched as the ball came down to him from up on high as if it were a lightning bolt thrown from Olympus. Sutton jumped and took a swat at the football, but it went just over his hand.

The ball landed on Phelan's chest, and he pulled it in, rolled over, got to his feet, and put his arms up in the air. Then he was surrounded by all those teammates, and they all celebrated as an uncontrollably happy and slightly jealous Gary Gulman watched in Lynnfield.

"Caught by Boston College!" announcer Brent Musburger shouted. "I don't believe it! It's a touchdown! The Eagles win it!"

| | | | | |

FIVE YEARS LATER, GARY GULMAN WAS RECRUITED TO PLAY
football at Boston College. It didn't work out. Gary tells some great
stories about how football wasn't for him.

"How would I pull this off?" he wrote in his memoir, *Misfit*, of his
thoughts after the gentlemanly Jack Bicknell offered him a Boston
College football scholarship. "Maybe I'd outgrow Mister Rogers. Maybe
I won't cry every time I heard John Denver's 'Sunshine on My Shoulders.' Maybe someday I won't run to the TV when I heard the first few
xylophone notes of *Sesame Street*. Maybe someday I won't need to sleep
with the light on after watching *Ghostbusters* or *Gremlins*."

He didn't play football for long. Instead, Gary stayed Gary. But before
he left football, he did go through the Boston College playbook looking
for that play, 55 Flood Tip.

"It wasn't in there," he would say.

Why not? Maybe they had stopped running it by then. Maybe they
changed the name. Whatever the reason, the play wasn't in there; it
was gone, a happy memory that, like childhood, could never be re-
peated.

NO. 14:

THE HAIL MARY

"I closed my eyes and said a Hail Mary."

—ROGER STAUBACH

—

DECEMBER 28, 1975

By the time Dallas quarterback Roger Staubach dropped back to throw on that chilly winter day in Minnesota, the Hail Mary play already had a long and rich history in football.

The first Hail Mary, as best as we can tell, was some undisclosed play that Knute Rockne's Notre Dame team ran in 1922 against Georgia Tech. Sleepy Jim Crowley, one of Notre Dame's famed Four Horsemen,[*] told the story (and told it and told it for the next half century) this way: Notre Dame faced a critical fourth-down play. Noble Kizer—a Presbyterian—suggested they pray first. They did, and Notre Dame scored.

A little later, Kizer again suggested they pray and once again they scored.

"Say," Kizer said when the game was over, "that Hail Mary is the best play we got!"

Roughly a dozen years later, we got what was probably the first Hail Mary pass play. This was Notre Dame too. In 1935, facing Ohio State, Notre Dame coach Elmer Layden—who had played on that 1922

---

[*] The original Four Horsemen of the Apocalypse rode in Revelation 6 of the New Testament. When Notre Dame beat Army in 1924, the grandest sportswriter of the day, Grantland Rice, wrote, perhaps, the most famous sports column lede ever: "Outlined against a blue-gray October sky, the Four Horsemen rode again. In dramatic lore they are known as Famine, Pestilence, Destruction and Death. These are only aliases. Their real names are Stuhldreher, Miller, Crowley and Layden."

team—called the secret Hail Mary play, and Bill Shakespeare completed the game-winning touchdown pass to Wayne Millner with thirty-two seconds left.

For thirty or so years after that, there were various Hail Mary references. Before the 1941 Orange Bowl, for instance, Georgetown claimed to have several Hail Mary passes in their playbook. (They lost to Mississippi State 14–7 anyway.)

And by the mid-1960s, the term "Hail Mary pass" was commonplace ... but it was usually used derisively to describe desperation passes.* In 1969, for instance, Philadelphia's Norm Snead threw what Washington general manager Vince Lombardi disgustedly called a "Hail Mary" pass to Ben Hawkins at the end of the game. The pass was not even caught, but Washington was called for a pass interference penalty.

"A 'Hail Mary' pass," one Philadelphia sportswriter wrote, "is a desperation pass against hope."

Even Roger Staubach used the term dismissively; in 1973, the Cowboys beat the Rams in the playoffs and Staubach said that he'd been lucky to hit a couple of Hail Mary passes.

Then, three days after Christmas in 1975, Staubach dropped back to throw. And the Hail Mary became a whole other thing.

BELIEVE IT OR NOT, THE HAIL MARY PASS WAS PERHAPS THE *second*-craziest play of that final Cowboys drive. The Cowboys got the ball back with 1:51 left, down four to the Vikings, and Staubach looked a little spooked. This was before Staubach would become known as

---

* One of my favorite uses of Hail Mary passes came from Boston sportswriter Jerry Nason, who wrote a poem at the beginning of a column and used the term for rhyming purposes:

A throwback to the old 'Hail Mary'
Pass—John U to Raymond Berry

"Captain Comeback." This was also before the Cowboys became known as "America's Team."

All of that would come out of the Hail Mary.

Staubach fumbled a bad snap at the Dallas 31 and had to take a loss. He slammed the football into the turf in frustration. Then, with no receivers open, he was forced to throw the ball away on the next two plays. That made it fourth and 16 with forty-four seconds left. The end zone was 75 yards away. Hope seemed lost.

And then came the first amazing play. Staubach took a deep drop all the way back to the 14 and fired a long and dubious pass to the right sideline. He hoped it would find his star receiver, Drew Pearson, whom the Vikings had shut down all game long.

Somehow the ball did find him. Pearson pulled it in just as Minnesota's Nate Wright knocked him out-of-bounds. In today's game, it wouldn't be a catch because he didn't get two feet in bounds. But in 1975, the rule stated, "If a receiver would have landed in bounds with both feet but is carried or pushed out-of-bounds while maintaining possession of the ball, pass is complete."

The pass was caught for 25 yards, putting the ball at midfield.*

"That was the biggest play of the game," Pearson said.

Then with thirty-seven seconds left, Staubach dropped back. After the game, Tom Landry would insist that the Cowboys had practiced the play, but that was just Landry being Landry. Not only had the Cowboys never practiced it; the play hadn't even existed. It had no name. Staubach and Pearson had come up with the play in the huddle.

---

* Here's something wild from that play: After Pearson fell out-of-bounds, a Minnesota security guard named Dick Jonckowski let his emotions get the better of him and wandered over and gave Pearson just a tiny little kick. Jonckowski was suspended for two years. He went on to become a beloved Minnesota sports personality, and a half century later, NFL Films got Pearson and Jonckowski together. "Dick Jonckowski," Pearson would say, "the man who kicked me, became my friend."

"Do you have the energy to go deep?" Staubach asked.

"Yeah," Pearson said.

"Run it," Staubach said.

Staubach pump-faked left to freeze safety Paul Krause. He then threw the ball as high and as far as he could. Staubach said at his best he could throw the ball 60 yards in the air. In that cold air, with an icy wind, the ball went only 54 yards. Pearson had to slow down and go back to get the ball.

And that was why the play worked. Pearson was able to adjust to the ball better than Nate Wright, who fell to the ground. Or was pushed to the ground. We'll get back to that.

The ball almost slipped through Pearson's hands. He held on to it by jamming the ball between his right arm and right hip. Then he did a little sidestep dance into the end zone for the touchdown that won the game.

Immediately—and I do mean immediately—the Vikings screamed that Pearson had pushed Wright down. Krause instantly began pointing at Pearson, who looked back at him with a sort of sheepish "Who, me?" look. Then, when Pearson realized that the officials were not going to throw a penalty flag, he joyfully ran to the back of the end zone and flung the ball into the stands.*

"It was clear as night and day that Nate was pushed," Vikings coach Bud Grant said. This has been the Minnesota stance on the play for almost fifty years.

"If you look at the film," Staubach would say, "you can see Drew didn't push him. He just made a great play." This has been the Dallas stance on the play for almost fifty years.

NFL Films asked Roger Bennett, best-selling author and host of the

---

* While no flag was thrown, somebody in the crowd threw an orange on the field at the precise instant when Pearson caught the ball. If you watch the play even now on film, you will think it's a flag. Pearson thought that and "then I realized the flags don't roll."

Men in Blazers podcast, to explain why the Hail Mary is the greatest play in NFL history. I love what he said:

> "It's the essence of sports. It's the essence of everything that's great about America, to never give up, to always believe, to never stop trying, to always go on. And whenever I watch that play, the Hail Mary, the first one . . . you realize Roger Staubach did not just invent a word. He pretty much invented hope in sport."

NO. 13:

THE DRIVE

"Listen. Do you hear? That is the sound of ultimate suffering."

—INIGO MONTOYA, *THE PRINCESS BRIDE*

—

JANUARY 11, 1987

This will be a very short chapter.

In the 1986 AFC Championship Game, with the Denver Broncos trailing the home team Cleveland Browns by a touchdown, John Elway drove his team 98 yards through the cold and wind and desperate wails of a city hoping to win. In the drive, the Broncos converted on two third downs, one of those a third and 18. The final play in regulation was a 5-yard pass from Elway to Mark Jackson that darted through the Browns' defense at roughly the speed of sound.

The Broncos won the game in overtime on a Rich Karlis kick that I am still convinced did not go through the uprights.

That is all I can write. I was twenty years old then. I am fifty-seven now. I have never gotten over the Drive, and I know that I never will. John Elway still shows up in my nightmares.

NO. 12:

THE GALLOPING GHOST

"He is Jack Dempsey, Babe Ruth, Al Jolson, Paavo Nurmi and Man o' War. Put them together, they spell Grange."

—DAMON RUNYON

———

OCTOBER 18, 1924

In many ways, Harold "Red" Grange invented professional football. Well, maybe he didn't *invent* it, but he infused life into it when pro football was, as John Underwood explained in *Sports Illustrated*, "a dirty little business run by rogues and bargain-basement entrepreneurs."

"When I came into pro football," Grange said, "it was really a nothing game. I took quite a beating from the press and the different schools. Probably I would have been thought more of had I joined the Capone mob in Chicago instead of professional football."

He doesn't exaggerate. Grange was an American hero as a college football player at Illinois. He didn't drink. He didn't smoke. He didn't carouse or party. He was unceasingly friendly and modest. Grange was as big as any of the sports stars in that Golden Age of Sport. When he played his last college game against Ohio State, 85,500 fans showed up, the largest crowd to ever watch a football game up to that point.

"This man Red Grange of Illinois," Damon Runyon wrote, "is three or four men and a horse rolled into one."

He was America's hero . . . that is, until he decided to play football *for money*. He was promised $100,000 by agent C. C. Pyle, and he saw that as a pretty good deal. Nobody else thought so. Disillusionment spread across America. Grange's own Illinois coach, Bob Zuppke, tore him apart viciously at a school banquet.

"The Grange we know and the Grange we have watched for three years is now a myth," Zuppke said with Grange sitting in the crowd. "As time goes on, those runs will grow in length with the telling. Grange will pass on and be forgotten."

And then he shouted: "I tell you that no other $100,000 player is going to be on one of my teams."

Grange left the room in tears.

He simply couldn't understand the fury. Why shouldn't he make some money while he was the most famous football player in the country?

Grange signed with the Chicago Bears and went on a zany barnstorming tour that changed the trajectory of pro football. Before that tour, the NFL was a hodgepodge, twenty teams in towns like Rock Island and Hammond and Rochester and Akron and Duluth. Games might draw a few hundred people.

Well, thirty-five thousand came to see him in Philadelphia. Seventy thousand saw him play in New York; he might have single-handedly saved the New York Giants franchise. Grange met President Calvin Coolidge in Washington.* He met Babe Ruth in Boston. More than seventy-five thousand people piled in to see him in Los Angeles, including movie stars like Charlie Chaplin, Mary Pickford, and Douglas Fairbanks.

Later Grange would play in the movies himself.

The tour drained Grange. At one point he played eight games in eleven days. He played so many games and took so many hits and traveled so many miles that he was never the same electrifying runner he had been at Illinois. He did play in the NFL for eight seasons, but he was probably more effective as a defensive player than as a runner.

However, C. C. Pyle delivered on his promise and Grange made his $100,000.

Grange made professional football a viable game. But if you want to talk about Red Grange *the player*, you go to Illinois versus Michigan in October of 1924. That day Illinois dedicated its new $1.7 million,

---

* Grange and George Halas were introduced to the president as members of the Chicago Bears. "I'm very happy to meet you," Coolidge said. "I always did like animal acts."

sixty-eight-thousand-seat Memorial Stadium. Every seat was filled for the game. Michigan was the best team in the Big Ten Conference and had not yet given up a point that season.

Michigan kicked off. Grange caught the ball at the 5-yard line and ran to his right. At the 30, he suddenly cut back and left all but one of the Michigan players behind. The last Michigan player, Tod Rockwell, dived at him at the 5. "I remember this thing went through my mind," Grange said. "Wouldn't it be awful if this one fella tackled me here?"

The fella did not. Touchdown number one.

After a punt, Illinois got the ball back. At the 33, Grange took a hand-off. He ran left and then made one move, cutting back to his right, and he was gone, 67 yards. Touchdown number two.

After an exchange of punts, Illinois got the ball at the 44. This time Grange ran right, followed his blockers, and went 56 yards for a score. Touchdown number three.

After a Michigan fumble, Illinois got the ball at the Wolverines, 45. The Illini tried the same play, and it worked just the same: Grange ran right, followed his blockers, scored easily.

That made 4 touchdowns in twelve minutes covering 262 total yards. To that point, it was the greatest performance in football history. In many ways, it still is. America's leading sportswriter, Grantland Rice,* was so dazzled, he wrote one of his most famous verses:

Red Grange of Illinois

A streak of fire, a breath of flame,

Eluding all who reach and clutch;

A gray ghost thrown into the game

That rival hands may rarely touch . . .

---

* A year later, Rice would add even more to Grange's fame. After Grange ran all over Penn, Rice referred to him as the "Galloping Ghost," granting him one of the most famous nicknames in American sports.

NO. 11:
THE CATCH

"I thought it was too high. I mean, I'm not much of a jumper.
But I guess you jump as high as you need to go
when you're trying to go to the Super Bowl."

—DWIGHT CLARK

—

JANUARY 10, 1982

If there's one story that repeats again and again, it is that NFL scouts do not believe in magic. More to the point: They can't afford to believe in magic. They get paid for brutal honesty, clear-eyed judgment, unsentimental evaluation. Betting on things you can't see is, so often, a fool's bet; bet instead on the measurables: size, speed, strength, arm, performance.

Magic? No. Magic is for a night out in Las Vegas.

Magic has nothing to do with professional football.

And so NFL scouts just didn't get Joe Montana.

ON NEW YEAR'S DAY 1979, JOE MONTANA LED NOTRE DAME against Houston in the Cotton Bowl. It was a frigid day—cold days in Dallas somehow feel colder than elsewhere—and Montana had a nasty case of the flu. He shivered on the sideline. His body temperature dropped. In the first half, he threw two interceptions. Then he stayed in the locker room covered in blankets. The Notre Dame players were told he wouldn't play anymore.

Then, as the legend goes, the Notre Dame team doctor Les Bodnar—who was actually an orthopedist and, as such, roughly as qualified as your grandma to deal with the flu*—did the only thing he knew to do: He pulled out the chicken soup packets his daughter Beth had given him before the game. And he fed Joe Montana.

Montana came back out with 4:40 left in the third quarter. He was a wreck. Houston had built up a 3-touchdown lead. Then some stuff started happening. Notre Dame blocked a punt for a score. Montana ran for a touchdown. Suddenly it was 34–28 with 4:15 left.

Montana then fumbled and once again the game seemed over.

But with twenty-eight seconds left in the game, Houston coach Bill Yeoman made a somewhat bizarre call. Facing fourth and inches on their own 29-yard line, the Cougars went for the first down rather than punting. "We make a foot and the game's over," he said fiercely after the game, not mentioning that if they had punted, the game would almost certainly have been over too.

Houston did not make it. The Irish took possession and Montana drove Notre Dame down to the eight. And then, with two seconds left, here's what he did:

He rolled right.

He looked and looked for an open receiver.

He found one and fired the touchdown pass.

"The guy's Superman," said Kris Haines, who caught that touchdown pass. "In his mind, there was never even a doubt."

This is what English teachers call "foreshadowing."

Because what was that but magic? Montana's entire Notre Dame career was filled with it. But Joe Montana was on the smaller side, and his arm didn't wow you, and he seemed a little bit frail, and he made it all the way to the third round of the NFL draft.

That was when a guy named Bill Walsh took him.

Bill Walsh did believe in magic.

---

* "Does chicken soup cure the flu?" I used to ask my grandmother. "It couldn't hurt," she used to say.

| | | | | |

DALLAS LED 27–21 WITH FIVE MINUTES LEFT IN THE NFC CHAM-
pionship Game. This was the 49ers' first championship game in a decade. They had lost that last one to the Cowboys too. All game long, San
Francisco had looked entirely unready for this moment. Montana
threw three interceptions. Ronnie Lott committed two crushing pass
interference penalties. The 49ers lost three fumbles. It was a mess.

Yet they were still in it somehow, still had a shot.

All they had to do was drive the ball 89 yards against America's team.

In that moment, Joe Montana's arm strength didn't matter. He
dinked and dunked the 49ers and moved San Francisco down the field:
a run left, a quick pass, a reverse, a down and out, a short slant. He was
previewing the next decade in football—a decade filled with short,
precise, and, to some, infuriatingly unstoppable passes.

"Losing to Joe Montana always felt like getting knocked out in a pil-
low fight," Hall of Fame lineman Howie Long said.

Bill Walsh then called "29 Scissors," a play that he believed would
free Freddie Solomon in the corner of the end zone. The play worked
perfectly. Solomon broke open. Bill Walsh jumped high in the air and
screamed. "I thought that was the championship right there," he
would say.

Montana missed his target.

"Yeah, I did happen to see Coach Walsh's reaction," Montana told
Sports Illustrated. "He looked pretty disgusted."

After a good run, the 49ers were at the 5-yard line. There were fifty-
eight seconds left. Walsh called the play: "Right sprint option." It was
the same play that the 49ers had run in the first quarter when Montana threw an 8-yard touchdown pass to Solomon. This time, though,
Walsh expected Solomon to be covered.

Dwight Clark was the second option.

"Dwight will clear," Walsh told Montana. "He's going to break out and break into the corner. Got it? Get ready to go to Dwight. If you don't get what you want, you'll just simply throw the ball away. Not there, away it goes."

The play was 49ers perfection. It captured Walsh's strategic genius. It captured Dwight Clark's hunger to succeed. And it captured Montana's magic. He rolled right—just like he did in the Cotton Bowl—and he saw that Solomon was covered. Then he held on to the ball as Walsh said, stalling for as long as he could. He drew in the Cowboys' defenders, including the 6-foot-9 Dallas defensive end everyone called Too Tall Jones.

"I knew I was going to knock it down," Jones would say.

He might have knocked it down, except Montana faked the throw, causing Jones to prematurely jump. When Jones fell to the ground, Montana threw the ball high.

"He was definitely throwing the ball away," Jones would say.

"I still believe he was throwing the ball away," Dallas's legendary quarterback Roger Staubach would say.

"No," Montana would say simply.

No. He had seen Clark break free. He threw it high, trusting that Clark would go up and get it. How high was the ball? Here's one way to think of it. When *Sports Illustrated* ran the shot on their cover the following week, Clark's foot was at the bottom of the magazine and the football was covering up the *t* and the *s* in "Sports."

"I thought, 'Oh-oh, I can't go that high,'" Clark said.

But he did. He pulled it in. The 49ers then held the Cowboys in the final minutes and went on to win the Super Bowl, the first of four they would win with Joe Montana at quarterback.

NO. 10:

JERRY RICE

"It's to Rice now."

—BENGALS COACH SAM WYCHE WITH THIRTY-NINE
SECONDS LEFT IN SUPER BOWL XXIII

—

JANUARY 22, 1989

Maybe you've heard the John Candy story. With 3:04 left in the 1989 Super Bowl, the 49ers trailed the Cincinnati Bengals by 3. They had the ball at their own 8-yard line. In many ways, this was the Super Bowl moment that everyone had been waiting for since the start. There had never been a Super Bowl situation quite like this, with a team needing to drive the length of the field in the final seconds to win the game.

And this wasn't just any team. This was a team led by Joe Montana, Joe Cool, the master of such moments. The air was obviously fraught with anxiety and tension, and this could best be seen in offensive lineman Harris Barton, who was practically hyperventilating. And Montana, serene as ever in the middle of it all, gazed into the crowd, smiled, and said to Barton, "Hey, look, it's John Candy."

Hey, look, it's Canadian actor and comedian John Candy, star of such films as *Spaceballs* and *Planes, Trains and Automobiles* and *Splash*.

The story has been told again and again through the years to demonstrate just how cool a customer Joe Montana was.

But there was another legend in that huddle. The greatest receiver who ever lived—heck, the greatest football player who ever lived—was in that huddle. And ever since then, people have asked Jerry Rice if the story is true, if Joe Montana really said that thing about John Candy, if it really had a soothing effect on the team, if it was the bit of good mojo that sent the 49ers on the most famous drive in Super Bowl history.

And Rice is very clear about his answer: He has absolutely no idea.

See, Jerry Rice had gone into that place, a place where few athletes ever go, where he heard nothing except the play and saw nothing except the ball. He went to that place where, as he wrote in his book *Go Long!*, "the mind rejects any and all distractions."

Nobody in football history went to that place more often.

CHOOSING THE GREATEST FOOTBALL PLAYER EVER IS ABSURD. Choosing the greatest in any sport is pretty absurd,* but it's especially so in football, in which everybody's job is different. Jerry Rice didn't do what Tom Brady did, and Tom Brady didn't do what Jim Brown did, and Jim Brown didn't do what Lawrence Taylor did, and Lawrence Taylor didn't do what Anthony Muñoz did, and so on and so on forever.

Let's just put it this way instead: No player came closer to perfection than Jerry Rice.

He chased perfection with the single-minded fury of the Terminator. When Rice came out of Mississippi Valley State—where he had put up numbers so mind-boggling, they hardly seemed real—scouts were less than impressed because he ran a sluggish 40-yard-dash time. Two receivers were taken before him in the draft.

He came to his first practice with the San Francisco 49ers, and every catch he made, he would run it all the way out until he reached the end zone.

"I know many of the veterans thought I was crazy or that I was a hot

* Says the guy who wrote a book called *The Baseball 100*, which counted down the hundred greatest players ever.

dog trying to show them up," he wrote, "but it's the only way I know how to practice. Treat it like a game."

He practiced that way every time. He played that way every time. That's part of what separated Jerry Rice from everyone else. He never took a day off. He never took a play off. He never dropped passes (not even in practice). He prepared so thoroughly for every game that he developed a sixth sense. Cowboys quarterback Troy Aikman always remembered that in a 1992 Pro Bowl practice, he fired a pass to Rice, but the timing was off—Rice was not yet out of his break—and the ball was headed straight for his head.

"I was sure I was going to kill him," Aikman said.

Instead, Rice somehow *felt* that a football was speeding toward him, and he simply turned early and made the catch. "It wasn't so much that he just reached up and caught it," Aikman told *Sports Illustrated*. "It was that he didn't even flinch."*

At every other position in football, there's an argument to be made. Tom Brady has the strongest case for best quarterback ever with his untouchable winning record, certainly, but there will be those who argue for John Unitas or Joe Montana or Peyton Manning or Otto Graham or, soon enough, Patrick Mahomes. Jim Brown has Walter Payton and Lawrence Taylor has Dick Butkus and Reggie White has Bruce Smith or Deacon Jones or Gino Marchetti.

At receiver, though, there is one man all alone, Jerry Rice, with most receptions, most yards, most touchdown catches, most touchdowns period, most yards from scrimmage, most all-purpose yards. The argument begins with him and ends with him. Football has changed dramatically even since he retired in 2003: Passing games have been supercharged; receiving numbers have skyrocketed.

And still, there is one man all alone: Jerry Rice.

---

* People often credited Rice's otherworldly hands to the bricklaying work he did with his father, Joe, who used to toss him bricks. Jerry said catching those bricks did nothing for his hands. "Catching bricks," he said, "taught me the meaning of hard work."

| | | | | |

FOR ME, THERE WERE TWO MOMENTS THAT CAME CLOSEST TO
capturing the splendor of Rice. My favorite happened during Super
Bowl XXIX when the 49ers played the San Diego Chargers. The 49ers
were massive favorites in that game—the 18.5-point spread remains
the highest in Super Bowl history—but it was striking how confident
the Chargers sounded all week. Player after player, coach after coach,
acted as if they knew something about the game that was eluding
the rest of us. They seemed to have a secret plan for dealing with the
49ers' brilliant passing attack and a way to counteract the unstoppable
Jerry Rice.

By week's end, they almost had me convinced.

On the third play of the game—the *third* play—Jerry Rice broke
wide open over the middle of the field and scored a 44-yard touchdown, and it was like: *Oh yeah, that's right. There is no secret plan for
stopping Jerry Rice.*

The moment I've chosen, though, comes from the John Candy Super
Bowl, because it shows that Rice didn't even have to catch the ball to
beat teams. Rice was utterly incredible in that game. All week Bengals
defensive backs had been talking about him.

"He doesn't strike fear into my heart," Cincinnati's Eric Thomas said.
"Our whole secondary is as fast as he is."

"We're not going to let this guy beat us," Cincinnati's Lewis Billups
boasted.

Plus, Rice had a nasty ankle injury that had kept him out of two practices.

But . . . he was Jerry Rice. He caught 11 passes for a Super Bowl record
215 yards and a touchdown. In that remarkable final drive, he caught
three passes for 51 of the 92 yards covered. The big one came on a second down and 20 from the Cincinnati 45; he caught a ball over the
middle despite being guarded by three Bengals and then he ran away
from all three of them for a dazzling first down.

Then, with thirty-nine seconds left and the 49ers on the Bengals' 10-yard line, Rice beat the Bengals in a whole different way. He got in their heads.

"It's to Rice now," Bengals head coach Sam Wyche said to his coaches, though they already knew that. Everybody knew that the ball was going to Jerry Rice. The Bengals basically put everybody they had on him.

And then . . . the pass instead went to John Taylor, who had not made a single catch all game. The 49ers had called a play, 20 Halfback Curl X Up, that used Rice as a decoy. He went in motion and ran left. The defense went with him. Taylor was wide-open in the back of the end zone.

"I'm sure they thought the ball was going to Jerry," Taylor would say. "You can't blame them. That's what I would have thought too."

NO. 9:

REBIRTH

"It was indeed the loudest noise, the most fervent noise,
the happiest noise I ever heard at a sporting event."

—TONY KORNHEISER

—

SEPTEMBER 25, 2006

Does football matter? Yes, of course, football matters because we
invest so much in it. Football matters because of the community
and family we build around the game. Football matters because, at its
best, the game illustrates life at its most exuberant and most passionate and most emotionally heightened. Football matters because when
someone scores a touchdown in Knoxville or intercepts a pass in Eu-
gene or makes a great catch in Green Bay or gets stopped on fourth
down in Columbus or recovers a fumble in Kansas City or breaks into
the open on a punt return in Gainesville, countless people feel just a
little bit closer to heaven.

Sure. But does football matter?

In late September 2006, some fifty-five weeks after Hurricane Katrina devastated New Orleans, the Superdome opened again. New Orleans coach Sean Payton gathered the team together before practice. It
was two days before the Saints would play Atlanta on *Monday Night
Football*. Payton knew that he didn't need to say much. They all knew
the Superdome had been used as a public shelter, and it became a
symbol of the incomprehensible destruction of Katrina. Without air-
conditioning, the temperatures inside the Superdome rose into the
nineties. Parts of the roof were ripped off by winds. The plumbing system broke down. Food rotted. The stench, those inside said, was unforgettable.

There were those who predicted that the Superdome would never open again.

There were those who said that New Orleans would never recover.

Now the Dome smelled of fresh paint.

No, Sean Payton didn't need to say much, but he needed to say something because in two days the Saints would play a game unlike any other.

"My job as a football coach is to get you ready to play football," he began.

And then he stopped talking, and the Dome went dark, and on a screen a video began to play. This was the video that would play before the game. The camera zoomed through the streets of a recovering New Orleans, a city on the rise again, and people from all parts of the Big Easy welcomed the Saints back.

When the lights came back on, every Saint was crying.

Superdome manager Doug Thornton was there. He told Nola.com what Payton said next:

"Now you see those people there, they're going to be here Monday night. Those are the fans of New Orleans. They're going to be here Monday night, and we can't let them down. We're playing for them."

STEVE GLEASON WASN'T BIG ENOUGH TO PLAY PRO FOOTBALL. He wasn't strong enough to play pro football. He wasn't fast enough to play pro football. He knew all those facts intimately because people had been telling him so pretty much his whole life. Of course, he wasn't drafted. Of course, he was cut by Indianapolis. Of course, the Saints put him on the practice squad and, surely, never expected him to ever play in a game.

There are a handful of people in this world who believe in themselves so completely that every setback merely strengthens their resolve, every doubter simply makes them surer. Steve Gleason is one of those people. When told by a Stanford coach that he lacked the speed to play in the Pac-10 Conference, he simply signed with another Pac-10 school, Washington State, and became a starter and a star.

"Pound for pound," Washington State coach Mike Price said, "he's the best football player I've coached."

Gleason played with such wild abandon on special teams that the Saints simply had to keep him on the team. They would never be able to find anyone willing to run that hard and sacrifice that much for the sake of the team.

During the week before New Orleans played Atlanta, Saints special teams coach John Bonamego detected a weakness in the Falcons' punt game. Coaches watch thousands and thousands of hours of film in the hopes of finding such a flaw. Essentially, he noticed that when the protector—the guy standing a few yards behind the center in punt formation—lined up left, the center would block to the right. And vice versa. Bonamego realized if they could time it just right, they might be able to loop a player between them and get a clear path to the punter.

The player for such a job was, of course, Steve Gleason.

He'd already blocked three punts in his career.

So Bonamego showed him the film. Steve got it right away. "I remember in one of our special teams meetings, Steve, he was pretty much saying he was seeing the middle open up," said Curtis Deloatch, who had just joined the team as a backup defensive back. "He was like, 'We got a chance to block it.'"

THE NOISE IN THE SUPERDOME WHEN THE SAINTS KICKED OFF that Monday night, the first game in New Orleans since Katrina, well, it was indescribable. Perhaps there have been louder places—but surely there has never been a more enthusiastic sound, a more triumphant sound, a more hopeful sound.

"I'm vague on all details of that game, even who the Saints were playing," says Tony Kornheiser, who was part of the *Monday Night Football* announcing crew. "But I remember the sound, the grateful roar of fans who were alive, who had come through this, who had their team back and their stage back and were part of the action again."

"I vividly remember looking up at the crowd and thinking, 'It's impossible for us to lose tonight,'" Steve Gleason said.

The Saints forced a three-and-out—Saints linebacker Scott Fujita sacked Atlanta quarterback Michael Vick and forced a fumble on third down—and Bonamego immediately asked Payton to go for the punt block.

"Let's do it," Payton said.

He sent out the punt block team . . . but only ten men went out there. Bonamego grabbed Deloatch and told him to get in there. He ran in. He had no idea what he was supposed to do.

Gleason did. He looped around a teammate and raced directly at punter Mike Koenen. He timed it exactly right; there was nobody there to block him. He didn't dive at the punter but instead sort of fell forward in order to make his body as big as possible. He blocked the punt cleanly.

And waiting to fall on the ball for a touchdown? Curtis Deloatch. Sure.

And the sound in the Superdome went from indescribable to unforgettable.

THERE IS A STATUE OUTSIDE OF THE SUPERDOME NOW CALLED *Rebirth*. It is of Steve Gleason blocking the punt. Below it are ninety words.

> *On Monday, September 25, 2006, Steve Gleason was responsible for one of the most dramatic moments in New Orleans Saints history. He blocked a punt in the first quarter of the team's return to the Superdome following Hurricane Katrina. That night, the Saints*

defeated their rival Atlanta Falcons 23–3. It would kick-start an improbable run for a team that would go on to win the NFL South crown and play for the NFC Championship that season. That blocked punt that season symbolized the "rebirth" of the city of New Orleans.

IN JANUARY 2011, LESS THAN FIVE YEARS AFTER BLOCKING THE punt, Steve Gleason was diagnosed with ALS. Doctors gave him two to five years to live. As I write these words, he has just finished a book called *A Life Impossible*. His foundation, Team Gleason, has raised more than $40 million to assist people battling the disease.

"While my body has become a prison," he writes, "and I face seemingly impossible adversity and immense challenges every day, I have been able to survive and build a wonderfully possible life. I am free."

NO. 8:

THE HELMET CATCH

"We didn't treat them like some Greek myth."

—DAVID TYREE

—

FEBRUARY 3, 2008

Let's start with a simple fact you might know: No team has gone undefeated since the NFL went to a sixteen-game schedule in 1978.

Three have come close. The 1984 San Francisco 49ers lost one game, a heartbreaking 20–17 defeat to the Pittsburgh Steelers. Those 49ers led by a touchdown in the fourth quarter, committed a crushing pass interference penalty late, and blew the lead, and then their kicker Ray Wersching missed what would have been a game-tying 37-yard field goal with ten seconds left.

"I guess some people could say we beat ourselves today," a glum head coach Bill Walsh said after the game.

The next year, the Chicago Bears lost just one game all season, but they thoroughly earned that loss on a Monday night against red-hot Dan Marino and the Dolphins. Miami won that game by 2 touchdowns—the Bears scored late to make the defeat look a little less gruesome—and at halftime, supposedly, Bears head coach Mike Ditka and defensive coordinator Buddy Ryan nearly got into a fistfight.

More than twenty years passed before another team dared fly that close to the sun.

Say whatever you want about them, but the 2007 New England Patriots, unquestionably, were playing for more than a championship. They were playing for history. They were playing for immortality. They had their dreadful division wrapped up pretty much by the midway point of the season. They had the top seed in the conference locked up a month before the season ended.

Still, they played on for perfection. In the utterly meaningless last game of the season, Tom Brady threw forty-two passes as he got into a shoot-out with Eli Manning and the Giants. He played the whole game. All the starters did. Brady and the Patriots trailed by 12 points in the second half but wouldn't relent, wouldn't give in. They scored 3 straight touchdowns and won the game 38–35. That made them the only team to ever go 16-0. But their season wasn't over. And there was something larger at stake for them. Bill Belichick's Patriots had already won three Super Bowls. This season was about something more.

"Anyone who is a competitor at heart," Patriots owner Robert Kraft said, "strives for perfection."

The Patriots set countless records that year: Brady threw the most touchdown passes ever, Randy Moss caught the most touchdown passes ever, they scored the most points ever, they had the largest point differential ever, and so on.

The Patriots won their two playoff games. They were never in any danger of losing those games, but, looking back now, you can see they also didn't win either one overwhelmingly. The oddsmakers installed them as 12-point favorites over the Giants in Super Bowl XLII.

The Giants' defense was much too good that day to allow that sort of blowout. But Tom Brady did throw a late touchdown pass to Randy Moss to give New England a 14–10 lead. The Giants coughed and wheezed up the field and faced a second down from their own 44-yard line with 1:20 left.

And that left the floor to Eli Manning and the Giants.

ELI MANNING WAS THE KID BROTHER. THIS WAS MORE THAN HIS family status—younger brother to one of the greatest quarterbacks who ever lived, Peyton Manning; it was his ethos, his persona. He was the kid brother: a little cocky, a little mischievous, a little bit wobbly, perhaps.

He could do some amazing things. But people did wonder what he had inside. Back in college at Ole Miss, playing against LSU in the biggest game of his life, he fell down on a fourth down. He came to the NFL and had more shaky moments than stellar ones. In 2007, he led the NFL in interceptions. Now he was trying to beat the unbeatable Patriots.

"That's *just* where you want to be," Manning would say.

OK, but he said that *after* the game. How did he feel right then? On second down, he dropped back to throw and looked for receiver David Tyree. Well, it's not strictly accurate to call Tyree a "receiver"; he had caught only four passes all season. He was a special teams guy, a darned good one, a Pro Bowler in 2005, but the Giants barely used him as a receiver.*

So it was no surprise that Manning and Tyree were not on the same page. Manning was pressured by a blitzing Rodney Harrison, and on trust, he threw to the sideline where he expected Tyree to be. Tyree, meanwhile, had turned up the field. The only person standing there when the ball arrived was New England cornerback Asante Samuel.

Samuel would take a lot of heat for not intercepting that pass. And you can understand why: Samuel was a ball-hawking cornerback who led the league in interceptions twice. But the ball was wild and high and very close to the sideline; it would have taken a special effort to intercept that pass. It would not have been impossible. And it would have been a great play.

Samuel did not intercept the ball and end the game.

A fuming Manning screamed at Tyree—"That's about as demonstra-

---

* The *Edmonton Journal* was one of the few newspapers that made special mention of Tyree going into the game, but they referred to him as "kicker David Tyree."

tive as you're going to see Eli Manning," announcer Troy Aikman said—and then the Giants faced third down with hope still flickering.

Just *where you want to be.*

Manning took the third-down snap and was almost immediately engulfed by New England defenders. Linebacker Adalius Thomas circled around his blind side and grabbed at Manning's shoulder pad. Richard Seymour and Jarvis Green both grabbed him from behind. It looked like a zombie movie scene in which countless dead arms reach up out of the ground to grab our hero.

At one point, Manning's momentum was stopped enough that an official might have been tempted to whistle the play dead. But Manning kept wriggling and moving just enough, and then, somehow, he was free and he ran backward into open space. He prepared to throw the ball out-of-bounds when he saw that guy David Tyree running over the middle.

Manning knew, even as he was in the process of throwing the ball, that he was doing exactly what a quarterback should never do: throwing the ball back over the middle into coverage. But he also knew that those were desperate times, and the Giants would not beat the unbeatable team unless they did something dramatic and startling.

"I thought we needed a play" is how he put it.

DAVID TYREE GREW UP IN MONTCLAIR, NEW JERSEY, A TWENTY- five-minute drive (in moderate traffic) from the Meadowlands. It's true that he had not been much of a factor as a receiver all year, but for some reason the Giants seemed to believe that he offered a matchup problem for the Patriots. That week, he practiced more as a receiver than he had all year.

In the Friday practice, he dropped just about every ball that came his way. One ball conked right off his helmet and fluttered away.

Giants coach Tom Coughlin said: "At one point Eli goes over, puts his arm around David, says, 'Don't worry, David. When we need you, you'll be there.'"

And sure enough, early in the fourth quarter, with the Giants down, Manning hit Tyree on a 5-yard touchdown pass. It was Tyree's first touchdown in more than a year.

Now there he was, with Manning's somewhat wobbly pass coming his way and Patriots all around him. Tyree realized he was going to have to jump as high as he could go to catch it. And jumping wasn't necessarily his strong suit, which was part of why he was a special teams player in the first place.

Up he went. He felt Harrison on his back. He reached up with both hands and caught the ball. Just as he caught it, Harrison whacked at it with his right hand, knocking the ball loose. Tyree then jammed the ball against his helmet and, in his own words, "held on for dear life.

"I just wouldn't let go," Tyree would say.

"That catch was impossible," Eli would say.

The catch did not win the game for the Giants. They still had to score, which they did four plays later, on a 13-yard touchdown pass from Manning to Plaxico Burress.

And that was it. The Giants beat the only team to ever go 16-0 in the regular season. They had pulled off one of the most unlikely upsets in Super Bowl history on one of the most unlikely plays in Super Bowl history. And the Patriots?

"Now we go down as 18-1," the Patriots' Ellis Hobbs said. "And that is one big zit."

NO. 7:

KICK SIX

"I knew they had big guys on the field.
And I knew I could outrun them."

—CHRIS DAVIS JR.

—

NOVEMBER 30, 2013

How do you explain the Alabama-Auburn rivalry? Here's one story: When Bear Bryant died in 1983, the state fell into mourning. Bear was everything in Alabama, of course: the man who made Alabama football, conqueror of six national championships and fourteen conference championships and more victories than any coach who ever lived.

"The man was a saint," one tearful Alabama fan said to another.

"Hell, he wasn't no saint," the other replied. "A saint wouldn't have lost that Auburn game in '72."

That's right. There were still Alabama fans then—there are still Alabama fans now—who had not gotten over the 1972 Auburn game when the Crimson Tide blew a 16–3 lead in the final six minutes by allowing Bill Newton to block not one but two punts, both for touchdowns.

"Hateful and eternal," writer Tommy Tomlinson says of the rivalry. "The fans go to the same high schools, worship at the same churches, eat at the same diners—they can't escape each other. And they live in a state where nothing else matters as much. It's all day, every day, year after year."

"A less bloody Hatfield versus McCoy," says *Esquire* editor Brian O'Keefe.

In his book *Rammer Jammer Yellow Hammer*, author Warren St. John tells of an Alabama fan named Donnie who once went up to Navy rear admiral Isaac Richardson and asked him how much it would cost to "nuke Auburn."

There are countless such stories. This is a rivalry that sort of goes back to 1893—"sort of" only because they didn't play each other for more than forty years for a dozen petty reasons that reflected just how much people at those two schools loathed one another.

"Nothing matters more than beating the cow college on the other side of the state," Bear Bryant bellowed.

"About sixty minutes," Auburn coach Pat Dye said when asked how long it would take him to beat Alabama.

Every Iron Bowl—as the rivalry is called—matters, but the 2013 game stands out. From 2009 to 2012, Auburn and Alabama won all four national championships. First, it was Alabama in 2009; that was Nick Saban's first national title with the Crimson Tide. Then, in 2010, Auburn won behind their superhero quarterback, Cam Newton (overcoming a 24–0 deficit against Alabama along the way). Then Alabama won the next two (outscoring Auburn 91–14 in those Iron Bowls).

In 2013, Alabama was undefeated and No. 1 in the nation, Auburn had one loss and was No. 4 in the nation, and the winner would go to the conference championship game and probably the National Championship Game too.

Alabama came into the game as a 2-touchdown favorite, and the Crimson Tide seemed on the brink of putting that game away at least a dozen times. Amari Cooper, one of the best receivers in America, dropped a sure touchdown pass. Alabama kicker Cade Foster missed two field goals (one on a bad snap) and had a third kick blocked. Alabama also got stopped on a fourth and 1 deep in Auburn territory, probably because Saban didn't want to try any more field goals.

Alabama did lead by a touchdown—a 99-yard touchdown pass from quarterback A. J. McCarron to Cooper did the trick—with less than a minute left. Auburn was driving, though, and with thirty-two seconds left, Auburn quarterback Nick Marshall flipped a 39-yard touchdown pass to Sammie Coates to tie the game.

Alabama then went on a wild, final desperation drive and Alabama's T. J. Yeldon got out-of-bounds at the Auburn 39. At first the officials said the clock had expired and they were ready to start overtime. Saban went bonkers. He screamed at the officials to review the play, and they did. After some time, the referee announced: "After review, the runner's foot touched out-of-bounds at the 39-yard line with one second on the clock."

You can probably find Auburn fans wearing T-shirts with those words on them.

Saban's choices for the final play of regulation: to try a Hail Mary pass or to let his kicker go for a 57-yard field goal. Everyone—and I mean everyone—thought he would try for the Hail Mary; after all, he had a Heisman Trophy candidate at quarterback in McCarron and a bunch of talented receivers, particularly Cooper.

He decided to kick. He knew Foster probably didn't have the leg for such a long kick. So he went up to a player wearing No. 99—a freshman kicker named Adam Griffith—and said: "You're going to kick the next one. What's your cutoff? Fifty-eight? Fifty-nine? OK, cool."

And with that, Adam Griffith jogged onto the field to try a 57-yard field goal.

Let's pause for just a moment here because Griffith's story is something. He was born in Poland as Andrzej Debowski. He grew up in an orphanage. When he was thirteen, Tom and Michelle Griffith asked to adopt him and take him back to Calhoun, Georgia, a small town in the northwest corner of the state. He was reluctant and, as he expected, hated it in Georgia at first. He knew no English and had no friends. But then his soccer coach suggested he try kicking field goals. He was terrific and became the No. 1 high school kicker in the country. He signed with Saban and Alabama.

He'd made long field goals in practice. Saban sent him out there.

Auburn coach Gus Malzahn doubted that Griffith—even with his strong leg—could come off the bench cold as a freshman and make a 57-yard field goal in the Iron Bowl. So he countered Saban's move with his own: He sent senior defensive back Ryan Smith to stand in the end zone in case the kick was short.

Then a brainstorm hit. He called time-out and replaced Smith with his dynamic punt returner, Chris Davis Jr.

"Ryan Smith was actually mad when coach called time-out and told us to switch," Davis would say.

Griffith's kick was high but well short.* Davis caught it in the back of the end zone. And he began to run.

"No!" said the marvelous announcer Verne Lundquist of the kick missing. "Returned by Chris Davis. Davis goes left! Davis gets a block! Davis has another block! Chris Davis! No flags! Touchdown, Auburn! An answered prayer!"

An answered prayer. The truth is, none of the Alabama players even had a chance to tackle Davis. It wasn't a unit prepared to stop an electrifying kick returner. The only player who had even the longest shot was Alabama holder Cody Mandell, but he could barely get a hand on him.

"First time I've ever lost a game that way," Saban said. "First time I've ever seen a game lost that way."

"When I was in the end zone, I took a look back," Davis said, "and I thought, 'What just happened?'"

---

* While Griffith's Kick Six was short, two years later Griffith made five field goals in the Iron Bowl as Alabama beat Auburn. "If it was any other team, I'd be like, 'It's just another team,'" he said. "But this is Auburn."

NO. 6:

THE ICE BOWL

"By any yardstick, it is indeed cold."

—CBS ANNOUNCER RAY SCOTT

DECEMBER 31, 1967

The statistics of quarterbacks in the 1960s will never look impressive to us—not after Marino and Fouts and Manning and Brees and Mahomes lit things up—but even with that caveat, Bart Starr's statistics are particularly tame. He never threw more than sixteen touchdown passes in a season. He never threw for 2,500 yards in a season.

"How's five world championships in seven seasons?" his teammate and friend Bill Curry asks me with just a little edge in his voice. "How's that for a statistic?"

This is how friends talk about Bart Starr. They are fiercely protective of him and his particular kind of greatness. See, even in his time, Starr wasn't as celebrated as flashier quarterbacks like John Unitas and Joe Namath and Sonny Jurgensen, among others. He was overshadowed by his coach Vince Lombardi. He was the trigger for the Packers' famous sweep play, which hardly left much room for him to shine. He was viewed often as the friendly but bland traffic cop of the Green Bay Packers, with his job being to prevent accidents and avoid mistakes.

This was Lombardi's own view when he took over the Packers job. "When I first met him," Lombardi said, "he struck me as so polite and self-effacing that I wondered if maybe he was too nice a boy to be the authoritarian leader that your quarterback must be."

Or as Packers lineman Jerry Kramer said: "If you think back, Bart Starr was methane. He was colorless, odorless, tasteless, and virtually invisible. We didn't know who Bart was then."

He revealed himself slowly, patiently, through a thousand small moments. Kramer would often tell the story of the time the Bears' ferocious linebacker Bill George took a cheap shot at Starr—a forearm to the head—splitting his lip and making him bleed profusely.

"That ought to take care of you," George yelled.

"Fuck you, Bill George," Starr screamed, the first (and only?) time that Kramer ever heard him swear. "We're coming after you!"

And Starr led the Packers right down the field for a score.

He was always displaying his steel in unexpected ways. Even Lombardi felt it. Lombardi was famous for the fury he unloaded on his players, and for a time Starr was one of his favorite targets. Starr finally went to see Lombardi in his office and closed the door.

"I told him, 'I can take all of the chewing out you can give out,'" Starr would say. "I said, 'I know your personality. That doesn't bother me.'"

Then he went on: He said he could not lead that team if the players saw Lombardi belittling him. And he offered a deal. He told Lombardi that anytime he wanted to lambaste Starr, he should feel free to do so, but *only* behind closed doors in his office.

Lombardi nodded. He never criticized Starr in front of the team again.

NOBODY, NOT EVEN TOM BRADY, WON BIG GAMES LIKE BART Starr. He became a full-time starter in 1961, and the Packers won the title that year and again the next and then again in 1965, '66, and '67. He played in nine postseason games over that stretch of time. The Packers won all nine of them.

The crescendo was the Ice Bowl, the 1967 NFL Championship Game against Dallas. There have been plenty of cold NFL playoff games—the Cleveland-Oakland Red Right 88 game in 1981, the Chargers-Bengals Freezer Bowl game in 1982, the Seahawks-Vikings wild card game in 2016, the Chiefs-Dolphins game at Arrowhead in 2024—but this was the coldest, both in temperature (–13 at kickoff, much colder when the game ended) and in legend. Cowboys quarterback Don Meredith would recall getting his wakeup call and the woman saying, "Good morning! It's seven o'clock and sixteen below."

"Sixteen below what?" Meredith asked.

"Step outside, honey," she said, "and you'll find out."

It was so cold that Cowboys receiver Bullet Bob Hayes, who had grown up in Florida, ran with his hands stuffed in his pockets when running plays were called.

It was so cold that Lombardi's great pride—the so-called electric blanket he had installed below the turf at Lambeau Field to prevent freezing—was rendered useless. The field was a choppy sheet of ice. Dallas's Doomsday Defense sent Starr crashing into the rock-hard field eight times. On one of those sacks, Starr fumbled, and Dallas's George Andrie scooped up the ball and scored.

With a little less than five minutes left in the game and the Cowboys leading 17–14, Starr took the field for what he knew would be, one way or another, the decisive drive.

"Don't let me down!" a manic Ray Nitschke screamed at Starr.

Starr led the Packers on a methodical march, mixing runs and short passes. Those were the days when quarterbacks called all the plays. Few were shrewder than Starr. He connected with his running back Donny Anderson for a key first down. He hit Chuck Mercein for 19 yards. Then Starr made a gutsy call: He called a trap play up the middle, gambling that Dallas's Bob Lilly, one of the best defensive tackles ever, would follow the pulling guard. Lilly followed, and Mercein bulled his way to the 3. Anderson then powered his way to the 1 and a first down.

What followed is now legend.

On first down, Starr gave an inside handoff to Anderson, who slipped on ice and was spun around for no gain.

On second down, Starr himself slipped a little on the snap and gave the ball to Anderson again. He couldn't get any traction and fell into the pile: again no gain.

Sixteen seconds remained. The Packers called their last time-out.

Starr went to the sideline. The situation was clear. If the Packers ran the ball again and didn't get in, they'd have to race on the field goal unit and try a game-tying kick. Was there enough time for that? With the field in the condition that it was in, Lombardi was dubious.

He decided to go for it anyway.

"The whole world loves a gambler," he famously said. "But not when he loses."*

Lombardi called the 31 Wedge, the Packers' best short-yardage play, with a running back crashing in behind Kramer. Starr, as unselfish a player as anyone in NFL history, shook his head no. He said Anderson couldn't get to the line without slipping. "I'm already standing up-right," he said. "I can shuffle my feet and lunge in."

Lombardi looked at his man and nodded.

"Run it," Lombardi said. "And let's get the hell out of here."

Starr took the snap, Kramer shoved the Cowboys' Jethro Pugh back just enough, and Starr lunged in for the touchdown that won the game and Vince Lombardi's last NFL Championship.

When asked about the guts it took to call his own number in that moment, Starr, as always, modestly demurred. "We sort of ran out of things to do," he said.

---

* We have to mention here that had Bart Starr failed to score on the play, the Packers would probably not have had enough time to kick the game-tying field goal, and Vince Lombardi's final game with the Packers would have been forever remembered as one he lost because of an extremely questionable coaching decision. Such is the tissue-thin difference between legend and catastrophe.

NO. 5:

THE PLAY CALL

"Terrible call."

—TORRY HOLT

"That's a terrible play call. #Awful."

—SHANNON SHARPE

"DUMBEST PLAY CALL IN THE HISTORY OF NFL FOOTBALL."

—DWIGHT CLARK

"Would you send the bunt signal in to the Babe?"

—BRIAN DAWKINS

"That was the worst play call in Super Bowl history."

—DEION SANDERS

"Worst play call I've seen in the history of football."

—EMMITT SMITH

—

FEBRUARY 1, 2015

The play call follows Pete Carroll around like a deeply loyal stray dog. Carroll tries to shoo it away with detailed explanations and keen insights into his thought process. He will throw in an occasional burst of righteousness. But the play call won't leave. Forever, there will be twenty-six seconds left in Super Bowl XLIX, the Seattle Seahawks will be at the New England Patriots' 1-yard line, and Mr. Beast Mode himself, Marshawn Lynch, will be standing in the backfield, ready to go smashing.

Marshawn Lynch will never get that ball. Not ever.

Instead, Seahawks quarterback Russell Wilson will take the snap, turn to his right, and almost instantly throw toward Ricardo Lockette, who is running a shallow cross toward the middle of the end zone.

Lockette looks open for an instant. Perhaps. But before the ball is even out of Wilson's hand, Patriots rookie Malcolm Butler will come crashing down and his left shoulder will crash into Lockette's right shoulder as the ball arrives. Lockette goes flying. Butler intercepts the pass. The Seahawks lose. Every single time the call happens, the Seahawks lose.

"I'm sorry," announcer Cris Collinsworth says, "but I can't believe the call."

"Me neither," Al Michaels says.

"I cannot believe the call," Collinsworth continues. "You've got Marshawn Lynch in the backfield, a guy that has been borderline unstoppable in this part of the field. I can't believe the call."

All across America, in that precise moment, countless people are shouting and texting and posting the exact same thought. *I cannot believe the call.*

When Pete Carroll sees that the ball was intercepted, he shouts, "Oh no!" He drops his headphones before the players even hit the turf. He knows. The play call is his now forever and ever, and there is absolutely nothing he can do about it.

LET'S GET A LITTLE MORE TECHNICAL FOR THIS ONE AND GO back to the 2013 AFC Championship Game between the Patriots and the Broncos. In that game, Peyton Manning twice drove Denver down inside the 5-yard line. Both times the Broncos ran a play-action pass and Manning was able to find a wide-open receiver for the touchdown.

Bill Belichick was outraged. All season long, when teams had gotten within a few yards of the end zone, they were throwing touchdown passes. It drove Belichick bonkers. As soon as the season ended, he brought his whole defensive staff into a room before the sun was even up, and he roared that he was not going to go through all that again. One of the coaches in that meeting was Michael Lombardi.

"Each time the famous coach brought up his team's horrendous goal line defense," Lombardi wrote in his book *Gridiron Genius*, "his mood increasingly matched his surroundings: dark, cold, and ominous. All the men in the room were terrified, myself included."

Fear sometimes sparks innovation. The problem was plain: Traditional goal line defenses are created to stop the run. But NFL teams don't run the ball nearly as much around the goal line. They will put in extra receivers and run a variety of patterns, and a traditional goal line defense simply can't handle it.

So the Patriots' coaches, led by Belichick, fashioned a special goal line defense in which they would replace their Pro Bowl safety Devin McCourty with a quicker cornerback. That would give them three cornerbacks and allow them, perhaps, to match up better when opponents tried to throw near the end zone.

They called the defense, naturally, Goal Line 3 Corners.

Lombardi wrote that the Patriots didn't run Goal Line 3 Corners all season. But the week of the Super Bowl, Belichick insisted they practice it. He just had a hunch. And while running Goal Line 3 in the Friday practice, a receiver cut underneath and was wide-open for a touchdown.

"Malcolm!" Belichick shouted at his rookie corner, Malcolm Butler. "You've got to be on that!"

MALCOLM BUTLER THOUGHT FOR SURE THAT HE WOULD BE THE goat of the Super Bowl. Not the GOAT, Greatest of All Time, like Tom Brady, but the goat, the guy who cost them the game. It had been quite a ride for him. He went undrafted out of West Alabama. New England was the only team that even offered him a tryout. He beat crazy odds to make the team as a special teams kamikaze. As the season went on, he started playing more on defense.

And there in the Super Bowl, he was suddenly on the field with the game on the line. He was covering Seattle's Jermaine Kearse, and he had sublime coverage, and the ball was thrown, and he leaped up and knocked the ball away . . . only he didn't knock it away. Somehow it defied gravity, popped up straight in the air, and fell straight down. Kearse, who was falling backward, reached out his right hand, popped the ball back in the air and then reached up both hands and pulled it in at the 5-yard line.

"It was devastating," Butler said. "I came out after that play. I wasn't feeling too well."

On the next play, Marshawn Lynch blasted through the defense for 4 more, getting the ball down to the 1.

And then three things happened at once.

1. **The Patriots called Goal Line 3 Corners, sending Butler back in the game.**
2. **Pete Carroll saw that the Patriots had a goal line defense and he decided it would be hard to try to run against it. He concurred with his offensive coordinator, Darrell Bevell, and they sent in the infamous pass play.**
3. **Marshawn Lynch stood in the huddle with the rest of the team and learned from Wilson that the Seahawks were not going to give him the ball. "I was looking at nine other guys, and they looked at me like, 'What the fuck just happened?'" Lynch later told Shannon Sharpe.**

What happened was that Belichick had baited Carroll into going away from Lynch and trying a pass against what he thought was a typical goal line defense. The Patriots knew exactly what was coming. Cornerback Brandon Browner knew his job was to jam Kearse hard at the line and not let himself get pushed back into Butler's lane. Butler knew his job was to crash in and beat Lockette to the ball.

And it happened just like that.

In the years that have passed, Lynch has made it perfectly clear how angry he remains about not getting the ball. "They took a dream away from me," he said. Other Seahawks have spoken angrily about it too. Amateur analysts have gone round and round and round about it; some do think the decision to pass might have been fine, but the Seahawks should have come up with a more innovative play. A few think the play call was sound and the result was unlucky and those are just the breaks.

But most, yeah, most still hate the call.

Pete Carroll himself keeps trying to explain—he talks about match-ups and situational thinking and the unlikeliness of an interception and how the Seahawks had only one time-out and so on—but words won't make it go away. One yard to go. Super Bowl on the line. The play call shadows Pete Carroll forever.

NO. 4:

THE IMMACULATE RECEPTION

"You talk about Christmas miracles.
Here's the miracle of all miracles."

—ANNOUNCER CURT GOWDY

—

DECEMBER 23, 1972

Here are one hundred facts about the Immaculate Reception.

1. The Steelers trailed Oakland 7–6.
2. There were twenty-two seconds left in the game.
3. It was fourth down and 10.
4. The Raiders had taken that lead when quarterback Ken Stabler, nobody's idea of a sprinter, coughed and wheezed and sputtered 30 yards for the touchdown.
5. This was the first home playoff game ever for the Pittsburgh Steelers.
6. It was only the second playoff game ever for the Steelers, home or road.
7. They'd lost their only other playoff game 21–0. This should give you an idea how bad the Steelers' history was.
8. Steelers coach Chuck Noll sent in a pass play called "66 Circle Option."
9. The intended receiver on the play was a rookie named Barry Pearson, who was playing in his first NFL game and had never made a single NFL catch.
10. "We didn't have any big play threats then," Steelers quarterback Terry Bradshaw explained.
11. The Steelers' one dangerous offensive player, running back

Franco Harris, did not have a passing route on the play. He
was supposed to stay in and block.

12. Harris was a rookie, but he was already the most popular
    player on the Steelers.

13. A group called "Franco's Italian Army" had formed to cheer
    him on.

14. Oscar-winning composer Henry Mancini asked to be a
    member of Franco's Italian Army.

15. So did Frank Sinatra.

16. Before the game, Sinatra sent a telegram to the Steelers that
    read: "The following is an order: 'Attack! Attack! Attack!'" He
    signed his name "Colonel Francis Sinatra of the Franco
    Italian Army."

17. Some Steelers fans left before the play. Franco's Italian Army
    stayed.

18. Bradshaw dropped deep into the pocket and looked deep for
    Pearson, but he wasn't open.

19. Raiders defensive end Tony Cline charged in and reached out
    his hand to grab Bradshaw.

20. Bradshaw rolled to his right to get away.

21. Franco Harris, without a pass pattern, didn't block anybody.
    Cline ran right behind him.

22. "I guess I didn't block that well," Harris said.

23. Bradshaw sidestepped Oakland's Horace Jones and then
    threw the ball just as Cline came in to clobber him.

24. Bradshaw was knocked hard to the ground and Cline piled on
    top of him.

25. Bradshaw didn't see anything that happened.

26. The ball headed for Pittsburgh's Frenchy Fuqua, a marvelous
    character.

27. Frenchy's real name was John, but when he was at Morgan
    State, he nicknamed himself the "French Count." This was
    shortened to "Frenchy" for convenience.

28. Frenchy Fuqua was a famously snappy dresser. His best-known accessories were platform shoes with transparent high heels.

29. Fuqua would fill those heels with water and put goldfish in them.

30. Fuqua headed over the middle. His eyes were trained on the ball.

31. Fuqua did not see Oakland's Jack Tatum come crashing at him.

32. The two collided at roughly the Oakland 33-yard line.

33. Jack Tatum was famously called "Assassin."

34. He was first called the "Assassin" while playing at Ohio State, but it wasn't until he played with Oakland—for Al Davis's hard-hitting team—that the nickname really stuck.

35. The pass hit someone and then ricocheted backward a full 10 yards.

36. The ball might have hit Fuqua.

37. It also might not have hit Fuqua.

38. Because of the rules at the time, it matters whom the ball hit last.

39. As the ball was thrown, Franco Harris had in his mind the voice of his old Penn State coach Joe Paterno, who said, time after time, "Go to the ball."

40. So Harris went to the ball.

41. At least, that's how he remembered it.

42. Raiders linebacker Phil Villapiano was shadowing Harris on the play, and he had a different memory. He didn't think Harris went to the ball at all.

43. "Franco comes jogging down the field, half speed," Villapiano said. "I'm jogging half speed with him. I saw Bradshaw make the throw. I shot over to make the tackle."

44. "Meanwhile, Franco," Villapiano continued, "drifted over there somewhere. The ball went right to him."

45. Villapiano's conclusion: "Had I been as lazy as Franco, that ball would have come to me."

46. Either way, Harris reached down and caught the ball at the 43.

47. NFL Films' legendary cameraman Ernie Ernst trained his camera on Franco throughout and got the iconic shot of Harris pulling the ball in, which you've probably seen a million times.

48. If not for Ernst, there might have been a controversy over whether Harris actually caught the ball or not. It was very close, but Ernst's angle shows he did catch it.

49. There was nobody in front of Franco as he ran.

50. "I lost all sense of consciousness," Franco would say.

51. Bradshaw, meanwhile, still had not gotten up.

52. "I didn't see anything, but I heard a roar," Bradshaw would say. "And I could tell this was a good roar."

53. Villapiano saw the whole thing happen; he was one of the few on the field who did.

54. He chased Harris and, to this day, believes he would have made the tackle and put an end to the whole thing.

55. Except . . .

56. Pittsburgh's rookie tight end John McMakin dived at the back of Villapiano's legs, a totally illegal block. And it knocked Villapiano off course.

57. "What's he got to lose?" Villapiano would say. "They're going to lose the game anyway. It's the biggest clip ever. No clip called."

58. In the Tom Hanks movie *That Thing You Do!*, the pizzeria where the band gets its first gig is called "Villapiano's."

59. Tom's son Colin Hanks is pretty sure the place was named for Phil.

60. Harris kept on running.

61. The last Raider with a chance to tackle him was Jimmy Warren, who desperately reached out at about the 9-yard line.

62. Harris stiff-armed him to the ground and ran into the end zone for the touchdown.

63. It was the first playoff touchdown in Pittsburgh Steelers history.

64. The Steelers led 12-7.

65. There were five seconds left on the clock.

66. Fans poured on the field and jumped on Harris and teammates.

67. One fan stole the helmet of Steelers defensive end Dwight White.

68. A dazed Terry Bradshaw ran around and repeatedly screamed at anyone who would listen, "What happened? What happened?"

69. Raiders' owner Al Davis ran through the press box screaming at NFL officials that the play was illegal.

70. When he got no satisfaction, he sat in the corner and put his face in his hands.

71. One Pittsburgh reporter timed him sitting there for twenty-nine minutes.

72. Why was Davis screaming? Well, here is where an obscure and outdated rule comes into play.

73. In 1972, Rule 7, Section 5, Article 2, Item 2c, stated, "Any forward pass (legal or illegal) becomes incomplete and ball is dead immediately if pass is caught by any A player after it has touched ineligible A player or second eligible A, and before any touching by B."

74. In clearer English, that means that if the ball touched Fuqua last, Harris would not be allowed to catch it.

75. If Fuqua touched it and then Harris—with no Raiders player in between—the ball should have been called dead, and the Steelers would have been penalized a loss of down.

76. That would have won the game for the Raiders.

77. It's a dumb and confusing rule and you can understand why the NFL got rid of it.

78. But it was a *big deal* in 1972.

79. Jack Tatum insisted he had not touched the ball.

80. "I ran out on the field," Raiders coach John Madden said. "The officials say, 'We don't know what happened.' I say, 'I know you don't know what happened. I'll tell you what happened.' I said, 'It hit Frenchy Fuqua illegally.' Well, they told me to get the hell off the field."

81. "We got taken," Al Davis said. "The word is stronger than that."

82. And what did Frenchy Fuqua have to say? Well, that's the fun part. He's had a lot—and absolutely nothing—to say about it for the last half century.

83. "Did I touch the ball?" he would ask Rotary Club after Optimist Club after high school sports banquet crowd. Then he'd smile happily and give no answer.

84. The Raiders' Raymond Chester said that Fuqua came into the Raiders locker room after the game and admitted he did touch the ball.

85. For a fifty-year-anniversary documentary, Fuqua admitted that he did touch it. *But* . . . he insisted it then touched Tatum.

86. "The ball did hit me. In my hand," he said. "And if Jack hadn't been so aggressive, the game would have been over. But it hit him in the shoulder pad. The ball would not have gone as far as it did back the opposite way if the ball had only hit my hand."

87. That actually makes sense. When you watch the play, you see that Tatum was the only one who could have knocked the ball backward that far.

88. And if you don't trust me, trust John Fetkovich, a former professor at Carnegie Mellon, who agreed with me. He did a

detailed study of the film—and threw some footballs against a brick wall—and concluded that the ball had to have bounced off Tatum.

89. Of course, Carnegie Mellon is in Pittsburgh.

90. The Raiders remain unconvinced.

91. "The play bothered me then," Madden said. "It bothers me now. It will bother me until the day I die."

92. The *Pittsburgh Press*'s Phil Musick started his story the next day like so: "The God of all the losers who have ever been smiled down through a ghostly gray sky yesterday, and in the last desperate seconds of a mean, bitterly fought football game, did truly wondrous things."

93. Pittsburgh's legendary sportscaster and writer Myron Cope popularized the play's name, the "Immaculate Reception."

94. "December 23," he announced a day after the catch, "will henceforth be celebrated as the Feast of the Immaculate Reception."

95. Myron Cope, incidentally, was Jewish.

96. Oakland's George Atkinson nicknamed the play the "Immaculate Deception."

97. In a book called *Immaculate: How the Steelers Saved Pittsburgh*, the authors Tom O'Lenic and Ray Hartjen essentially credit the play for altering the future for the whole city of Pittsburgh.

98. The *Pittsburgh Post-Gazette* concurred and called the Immaculate Reception the "play that changed a city."

99. In 1994, a statue of Franco Harris making the Immaculate Reception was commissioned and unveiled at the Pittsburgh International Airport.

100. Almost twenty years later, by popular demand, the statue was moved to a more prominent spot because people coming through Pittsburgh would complain that they didn't get to see it.

NO. 3:

JOHNNY U AND THE GREATEST GAME

"I'm not a gambler. You're not risking anything
when you know where you are passing."

—JOHNNY UNITAS

———

DECEMBER 28, 1958

In 1955, Johnny Unitas caught a bad break. He was drafted in the ninth round by his hometown team, the lamentable Pittsburgh Steelers. They didn't understand him.* The Steelers didn't really get anybody in those days. In short order, they had released Hall of Famers John Unitas and Len Dawson and they failed to draft Lenny Moore and Jim Brown and they traded away the pick that the Bears used to take Dick Butkus.

"This is professional football?" Unitas asked on his first day in Steelers camp.

The Steelers cut him shortly after that. He pocketed the bus fare, hitchhiked back to Pittsburgh, and got a job on a construction crew. He also played for a semipro team called the Bloomfield Rams for six bucks a game. It might have ended like that except the Baltimore Colts caught wind of a promising prospect on the Rams. It wasn't Unitas. It was a guy named Jim Deglau. But they thought they might as well look at Unitas too.

═══════════════════════════════

WAS THE 1958 NFL CHAMPIONSHIP GAME TRULY, AS IT HAS BEEN called countless times, the "Greatest Game Ever Played"? Probably not,

———

* Tim Rooney, son of Steelers owner Art Rooney, loved Unitas and sent his father a long letter about how he was the best passer in camp and the coaches were just missing out. There are many legends surrounding that letter, my favorite being that the old man sent a postcard back from a racetrack saying, "I pay my coaches to make those decisions."

no. But it was something bigger than that: It was the most perfect storm in football history.

Think of it. The NFL was just beginning to work its way into the American consciousness. The game was played at Yankee Stadium in New York. There were stars all over the field, players whose names still ring through the years—Unitas, of course, but also Frank Gifford and Lenny Moore and Sam Huff and Jim Parker and Emlen Tunnell and Gino Marchetti and Don Maynard and Artie Donovan and Andy Robustelli and Raymond Berry and Roosevelt Brown. They are all in the Hall of Fame. Two of the greatest coaches in pro football history, Vince Lombardi and Tom Landry, were offensive and defensive coordinator for the Giants. The legendary announcer Pat Summerall was kicking for the Giants.

Rosey Grier and Jack Kemp were there too.

The president of the United States, Dwight Eisenhower, was among the 45 million or so Americans watching the game on television, the largest audience ever to see professional football at that point.

And with 2:20 left,[*] the Giants up 3, the Colts got the ball at their own 14-yard line. That was when Johnny Unitas became Johnny Unitas.

To begin with, the Giants didn't *have* to punt there. Football history, all history, turns on the smallest decisions. Frank Gifford had been stopped just inches shy of the first down by Gino Marchetti.[†]

"I made it! I made it!" Gifford shouted.

"Why don't you shut up?" the Colts' Art Donovan yelled.

The spot was the spot—that was long before replay review—and the Colts faced a fourth and inches from their own 43. Giants coach Jim Lee Howell, in a decision he would come to regret, chose to punt.

---

[*] Roughly. The Longines clock on the scoreboard above the end zone was not the most precise in the world.
[†] Marchetti fractured his ankle on the play; he was taken off the field on a stretcher. He famously refused to go the locker room for treatment. Instead, tough man that he was, he sat on that stretcher on the sideline until the end of the game.

"My wife tells me never to punt," he said sadly.

Unitas jogged out in his soon-to-be-famous high-tops. He'd led the NFL in touchdown passes in 1957 and '58, but he wasn't yet really known outside of Baltimore. "This Unitas is a gambler, a courageous and daring passer," Washington owner George Preston Marshall warned. "You don't want to be up against him when the chips are down."

There was no such thing then called the "two-minute drill." Johnny Unitas would have to invent it. After two incompletions, he faced his first critical pass—and he connected with Lenny Moore for a first down.

Then he threw a pass over the middle to Raymond Berry for 25 yards. It was a quintessential example of the supernatural connection they felt for each other; Berry was supposed to run to the sideline. But he noticed an opening in the Giants' defense and cut inside instead. And Unitas noticed the exact same thing at the exact same time.

"I know people say that John and I had a special connection, and I think we did," Berry would tell me years later. "But the truth is, John had that connection with everybody because he saw everything on a football field."

Next play, Unitas went back to Berry for 15 more. The field was dust and dirt, barely any grass at all; the sky was dark gray. You could almost feel the chill coming through your black-and-white television. Unitas's once white jersey—with the now famous blue "19" on the front and back—was the color of a rain cloud. Without huddling, he took the next snap, backpedaled, and once more found Berry, this time standing alone. Unitas hit him in the chest with the pass, and Berry turned it up and made it to the Giants' 13.

There were fifty seconds remaining and the Colts raced their kicking team on the field. In 1958, even a 20-yard field goal was no sure thing. The Colts' kicker, Steve Myhra, was a 6-foot-1, 237-pound guard and linebacker who happened to kick. The next year, he'd miss four of the six kicks he tried from between 20 and 29 yards.

He made this one. He leaped for joy. You can find the kicking shoe he was wearing in the Pro Football Hall of Fame in Canton.

Most players on the field thought the game was a tie and it was over.

But years earlier, the NFL had written a rule that had never come into play before: A playoff game could not end in a tie. And now there would be the first sudden-death overtime in NFL history.[*]

JOHNNY UNITAS LOST THE COIN TOSS. HE CALLED TAILS. THAT could have been the decisive moment of the game; the Giants would get the ball first and all they needed to do was score a field goal and the championship was theirs.

But the Giants were not in the right headspace for the moment. Giants quarterback Charlie Conerly talked on the sideline about how he was too tired to go on. And sure enough, the Giants went three and out and punted the ball away.[†] Unitas and the Colts started on their own 20.

There was little doubt about what would happen next. Unitas, with no time constraints, mixed his play calls as only he could, surprising the Giants each time. When they expected the run, he fired a pass to Berry. When they looked for a pass, he slipped an inside handoff to Alan Ameche for 23 yards, the big play of the drive.

The Colts moved inside the New York 10, easy field goal range, and the Giants thought for sure he would play it safe. That was when he sketched out a play in the dirt, dropped back, and lofted a pass to the sideline where receiver Jim Mutscheller had broken free from his

---

[*] There has been a sixty-four-year effort to make the pro-football playoff overtime rules equitable. From 1958 to 2010, NFL overtimes were strictly sudden death: The first team that scored won. Many thought this wasn't fair, so for the next thirteen years the rule was a bit more confusing: If the team that got the overtime kickoff scored a touchdown, they won, but if they scored a field goal, then the game went on. Finally—as first seen in the 2024 Super Bowl—the rule was changed so that both teams are guaranteed to get the ball at least once in overtime.

[†] This was the second time in a row that the Giants punted the ball away on fourth and 1. Howell should have listened to his wife.

defender. Mutscheller could not quite balance himself after he caught the ball, and he went out-of-bounds at the 1.

"What makes you such a gambler?" a reporter asked Unitas.

"I'm not a gambler," he said. "You're not risking anything when you know where you are passing."

All that was left now was for Unitas to call "16 Power." Ameche blasted off right tackle, where Lenny Moore—not known for being a legendary blocker—took out a Giant with a sweeping block. Ameche fell forward into the end zone for the game-winning touchdown, and the crowd poured onto the field to mob him.

PEOPLE HAVE LONG SAID THAT AMECHE'S TOUCHDOWN WAS THE birth of pro football as America's game. Maybe. One thing's for sure, though: It birthed the legend of Johnny Unitas. He played on for fifteen years, won three MVPs, and set all sorts of records, but none of that captured what he represented. After Unitas, being an NFL quarterback meant something different.

"When John Unitas was on a football field, he had only one thing in mind," Berry said. "He wanted to put the ball in the end zone. He did not think about statistics or history or fame or any of that nonsense. He thought about putting the ball in the end zone any way we could."

There's one Unitas story I particularly love. He was famously uninterested in his own fame. Long after he retired, the Pro Football Hall of Fame asked if they could display one of his famous high-top shoes. Unitas politely declined. He had only one pair left, he said. And he needed those for when he was mowing the lawn.

NO. 2:

THE PLAY

"We simply won the game. It's tragic that a Cal-Stanford game had to come down to this. In our hearts and in our minds, we know we won the game."

—STANFORD COACH PAUL WIGGIN

NOVEMBER 20, 1982

Here is the transcript of California's radio announcer Joe Starkey calling the Play:

"Well, this is some show, I'll tell you. And now the Bears are in a seemingly impossible situation. They have only one time-out left. They pretty well have to run it back to save the game, and boy, talk about a heartbreaking way to lose. . . .

"All right, here we go with the kickoff. Harmon will probably try to squib it, and he does. Ball comes loose, and the Bears have to get out-of-bounds. Rodgers along the sideline. Another one. They're still in deep trouble at midfield. They tried to do a couple of— The ball is still loose as they get it to Rodgers. They get it back now to the 30. They're down to the 20. Oh, the band is out on the field! He's gonna go into the end zone. He got into the end zone! Will it count? The Bears have scored but the bands are out on the field.

"There were flags all over the place. Wait and see what happens. We don't know who won the game. There are flags on the field. We have to see whether or not the flags are against Stanford or Cal. The Bears have made some illegal laterals. It could be that it won't count.

"Everybody is milling around on the field . . . and the Bears have won! The Bears have won! The Bears have won! Oh, my God, the most amazing, sensational, dramatic, heartrending, exciting, thrilling finish in the history of college football. California has won the Big Game over Stanford! Oh, excuse me for my voice but I have never,

never seen anything like it in the history of any game I've seen in my
life. The Bears have won it!"

Now ask yourself the question.

Do you have *any idea* what just happened?

Well, you can probably pick up that California beat Stanford in what they called the "Big Game." You might guess that they returned that kickoff somehow. You definitely know that the band was on the field. But other questions—such as "What happened?"; "Who scored?"; "How did they score?"; "Wait, what happened?"; and "What happened?"—are not really answered.

When he went home after the game that day, Starkey kept thinking, *I screwed it up.*

"That scared the heck out of me," he told SFGate forty years later. "Because I knew instantly this was a big deal and it would be on the record for a long time to come.... But my rule has always been, you call the play and apologize later."

The funny part is that the call is now legendary, one of the most famous in the history of football. I think it's because, while, no, Joe Starkey didn't give many details, he got to a larger truth with the tenor of his voice. The Play was chaos. And it was, indeed, the most amazing, sensational, dramatic,* heartrending, exciting, thrilling finish in the history of college football.

AS WE GO ON A TOUR OF THE PLAY, WE BRING ALONG OUR OLD friend Ed Price. Ed was a student at Stanford when the Play happened. He was at the game. He has the ticket stub to prove it.

He keeps that ticket stub in a safe.

---

* Some people heard "traumatic" instead of "dramatic," and you know what? The Play was that too, particularly for Stanford fans.

The Big Game, Stanford versus California, was first played in 1892,[*] making it the oldest football rivalry in the West. Since the 1930s, the winner of the game has received the Stanford Axe, which has its own long history going back to apparently being used at an 1899 Stanford pep rally to chop up a straw man dressed in Cal Blue and Gold.

This was the eighty-ninth Big Game, and it was played at California Memorial Stadium, and Cal seemed to have it pretty well wrapped up.

Ed would like to weigh in to say that in the second quarter, Cal's Mariet Ford "caught" a touchdown pass to give the Bears a 10–0 lead. "The ball went right through his hands, hit the turf, and he caught it on the way up," Ed says. "The only people who could see clearly what happened were in the Stanford section. It was ruled a touchdown."

With Cal up 19–17 and just 1:27 left, Stanford got the ball at their own 20. Stanford's quarterback then was a guy named John Elway, who . . . well, we don't talk about Elway, no, no, no.[†] But he took Stanford on one of the truly great drives in college football history—a drive that included a fourth-and-17 pass from their own 13-yard line. On that play, Elway dropped back to his own 2 and fired a let-'er-rip 29-yard rocket ship of a pass to Emile Harry.

Ed insists that Harry could not have dropped it even if he had wanted to. "If he didn't catch it," Ed says, "the ball would have stuck in his pads or gut anyway."

That drive ended with Mark Harmon's[‡] 23-yard field goal with eight seconds left. That should have wrapped up a bowl bid for Stanford. It might have won the Heisman Trophy for Elway. But, as mentioned above, there were eight seconds left.

Harmon set up for the kickoff. Cal was so stunned by what had just happened that they had only nine players on the field to return. In a

---

[*] Stanford's student manager for that first game? Future president Herbert Hoover.
[†] See No. 13 for details.
[‡] This is not the Mark Harmon who played quarterback for UCLA in the early 1970s and then became a popular actor, probably best known for his role as Special Agent Gibbs on the television show *NCIS*.

panic, they sent in two more at the last possible second, but in their haste they failed to put five players on the line. The officials missed it.

Harmon squib-kicked the ball and Cal's Kevin Moen fielded it at the Cal 45. He took about three steps, realized that there was nowhere to go, and threw an overhand lateral to Richard Rodgers.

Rodgers was not expecting the ball. But he was a wide receiver and so he instinctively caught it and found himself surrounded by three Stanford players. He heard his name—"Hey, Rich"—and turned and shoveled the ball back to the voice, which belonged to a Cal freshman named Dwight Garner.

Garner had dreams of scoring the game-winning touchdown. Those dreams were shattered when he ran into, as he recalled, twenty Stanford players at least. It was more like six Stanford players and one of them, Dave Wyman, was so sure that he had seen Garner's knee hit the ground that he started to run off the field, shouting, "Bowl, Baby!" His teammate Kevin Lamar punched his fist in the air.

"The ball game is going to be over with the tackle made at midfield," Stanford announcer Ron Barr told his radio audience.

That was when the Stanford band began to make their way onto the field.

Garner, though, flipped the ball back to Rodgers . . . and no whistle was blown.

That was when Joe Starkey yelled, "The ball is still loose!"

Rodgers found himself in some open field, and he ran the ball to the Stanford 45. When defenders closed in on him, he made a smooth pitch to Mariet Ford—the very man who had dropped/caught the touchdown pass back in the second quarter—and he was in the clear all the way to the 27-yard line.

Then Ford, just as he was about to be tackled by three Stanford players, blindly flung the ball over his right shoulder. It was caught by Kevin Moen at the 25. You can do the math: Release the ball at the 27, caught at the 25—that seems like a forward lateral.

But no official was looking for forward laterals.

Because by now the Stanford band in all its glory was on the field.

"I saw the band," Moen would say. "But I couldn't see the end zone."

There was one Stanford player, sophomore Darrell Grissum, and, like, a hundred members of the band between Moen and that end zone. Grissum, who would go on to become a pastor, was knocked out of the way by Cal's Wes Howell, probably an illegal block, but, you know, at that point, the Play was just sheer lawlessness.

Moen ran toward the end zone, as the panicked Stanford band members tried to get out of the way. It looked like a scene from a Godzilla movie. Finally, Moen crossed the goal line and he jumped in the air— he thought he could fly, but he couldn't fly—and he came crashing down on a 5-foot-6, 148-pound trombone player named Gary Tyrrell.*

The officials took a long time to figure out what had just happened.

It's probably fair to say they never really did. Cal won anyway.

Ed again: "I remember the officials gathered in a circle at midfield, and the place went quiet, waiting for their ruling. Then the referee came out and signaled touchdown. And the place went nuts. And my friend and I just bolted out of there and beat the traffic to the BART home because the rest of the Stanford fans just stood there, jaws open, for another five minutes."

There have been other amazing plays, other sensational multilateral kickoff returns, other dramatic and heartrending and exciting and thrilling finishes to football games. But Joe Starkey got it right the first time. This is the most. Most what? It is the most everything.

---

* Tyrrell would go on to become something of a Bay Area legend for his sense of humor about the Play. For years, he brewed a beer he called "Trombone Guy Pale Ale."

NO. 1:

MADDEN'S LAST GAME

"I'm the luckiest guy in the world. I never really had a job. I was a
football player, then a football coach, then a football broadcaster. . . .
Never once did it ever feel like work."

—JOHN MADDEN

—

FEBRUARY 1, 2009

*I*f I may step out of the background for a moment, now that we're at the
end: I know this might be a shocker at No. 1. Lists like these always put
the Immaculate Reception as the No. 1 moment in football history, and, sure,
that's fair. That moment was awesome. There are those who might put the
Play as the No. 1 moment in football history and that too makes perfect sense.
The Catch, the Helmet Catch, Kick Six, the Hail Mary, the Greatest Game
Ever Played—you can make a case for any of them and, yes, a hundred more.

But this is a book called Why We Love Football. And on one day, John
Madden announced his last game, James Harrison made the most absurd
play in Super Bowl history, and Santonio Holmes made the greatest catch in
Super Bowl history. The Arizona Cardinals almost made a remarkable comeback too.

Football, I think, is our most emotional game. It takes us fans to the mountaintop, and it tears our hearts out. It lifts us and crushes us, thrills us and
revolts us, leaves us empty and leaves us wanting and leaves us breathless.
All of it was there on display one Sunday in February of 2009, and that, for
me, is the No. 1 moment.

AL MICHAELS ALMOST TEARS UP TALKING ABOUT THAT LAST
game with John Madden. It's not only because of what Madden meant

to him and meant to professional football, though of course that's a part of it.

Also, that broadcast—the crazy first-half closing act, the wild ending, all of it—well, it's the most wonderful sports ever felt to him. He was there, of course, when the United States hockey team beat the Soviets in 1980, when he made his eternal call: "Do you believe in miracles? Yes!"

He was there in 1986 when the Boston Red Sox and California Angels played Game 5 of the American League Championship Series, a baseball game for the ages. He was there for Kentucky Derbies and Sugar Bowls, Indy 500s and NBA Finals, World Series and Stanley Cup Finals and ten other Super Bowls.

But Super Bowl XLIII—Pittsburgh versus Arizona in Tampa, John Madden's last game—well, that was the pinnacle.

"That game felt so right in so many ways," he says. "There was the greatest feeling I've ever had working out of a booth. I thought I hit every note, which I rarely do. John Madden had a spectacular game. The truck had a spectacular game. The game was great. You had two off-the-chart iconic plays. You had Bruce Springsteen at halftime."

He pauses.

"And then it turns out to be John's last game."

He pauses again.

"It was just perfect," he says. "Life was good."

HOW DO YOU EVEN BEGIN TO DESCRIBE JOHN MADDEN'S IMPACT on professional football? He was the Raiders' coach for so many of their magical moments—the Holy Roller, Ghost to the Post, the Sea of Hands, Willie Brown's return—and in his ten years working for Al Davis, his team never had a losing record.

He was one of football's great pitchmen, appearing in America's living rooms. He burst through the wall to get them to fully grasp the

allure of Lite Beer from Miller. He punched the words "Tough-actin'
Tinactin" to emphasize just how easy it can be to deal with athlete's
foot.

He was the driving force behind the biggest sports video game to
ever hit America, *Madden NFL*. He was the one who insisted that it feature
eleven players on each side just like real football. When the people
at EA Sports told him that was impossible, he shrugged. "I'm not putting
my name on it if it's not real," he said. He gave the programmers
the Raiders' actual 1980 playbook, and he personally provided the
commentary. More than 130 million copies of the game have sold over
the years, and multiple generations of fans have learned the game from
playing *Madden*.

Finally, mostly, there was John Madden the announcer. Before him,
the game's television broadcasters were mostly dignified, steady, deep-
voiced gentlemen. Football was a serious game, and it was meant to be
called by serious men. And here comes John Madden and all the sound
effects and BOOM! the quarterback throws when you're not expecting
it and WHAP! the linebacker comes in and knocks the ball down and
BANG! the guard pulls around and smashes into a safety and DOINK!
the kick hits the upright.

All the while he scribbles the play furiously on the Telestrator. Madden was the Picasso of the Telestrator. Then he's talking about a pigeon
standing on the sideline. Then he's teaching America about the inner
game, the stunts and pulls and blitzes and play actions and loops and
all these other things that were once kept inside the meeting rooms.

And he did all of it with a joy that lifted everybody higher.

"When the game is in doubt, he analyzes," the television critic Nor-
man Chad wrote. "When the game is a rout, he amuses."

❝I think a guy makes a play like that, you've got to give him a touchdown. They can look at it inside out, upside down, but James Harrison got a touchdown there.❞

—JOHN MADDEN

THERE WERE, AS AL MICHAELS SAID, TWO OFF-THE-CHART iconic plays in Super Bowl XLIII. Both deserve their own chapter, but lifelong Steelers fan and NBC late-night host Seth Meyers convinced me that they belong together, that they are inseparable.

The first play happened at the end of the first half. Pittsburgh led 10–7, but Arizona had driven the ball to the 2-yard line. Eighteen seconds remained in the half, and it seemed sure that Arizona would at least tie the game.

That was when James Harrison made a play that made no sense. Harrison was a blitzing linebacker. That was his whole job. He was a pass rusher. He was a dream crusher.

He wasn't a pass defender.

Everybody knew that Harrison would go after Arizona quarterback Kurt Warner on that play, and "everybody" included the Steelers' defensive coordinator, Dick LeBeau, who had called for an all-out blitz. With so much on the line, Harrison was definitely coming.

Only . . . he didn't come. He intended to come, but then this thought bolted through him the way it does for only the greatest players: *I'm not getting there in time.* Harrison realized that Warner was going to make an immediate pass, nullifying his pass rush.

And so, instead, he chose to gamble—he faked the rush and then dropped back into coverage, anticipating the quick slant pass to receiver Anquan Boldin. When he dropped back, he saw Warner's eyes, and he thought that the gamble had failed, and Warner was going to throw the ball elsewhere.

But Warner did not see Harrison. He tried the slant pass. Harrison intercepted the ball at the goal line. Then he began a long journey.

Harrison was not a runner. His teammates knew that, which is why Pittsburgh's Deshea Townsend, who had returned punts at Alabama, raced over and reached for the ball. Harrison slapped his hand away. He wasn't giving this one up.

"Go block somebody!" he shouted.

"The best thing about that play," says Meyers, who was at *Saturday Night Live* at the time and was in the crowd that day, "is it's *SO* long. You get to see the entirety of that wonderful 2008 defense."

He's right. The play lasted eighteen seconds, and it just kept getting more and more absurd. A few Steelers tried to make blocks, a few Cardinals tried to make tackles, and Harrison just kept on trucking. He sidestepped Tim Hightower, who was on the ground. He high-stepped over Arizona's Mike Gandy, who had dived at his feet.

Then, right at the goal line, receiver Larry Fitzgerald grabbed him from the right and another receiver, Steve Breaston, slammed into him on the left and he fell headfirst into the end zone. The moment was pure madness. What even happened?

Here's what happened: Pittsburgh had just scored the wildest touchdown in Super Bowl history.

And the proof was Harrison splayed on the ground in the end zone, desperately trying to catch his breath.

"He's gonna need nine IVs!" Santonio Holmes yelled happily on the sideline. "Tell them to get the IVs ready. He's gonna need them!"

He didn't need IVs, but he did need oxygen: "He's really enjoying that oxygen, isn't he?" John Madden said. Up in the stands, Seth Meyers watched in shock and wonder and was instantly inspired to write a *Saturday Night Live* sketch in which an out-of-breath Kenan Thompson, as James Harrison, tried to retell the story of the run.

"Still, it must have been exciting," Meyers said.

"Exciting to what?" Keenan Thompson said. "To meet Jesus? Because while I was lying in that end zone, he came down. And he said, 'James, you ready to go?' And I'll never forget, I said, 'Yes!'"

"That sketch wrote so fast," Meyers says. "I wish there was a tape of me with a dumb grin on my face, pounding the keys."

But, as Meyers says, he couldn't have written that sketch if not for off-the-chart iconic play number two.

> **❝ When Santonio Holmes had to make the play, he made it. When Ben Roethlisberger had to make the play, he made it. They were both perfect. ❞**
>
> **—JOHN MADDEN**

THERE WAS 1:02 LEFT IN THE SUPER BOWL. PITTSBURGH WAS ON the Arizona 6-yard line, and the Cardinals led 26–23. The Cardinals had trailed 20–7 going into the fourth quarter when the Cardinals' brilliant receiver Larry Fitzgerald took over.

Fitzgerald had been utterly unstoppable all postseason. He played four games and had 100 yards receiving in all four. He scored at least 1 touchdown in all four games. He caught three touchdown passes against Philadelphia in the NFC Championship Game.

Then, in the fourth quarter against the Steelers, he came alive again. He scored the touchdown that pulled Arizona within 6. He turned a short crossing pattern into a dazzling 64-yard touchdown that gave Arizona the lead and that seemed destined to become a part of Super Bowl lore.

What a play. What a game. What a day. Up in the announcers' booth, Al Michaels sat next to his friend John Madden and felt hyper-focused, as if everything was moving in slow motion for him. In the crowd, Seth Meyers sat stunned but still hopeful: His Steelers hadn't let him down all year. The echoes of Bruce Springsteen's titanic halftime show still rang. More than 100 million people watched on television.

When the NFL was founded, that was roughly the population of America.

Eighty-eight years of professional football had led to this.

And the Steelers drove down to the 6, and in the huddle Santonio Holmes told his teammates, "We need this play, man! Let's win the championship here!" His job was to break for the left corner of the end zone. He was sure that he'd be open.

He was open. Pittsburgh quarterback Ben Roethlisberger pumped right, drawing the safety over, and then fired it to Holmes, who leaped up high and raised his arms and shifted his body to be sure to get both feet in bounds and . . .

. . . and the ball went right through his hands and fell incomplete.

Holmes fell to the ground and began to talk to himself. "Dude," he said, "you suck. You just blew the game."

He went back to the huddle and would always remember Roethlisberger side-eying him. And then Roethlisberger made the call: "62 Scat Flasher."

They were going back to Holmes, this time in the right corner of the end zone. He stumbled off the line but managed to maintain his balance ("Dude, you can't fall," he told himself) and then he cut to the corner. Roethlisberger looked right, held the ball, looked left, held the ball, then pointed to the corner of the end zone. And then he fired.

There were three Cardinals there . . . and Santonio Holmes.

The throw was so precise, so pinpoint perfect, that it zipped by rookie Dominique Rodgers-Cromartie, went just over the outstretched fingertips of Ralph Brown, and was out of reach for Aaron Francisco. That left only Holmes.

As good as the throw was, the catch was even better. Holmes leaped up in a mirror image of the previous play, raised his arms, pulled the ball, and somehow tapped both his feet in bounds. Considering the degree of difficulty, the game situation, and the fact that dozens of cameras were pointing at him to catch even the slightest bobble or mis-step, it's the greatest catch in Super Bowl history.

"Unbelievable!" John Madden shouted out.

Unbelievable. Up in the crowd, Seth Meyers raced to a nearby televi-sion to see the replay, then went back to report to his family that the ball had definitely been caught. The Steelers had the lead. And then the Steelers had the game.

"The best thing about Santonio's play, outside of it being the game winner," Meyers says, "is that it saved the Harrison play. Without that catch, Steelers fans would have been robbed of the joy of watching the greatest highlight in football history."

AL MICHAELS WILL NEVER FORGET THE DIVINE FEELING HE HAD leaving the booth after that game. He always left after games with at least one regret: one phrase he would have liked to take back, one in-sight he wished he would have thought of in the moment. That's the announcer's curse. But not this time. This time, it was exquisite, all of it, and John Madden's final words still resounded in his mind.

"Both of these teams played *so* well," Madden said. "And the gap be-tween winning and losing is the widest gap in sports. But they were so close, and they played so hard. Both teams, when they were down, they kept fighting and coming back.

"To me," he concluded, "this is the way football should be played."

EPILOGUE

I think now of a football story.

Years ago, I used to play a weekly chess match with a football superstar named Priest Holmes. He was a running back for the Kansas City Chiefs, and he was known throughout the country because he was not only a great player; he was the fantasy football star every person wanted on their team. He lit up the fantasy football scoreboard because he was the league's best rusher and because he was a fantastic pass catcher and because he scored touchdowns like nobody had scored them before.

In 2002, he scored 24 touchdowns though he missed 2.5 games with an injury.

In 2003, he set the record with 27 touchdowns.

Nobody else has ever scored 50 touchdowns over two seasons, and fantasy football owners were so grateful that they named teams after him—the Judas Priests and the Mobile Holmes and the Holmes Wreckers and so on. Priest would get a bucketful of thank-you letters every day, it seemed, and they didn't make much sense to him—he didn't really get the whole fantasy football thing—but he appreciated them just the same.

"I guess fantasy football made me a household name," he said.

Priest wasn't an easy guy to understand. He liked it that way. He had gone undrafted out of the University of Texas, and he willed his way onto the Baltimore Ravens and became a leader when they won the

Super Bowl. He went to Kansas City and became a fantasy football deity through sheer determination.* He didn't want distractions, and attention was a distraction. The media was a distraction. Even other players were a distraction. Teammates said he sometimes would go days without talking.

That was why I wrote the chess story. To break through. Priest loved chess. He believed in the power of chess. He started a chess club with the Police Athletic League of Kansas City for that reason. "All your life, you will have people tell you what you can and can't do," he told me. "These kids will have to hear that over and over again. But in chess, there are no limitations."

I played chess against Priest for the story. I lost. A week later, my phone rang. It was Priest Holmes. He wanted to play chess again. The next week he wanted to play again. And so it was: Every Friday before a game, I would sit down with Priest Holmes and play chess.

He always won. The pattern was usually the same: I would get an early advantage, he would go into himself—Priest was a very deliberate player—and he'd find his way out of danger and wait for my inevitable mistake and capitalize on it. Once, at an autograph appearance, someone asked him to scout me as a chess player.

"He's a good player," Priest said. "But he chokes."

We rarely talked football over the chessboard. But one time we did. And he told me this story: Early in a game, he ran the ball up the middle and into the secondary and he got absolutely leveled by a cornerback not known for his hitting. Just crushed. And the cornerback stood over Holmes and said, "I'll be here all day!"

And Holmes looked up and without smiling said, "No you won't."

"See that's the thing about football," Holmes said. "You can pretend for a little while. You can be a cornerback who comes up with a big hit

---

* At the end of the season, he would watch every single play he was involved in at least ten times.

early on. But when the fourth quarter comes around, cornerbacks turn back into cornerbacks. Everybody turns back into who they are."

Late in that same game, Holmes broke into the open field and saw that cornerback and saw him flinch just a little bit, which was all it took for Holmes to run through him.

"Did you say anything to him?" I asked.

He smiled. "You know why I love football?" he asked. "It's because you don't have to say anything at all."

ACKNOWLEDGMENTS

I assumed after writing *Why We Love Baseball* that I had a pretty good sense of how I wanted to write *Why We Love Football*. It turns out, I did not. The rhythms of football and baseball are so different in ways that are both obvious and indistinct. I started and restarted this book dozens of times. I kept waking up in the middle of the night thinking, *It's not working! This book doesn't feel like football!* My breakthrough came while spending a few days with Chris Willis at the offices of NFL Films in Mount Laurel, New Jersey. Chris is the head of the research library and one of the leading football historians in America. He's also one heck of a nice guy, and just by talking with him, watching legendary football moments with him, bouncing ideas off him, I slowly began to grasp what this book wanted to become and, yes, why I love football. I could not have written this book without him.

The same is true of the eminent football historian and author Michael MacCambridge, who has been a friend for twenty-five years, which means he will forgive me for calling him "eminent."

Many people have told me that my acknowledgments are always much too long, so I will wrap this up by generally thanking all the people who offered interviews, advice, tidbits, or support. I'm especially grateful to my editor, John Parsley, and the incredible Dutton team; to Sloan Harris, Tommy Tomlinson, Alan Sepinwall, Al Michaels, and Mike Schur for their direct contributions to the book; and, mostly, to Margo, Elizabeth, Katie, and our dog, Westley, who sometimes didn't bark when I was in the heat of writing.

INDEX

ABOUT THE AUTHOR

Joe Posnanski is the number one *New York Times* bestselling author of seven books, including *Why We Love Baseball*, *The Baseball 100*, *Paterno*, and *The Secret of Golf*, and has been named National Sportswriter of the Year by five different organizations. He writes at JoePosnanski.com and currently lives in Charlotte, North Carolina, with his family.